Writing Our Extinction

Post 45   Loren Glass and Kate Marshall, Editors
Post•45 Group, Editorial Committee

Writing Our Extinction

Anthropocene Fiction
and Vertical Science

Patrick Whitmarsh

Stanford University Press
Stanford, California

Stanford University Press
Stanford, California

Printed in the United States of America on acid-free, archival-quality paper

Library of Congress Cataloging-in-Publication Data
Names: Whitmarsh, Patrick, author.
Title: Writing our extinction : Anthropocene fiction and vertical science / Patrick Whitmarsh.
Other titles: Post 45.
Description: Stanford, California : Stanford University Press, 2023. | Series: Post·45 | Includes
    bibliographical references and index.
Identifiers: LCCN 2022046059 (print) | LCCN 2022046060 (ebook) | ISBN 9781503633001
    (cloth) | ISBN 9781503635548 (paperback) | ISBN 9781503635555 (epub)
Subjects: LCSH: American fiction—20th century—History and criticism. | American
    fiction—21st century—History and criticism. | Global environmental change in literature. |
    Extinction (Biology) in literature. | Geology in literature. | Ecoliterature, American.
Classification: LCC PS379 .W494 2023 (print) | LCC PS379 (ebook) | DDC 813/.54—dc23/
    eng/20230124
LC record available at https://lccn.loc.gov/2022046059
LC ebook record available at https://lccn.loc.gov/2022046060

Cover design: Jason Anscomb
Cover photograph: Unsplash / Ivan Bandura
Typeset by Elliott Beard in Minion Pro 10/15

For John Paul Riquelme

Contents

Acknowledgments

THIS BOOK BEGAN MANY YEARS ago as a presentation about the Fresh Kills Landfill (now a small portion of Chapter 1) that I delivered in a course on climate change for Boston University's Kilachand Honors College. Then still a graduate student working on a project that had nothing to do with the Anthropocene, I had no idea of the intellectual lengths to which that brief lecture would take me—the questions it would raise, and the insights it would invite. This book owes its existence to the many friends, colleagues, and family members who pondered these questions and insights with me and who nurtured them along the way, offering feedback, guidance, advice, and support.

To begin, I want to thank the faculty and colleagues who planted the roots of my research, those involved in Interdisciplinary Perspectives on Global Challenges: Climate Change, a course for the Kilachand Honors College: Anna Henchman (who asked me to join the class as a teaching assistant and has continued to encourage my scholarship since), Adam Sweeting, Neta Crawford, Leslie Kaufman, Nathan Phillips, and Carrie Preston. Their conversations, kindness, and the opportunities they made for me to participate in class instruction cultivated my fascination with the Anthropocene that informs the basis of this book. My tremendous thanks as well to my fellow teaching assistants, Aaron Ahlstrom, Katey Lesneski, Adelaide Lindseth, Michael Luke, and Kassidy VanGundy, without whom I would have drowned in ungraded papers.

Among the many people who read, engaged with, and otherwise offered feedback on this project—whether on excerpts, full chapters, or more—are Angela Allan, Jennifer Alpert, John Boonstra, Lucy Caplan, Samuel Dolbee, Morgan Day Frank, Reed Gochberg, Lauren Kaminsky, Laura Nelson, Catherine Nguyen, Briana Smith, Arianne Urus, and Duncan White. The scholarly community in Harvard's Committee on Degrees in History and Literature afforded multiple opportunities to share my work and elicit feedback, without which this book would not have found its balance. I want to thank the organizers and participants of the Mahindra Modernism Seminar, where I was able to test ideas from the project among a crowd that included John Lurz, John Plotz, and David Sherman. Katie da Cunha Lewin, Rachele Dini, Jason McEntee, Jay Shelat, Sarah Wasserman, and other participants in the MLA roundtable "DeLillo's *Underworld* at 25" helped me sharpen aspects of the project during its late stages.

Numerous conversations along the way have been essential to crafting this book. Early talks with Greg Chase, Pardis Dabashi, Jon Najarian, and Melissa Schoenberger convinced me this was a book worth writing. Their friendship has been a persistent comfort. Robert Chodat was an especially patient source of wisdom as I wrote, rewrote, and revised, and I have learned as much from his temperament as I have from his wealth of knowledge. Chance encounters with Takeo Rivera on the 86 bus provided encouragement as I developed my ideas, and my countless conversations with David Polanski over beers and books have been invaluable as I conceptualized the argument of *Writing Our Extinction*. I am also deeply grateful to James Toftness, who dedicated untold hours to reading my material, offering advice and assurances, and for being there when I needed a friendly ear. My thanks as well to Maria Christou and others involved in the podcast series *The Art and Artifice of Prediction*. Erica Wetter, Caroline McKusick, Gigi Mark, Catherine Mallon, Elspeth MacHattie, and the editorial team at Stanford University Press have been a crucial source of thoughtful guidance. I want to thank series editors Kate Marshall and Loren Glass for their support, as well as my anonymous readers for their kind and constructive remarks on my manuscript.

In the final months of revision, my graduate advisor, John Paul Riquelme, passed away unexpectedly. Even after I earned my doctorate, John Paul had persisted in his role as mentor, counseling on matters from the academic job market to classroom challenges to, of course, writing. He was a champion of this project from its inception, and his influence cannot be overstated. This book is dedicated to him.

I want to give thanks to my family, who have shared generously in my excitement and interests. Their love and support are in these pages. I couldn't have written a word without them.

And finally, the deepest thanks to my wife, Patty, who doesn't need to read this book because she has listened to me talk about all of it, every day, for years. Her selflessness, intelligence, and love are my greatest inspirations.

Writing Our Extinction

OVERVIEW
Reading Our Extinction

WHEN WE ENVISION THE PLANET, we often imagine ourselves as inhabiting a vertically oriented position in relation to the landscapes of the earth. We hover above, looking down; or, going even farther out, we picture the earth as a planet, a sphere floating in darkness. In other words, we conjure an overview, a perspective that introduces new dimensions and temporalities of earthly existence. Within this lofty framing, we wrestle with the simultaneous presence and absence of humankind. We encounter the power of technologies that enable such a view. We contend with the reality that ours is both a very old and a very recent planet: old by geological standards, yet recent by industrial ones. The earth formed billions of years ago as the result of slow cosmological processes, yet has recently entered a period of transformation wrought by human industrial expansion. The overview reveals conflicting imaginations of our planet, seen both as a place for humans and as a resolutely un-human and increasingly uninhabitable place.

To begin, I want to look at three distinct historical overviews, spanning one hundred fourteen years, that can elucidate the dynamics informing this book's argument. In 1847, Edgar Allan Poe conjures a dreamlike vision of the earth from an impossibly elevated point, casting the occupants of such a vantage as "earth-angels, for whose scrutiny more especially than our own, and for whose death-refined appreciation of the beautiful," God set in array "the wide landscape-gardens of the hemispheres."[1] The specifically non-technological beings of Poe's tale were "human once, but now invisible to humanity," a spectral residue of experience disenchanted from the planet's surface. Here, the vertical manifests as a perspective afforded by the transience of life—a passing into an ethereal existence somewhere in the upper atmosphere. An understudied and relatively unknown text in its author's corpus, "The Domain of Arnheim" bespeaks a consciousness of the planet more common among twentieth-century writers. For example, in 1961, as he flies over the United States in a commercial airliner, petroleum geologist Hollis Hedberg toys with a fanciful notion of subterranean travel. He envisions an upended landscape, a surface geography turned ninety degrees. His plane becomes a drill, its path a borehole, its journey the evolution of the earth. Not only are space and perspective suspended vertically—time is also.

A curious notion attends Poe's description of vertical imagination: that the arrangements of landscape are designed specifically for humankind's "deathful condition," its persistence as a species that dies.[2] It may seem odd to place the vaguely eschatological dimension of Poe's text alongside Hedberg's scientific reflections, until we consider the timescale to which Hedberg gestures. The more recent comment configures the earth as a text, its stratigraphy appearing as a narrative, but one that largely excludes human characters: "The history of the earth, with all its varied events, is written for us *only* in the sequence of rock strata making up the earth's crust. These strata carry the story, such as we can know it, like pages in a book" (italics in original).[3] Gazing down at the earth from an airplane window, Hedberg's vertical perspective affords him an impression of history dissociated from human civilization—a time that precedes humankind and will persist after its extinction. Despite the many historical developments that occurred between these two views of the earth, the remarks about them capture an emergent perspective in modern cultural consciousness. Both speakers fix their gazes upon a world made simultaneously miniature and magnificent, granular and grand, somehow for human experience and yet somehow not. Their orientations rescale their frames of reference; humanity shrinks while the planet expands. As this scalar shift takes place, natural and cultural forms collapse into each other. Aesthetic form bleeds into the perturbations of geography, civilization gives way to unimaginable terrestrial depths. The horizons of human history spill over into the deep reservoirs of planetary time.

Between these two remarks we can locate a third and equally revealing observation. In 1924, native Greenlander Arnarulunnguaq gazes down at a bustling New York City from the vantage of a newly built skyscraper, in awe of the "great plain of stones" below her.[4] People appear indistinct, less humans than insects, entities whose experience bears on an alternate reality. They are distant, alien to Arnarulunnguaq. They inhabit a different world. On one hand, readers might ascribe her alienation to the cultural gulf that separates her from the New Yorkers strolling the streets below. Yet on the other, Arnarulunnguaq explicitly connects this vision to a sense of human death, echoing the "deathful condition" of Poe's story: "I see things more than my mind can grasp; and the only way to save oneself from madness is to suppose that we have all died suddenly before we knew, and that this is part of another life."[5] In these moving and haunting lines, Arnarulunnguaq glimpses not only the brevity of human life in the geological timescale, and the tininess of humans on the planet, but the fragility of civilization itself: its propensity for self-destruction. In gazing from a skyscraper at the human figures strolling the streets of a metropolis, she can only conceive the vision as being from another world, a scene born from America's industrial imagination, a futuristic vista conjured by dead dreamers.

As literary episodes, these quotations do not seem to belong together; but as geological episodes, they are inseparable. Poe inhabits a nineteenth-century period of antebellum industrialization. Arnarulunnguaq speaks to us from between two World Wars, an Indigenous Greenlander witnessing the rise of the modern metropolis. Hedberg's geological flight of fancy (not to mention his physical flight over the country) is a postwar moment, captured as the geophysical sciences were accelerating at an exciting and alarming rate. If we adopt a view of geological time as one calendar year, the intimacy of these three speakers comes into focus, occupying as they all would the final second before the new year.[6] The calendrical model is helpful in scaling our perception of time, but it's also uncomfortably teleological, perhaps even apocalyptic— what happens after midnight? The bell's toll gives the impression of a rupture or shift, a sense of things irrevocably changing; but this impression elides the fact that things are already changing. The interrelations between humankind and the planet have led to significant ecological disruption. Our geophysical agency isn't necessarily shortening the lifespan of the planet, as the calendrical model suggests, but there are many reasons to assume it is shortening our time as a species on the planet. Geological midnight doesn't signify an end but an inflection point of industrial acceleration and scientific knowledge: the realization that our extinction may be traveling backward through time to meet us.

Juxtaposing Poe, Arnarulunnguaq, and Hedberg—three thinkers from very different historical situations—induces us to think at the planetary scale. Through their words and through blurring the cultural particularities that distinguish them, we feel ourselves being drawn outward and upward, away from the signposts of human modernity and into a stratosphere from which new topographies come into focus, as well as new relations between humans, systems, and the earth. It is from this figuratively elevated vantage that *Writing Our Extinction* begins its journey, which includes adventures into the subterranean depths and orbital flights of fancy, meditations on boreholes and atmospheric revelations. This book takes seriously the vertical imagination conjured by Poe, Arnarulunnguaq, and Hedberg, each iteration of which illustrates unique critical dimensions; but the postwar modality of Hedberg most helpfully telescopes the literary verticality of the late twentieth and twenty-first centuries, as I observe in the following chapters. The vertical perspectives of postwar literary fiction not only pitch us into defamiliarizing spaces and temporal experiences but also introduce new ways of approaching narrative and our sense of felt time. Moreover, vertical perspectives suggest that narrative may not be simply a textual phenomenon but a planetary one: the impressions and inscriptions left on the planet by extractive industries, jet propulsion and atmospheric technologies, settler colonialism, nuclear imperialism, and earthmoving projects. If, as Hedberg intuits, scientists might read the story of the earth "like pages in a book," then what would it mean for such a story to be written? For Hedberg, the answer lies with the processes of geological evolution and formation. The evidence in stratigraphic layers is analogous to sequences in a narrative of planetary time.

Poe and Arnarulunnguaq remind us of another aspect of such time. They acknowledge that the life of the planet and the life of humankind take place on incommensurate timescales. Our species will go extinct long before the planet perishes, barring some anomalous cosmic event; yet the incommensurability of these timescales does not mean they are unrelated. Human life unfolds in planetary time, even if it amounts to little, geologically speaking. As modern findings in earth system science have revealed, however, humanity's impact on the planet may very well amount to far more than anyone realized three centuries ago. Mid-twentieth-century innovations in science and technology have opened doors to new understandings of anthropogenic climate change and ecological crisis, and have revealed just how deeply entangled human systems are with geophysical ones. Insofar as these human systems—of industrialism, capitalism, colonialism, and imperialism—have produced new vectors of exploitation and energy consumption, they constitute a transformative dynamic, conveyed by this book's title. Human intervention now composes a planetary history—a script—in which humans are in danger of disappearing: a record of extinction written in geology, an archive of ongoing ecological disruption.

Despite its dour premise, the threat of extinction should not be read solely as a kind of eco-pessimism. Although planetary authorship often describes cultural and industrial practices that have seriously endangered life on earth and altered geophysical processes, it also implies the possibility of reimagining human existence. It allows writers and readers to postulate futures beyond the confines of capitalist realism by intuiting alternative realities of hopefulness and resilience embedded in the here and now. The dual poles of ecological endangerment and resilience correspond to concepts that I call the *overview* and the *underview*—concepts with which this book also begins and ends. Whereas I associate intimations of extinction and the hyper-rationalizing calculus of techno-industrial capitalism with an overview that is domineering, embodied in the eyes of orbital satellites, the underview implies a lived experience of ecological and social relations mobilized in opposition to hierarchical pressures from above. Throughout its chapters, *Writing Our Extinction* deals with several overviews and underviews imagined in numerous texts. Hardly a stable binary, these materials reveal perspectives from above and below to be indiscriminately perforated by competing cultural energies. The overview may often be thought of as a site of power, oppression, and domination, but its literary manifestations offer opportunities for identifying and challenging these associations. Likewise, although the underview may often be the locus of insurgent organization from below, it's also occupied by market forces, resource disparities, and environmental risks. Thus, *Writing Our Extinction*'s brief overview and underview sections provide not only a thematic prospectus and recap, respectively; they also signpost the complexity and oftentimes conflicted dynamics of the narrative fictions observed in the following chapters. It is through their extinctive expressions that these narratives also permit glimpses of resilient alternatives—alternatives by which, to paraphrase Walter

Explorer and Sputnik satellites, and the Apollo and Vostok programs, putting them in conversation with fiction published after 1960. Together, they make up a compendium of environmental disruption and damage, even as they precipitate the emergence of earth system science and an increasing awareness of anthropogenic climate change.[2]

Despite significant attention among literary critics to the intersections of literature and environmentalism, ecology, nuclear imperialism, settler colonialism, and technoscientific spheres of influence, the creative dynamic between postwar narrative fiction and styles of vertical imagining remains understudied. The resistance to a rhetoric of verticality is understandable, given its associations with elements of neoliberal politics: uplift, mobility, linearity, hierarchy, and progress. Vertical rhetoric often connotes success, ambition, promotion, climbing the corporate ladder, and orders of domination and subordination. Chains of command are vertical. Vertical management structures establish higher and lower orders of leadership. Moreover, the post–World War II sciences so central to this book remain inextricable from operational military endgames of obliteration: "we may say that in the age of bombing," Rey Chow writes, "the world has also been transformed into—is essentially grasped and conceived as—a target."[3] Literary critics and humanists have learned to be rightfully suspicious of vertical programs, which often reproduce heteropatriarchal academic models dominated by White men whose theoretical superstructures trickle down to women, people of color, and subaltern writers.[4] Practices of post-critical reading resist the vertical binary between surface and depth that characterizes Marxian and Freudian interpretive methods. These practices develop relational approaches to texts, positioning meaning as an interactive phenomenon between surface details.[5]

Recently, opportunities for vertical methodologies have begun to reappear. In a 2020 essay, Anna Kornbluh diagnoses recent trends such as postcritique and weak theory as symptoms of economic liberalization in higher education, and argues for reintroducing "insurgent figurations of the vertical," particularly dialectical ones, into critical discourse.[6] For Kornbluh, the vertical urgency responds to the condition of ecological crisis that has produced the very flattening she identifies in these recent trends. In a cruel irony, academic shifts toward horizontal methods haven't done away with vertical power structures as much as they have rendered ineffectual our ability to address them. *Writing Our Extinction* emphasizes postwar vertical culture for its ability to signal and illustrate a conflicted ecological consciousness. Even when verticality is bound up with troubling political motivations and power dynamics, its appearance in literary fiction tends to weaken these associations as much as it reinforces them, if not more so. As post-1960 writers explore the entanglements between verticality and planetary ecology, they reveal the ways that verticality itself troubles, and in some cases dissolves, its institutional foundations. Vertical perspectives reveal previously unknown vistas of planetary experience, displacing humankind within and throughout nonhuman scales of time and space. Seen from the vantage of geological time, the contours of human existence assume new forms. We come face to face with our un-human planetary past—what Quentin Meillassoux calls "ancestrality," the time before organic life—and our unsettlingly un-human future, or what Ray Brassier calls (in a fitting complement to Meillassoux) the "anterior posteriority" of extinction, its already-having-happened.[7] Such temporal immensities often manifest through vertical orientations, views of the world from above (the height of a satellite) and into the ground below (the earth's strata).

The vertical imagination in literature is not specific to the post-World War II moment, however, or even to the twentieth century. My point in focusing on culture and fiction after 1960 is not that the vertical imagination is a new development, but that it finds a wider and more profound purchase on the global consciousness via the circulation of materially reproducible planetary iconography such as *Earthrise*, the photograph taken in 1968 by Apollo 8 astronaut William Anders.[8] As recorded in the Apollo mission's flight transcript, Anders's remark upon seeing the earth through the spacecraft's window captures the un-homely sensation of seeing one's home planet from space: "Oh my god, look at that picture over there. That is the Earth coming up."[9] The repurposing of an ordinary phrase—that of watching the sun come up—casts a veil of uncanniness over the scenario. The comment frames the astronaut's extraterrestrial position within a familiar social context. A decade later, mythologist Joseph Campbell commented that Anders's photograph was "working its way slowly into our consciousness. One sees it in many places."[10] *Earthrise* was a visual component not only of a growing ecological sensibility but also of a material technological infrastructure of verticality.

This infrastructure spread earthward as well as spaceward as the geological and engineering sciences devised new methods for subterranean exploration, including new technologies for resource extraction. Industrial, military, and scientific endeavors to locate greater reserves beneath the planet's surface have redistributed political interests not only upon a cartographic (horizontal) plane but also along a geophysical (vertical) one. Writers such as Nigel Clark, Bronislaw Szerszynski, Jan Zalasiewicz, and Ian Klinke have outlined the emergence of a subterranean geopolitics since the mid-twentieth century, an expansive and complex history in which financial incentives, environmental desolation, and political power intersect.[11] The pursuits of the space race, geology, and atmospheric and nuclear sciences illuminate a set of new planetary frontiers that have emerged in the postwar decades: the famous *final frontier* and lesser known *deep frontier*.[12] Within the vertical frame of documents such as *Earthrise*, we can perceive the suggestive alignment of multiple vectors: the vertical perspective of midcentury science, the ecological consciousness of a burgeoning environmental modernity, and the growing necessity of massive amounts of energy. These techno-visual developments make up a planetary media ecology of unprecedented scale: a system of imaging and imagining that has cultivated a feedback loop of planetary impressions. As scientific propensities for vertical exploration sponsored technologies that enabled such exploration, those very technologies produced images—inscriptions—of vertical experience; and as these images and stories circulated, they formed a material basis for the vertical imagination that inspired such technologies in the first place. In the postwar era, verticality becomes a self-fulfilling prophecy of scientific expansion, giving rise to advancements in air and space travel, resource extraction, and nuclear experimentation, as well as a vertical thematics of cultural progress. I refer to these developments collectively as the *vertical sciences*.

The vertical sciences begin to emerge in the postwar years, metastasizing in the International Geophysical Year (IGY) of 1957–58 and culminating with *Earthrise* ten years later—a vertical decade that had an enormous impact on new media and perceptual technologies. The IGY was a landmark series of gatherings among scientists from around the world, participating in numerous studies and research programs for the purpose of expanding human knowledge about the planet. One of the most famous and widely visible pursuits of the IGY was the construction and launching of orbital satellites by the United States and Soviet Union. These programs served the dual purpose of providing geophysical data as well as windows on foreign affairs, giving rise to a network of visual technologies encircling the globe.[13] The import of this new planetary apparatus wasn't lost on writers of the time. Hannah Arendt cautiously remarked in *The Human Condition* (1958) that the launch of Sputnik marked a "step toward escape from men's imprisonment to the earth," and Alexander Marshack's popular account of the IGY, *The World in Space* (1958), notably mentions human efforts to "escape" the planet.[14] There emerges an ambivalent rhetoric of imprisonment and liberation around the vertical sciences in the decades following World War II, as the global community witnesses the *fait accompli* of rocketeer momentum.[15]

This momentum coordinates a series of overlapping phenomena that inform the emergence of post-1960 Anthropocene fiction: vertical perspectives on the planet, an increased attention to the ecological connectivity between human development and geophysical systems, and a sense of the earth as a script of humankind's accelerating extinction. Moreover, the vertical sciences were in many ways wedded to the increasing global demand for energy; as Benjamin Goossen notes, even the term *geophysics* was, at the time, often used to describe vertical practices related to "surveying and mineral scouting."[16] Hardly science for science's sake, environmental knowledge grew alongside policies of environmental exploitation. Theories of solar energy motivated the "conquest of space," highlighting science's colonial drive.[17] The proximity of financial incentives and knowledge of the earth gave rise to concerns over ecological precarity and anxieties about humanity's planetary existence: "I do not know whether you were frightened, but I at any rate was frightened when I saw pictures coming from the moon to the earth," Martin Heidegger revealed in a 1976 interview; "We don't need any atom bomb. The uprooting of man has already taken place. The only thing we have left is purely technological relationships. This is no longer the earth on which man lives."[18] Nearly two decades after Heidegger's comment, Paul Virilio further articulated the link between perspective and existential concern: "Today, when we are all so worried about the ecological balance of a human environment seriously threatened by industrial waste, would it not be appropriate to add to the concerns of *green ecology* those of a *grey ecology* that would focus on the postindustrial degradation of the depth of field of the terrestrial landscape?" (italics in original).[19] Virilio's remark conveys two complementary insinuations: that of worsening air quality on a global scale, which diminishes visibility, and the inauguration of techno-verticality, which abolishes the horizon. Verticality's aesthetic affordance lies in its ability to push readers and viewers toward new scales of experience, to reframe the object of their attention—especially when that object is humankind, or, more radically, the absence of humankind.

In addition to offering multiple close readings of key works, *Writing Our Extinction* provides an overview of the Anthropocenic consciousness that has increasingly occupied our vertical imaginations since 1960. Authors who participate in the development of this consciousness form a broad and diverse group: Thomas Pynchon, Don DeLillo, Tim O'Brien, Karen Tei Yamashita, Kim Stanley Robinson, Colson Whitehead, Reza Negarestani, Jesmyn Ward, and Hari Kunzru. As readers will note, there is an undeniable color line running through this group, and many of these writers draw our attention to ways in which the Anthropocene is economically, politically, and racially inflected. In other words, the Anthropocene does not describe a human-planetary dynamic authored by our species writ large, but a dynamic authored by specific practices and systems. What's more, novel writing itself is not innocent of such planetary authorship. As a cultural form predicated on industrialization, deforestation, and resource extraction, the postwar novel registers two kinds of inscription: one on the page, and one on the planet. It is no surprise that writers working after World War II begin acknowledging, to a greater extent, the entangled networks of narrative, verticality, and species precarity. The second half of the twentieth century is characterized by an intensifying awareness of destructive feedback loops that tie together cultural institutions and geophysical systems, and usher humankind toward mass extinction.

Extinction Humanities

As a topic of theoretical import, extinction complicates literary and intellectual conversations about environmental precarity on an industrially accelerating planet and poses a challenge to humanist study and social thought. Many fetishize extinction as the supreme motivator of human survival by any means, as depicted in countless mainstream disaster narratives. Others provocatively see extinction as a solution, such as the Voluntary Human Extinction Movement (VHEMT), founded by Les Knight in 1991.[20] Survivalism often valorizes the individual at the expense of collective and ecological interests, whereas VHEMT advocates for population control while mostly sidestepping the history of racial sterilization in the United States and elsewhere; yet both implicate us in crucial questions concerning extinction's role in our daily lives: what does it mean to confront our extinction? What stories can we tell ourselves about our extinction—a process whose closure we cannot possibly witness? How do we narrate our species' disappearance? "In a millennium or two," writes Don DeLillo in his 1973 novel *Great Jones Street*, "a seeming paradox of our civilization will be best understood by those men versed in the methods of counter-archaeology. They will study us not by digging into the earth but by climbing vast dunes of industrial rubble and mutilated steel, seeking to reach the tops of our buildings."[21] The paradox of DeLillo's passage lies in its imagining of simultaneous persistence and extinction—that some surviving, presumably educated humans (or a species capable of reading our ruins) will sift through cultural detritus to discern the "reasons for our demise."[22] The disappearance of humankind, DeLillo suggests, can be comprehended only by crafting a speculative, anachronistic subject that lingers beyond the scope of human time.

Such imagined disappearances frequently characterize what we might call the extinction humanities, a subcategory of the environmental humanities premised on what the end, and absence, of life on a mass scale means for human experience now. This speculative outlook exhibits a narrative valence; to make sense of our death, we must be able somehow to view the event after it has taken place. Sigmund Freud's theorized death drive is a notable precursor to the extinction humanities with its explanation for the posttraumatic habits of soldiers returned from war, who effectively suffered a dislocation of narrative control.[23] What Freud intuits in the individual psyche after World War I metastasizes during World War II into a collectively experienced social anxiety, informed by the emergence of a widespread material visual culture. Photographs of nuclear explosions, wartime atrocities, and the planet formed a visual program of postwar anxiety and apocalypticism. Furthermore, the global linkage of risks, and the capacity of new media technologies to transmit images of them, established an association between postwar precarity and planetary ecology: "The aesthetics, even erotics, of death is a long-running cultural concern in Western theory but one that today intersects with an emerging planetary consciousness," writes Joseph Masco in a perceptive analysis of Freud: "one that demands scaling local dangers up to the earthly sphere and back again."[24] The death drive assumes global proportions after World War II with the rise of the planetary media ecology: a worldwide information infrastructure by which various extinctive transmissions—from images of nuclear detonations to aerial photos of oil spills—circulate the earth.

The immediacy of extinction introduces a sense of lived futurity to everyday life. Such a concept of futurity is unique to our post-1960s contemporary moment, in which the consolidation of ecological knowledge, technoscience, and industrial acceleration have given rise to what Masco calls the "Age of Fallout," or "a way of recasting historical categories and periodizations to recognize the future-oriented planetary environmental consequences of historical and ongoing industrial activity."[25] Masco's fallout carries a powerful dual meaning: the fallout of nuclear war, but also the disorienting experience of living in the aftermath of disaster, in a world driven by consumption, contamination, and exploitation. The year 1960 marks the beginning of a broadening social awareness about large-scale eco-catastrophes, originating in works like Rachel Carson's *Silent Spring* (1962) and expanding like a mushroom cloud in Bill McKibben's *The End of Nature* (1989).[26] Coincidentally, *Silent Spring* was published in the year of the October Crisis, a singular moment in Cold War history that nearly escalated to violent conflict, and *The End of Nature* in the year of the fall of the Berlin Wall. These parallel histories form what might be called an archive of ongoing extinction, the slow engineering of humanity's nonexistence inscribed in planetary media. The Cold War and the increasing frequency of eco-catastrophes since 1960 are complementary narratives that orient humanity toward nonexistence, albeit according to different ideological investments and value systems.

It has been the tendency of industrialists and politicians to write off eco-catastrophes as anomalies—as bugs rather than features of capitalist development. Yet, if we adjust our settings, reframe the capitalist plot, and seriously consider the escalating intensity and frequency of such disasters, we find that progress quietly turns into precarity. Justin McBrien provocatively labels this account of precarity the Necrocene, arguing that the "history of environmentalism is the history of capitalism realizing its own principle of *becoming ex-*

tinction through the conceptual system of planetary catastrophism" (italics in original).[27] Precarity takes hold at a global scale, manifesting as an elemental function of postindustrial capitalism and producing what Virilio calls *"the delocalization of all accidents"*—the simultaneous experiencing (or witnessing) of calamity via the new planetary media ecology (italics in original).[28] Although Virilio's interest is in the virtual experience afforded by telecommunications, he compares the experience of delocalization to that of radioactive fallout: "while *radioactivity* [is] able to circulate with impunity from East to West, contaminating entire continents in passing, the electromagnetic transmission system of the *interactivity* of future information superhighways is part of the same phenomenon of global reach" (italics in original).[29] Like nuclear fallout, Virilio suggests, information follows complex and unpredictable paths, circumventing market barriers and state control.

Nuclear catastrophe and fallout produce a distinctly vertical scenario of postwar anxieties. Often detonated either belowground (as at test sites) or in the air above their targets (Little Boy, dropped by the Enola Gay, exploded hundreds of meters above Hiroshima), nuclear threats become a fixture of aerial and subterranean spaces. The Cold War fallout shelter introduces another element of extinctive verticality, carving out hollows in the planet where terrified citizens might gather in the event of an attack. Nuclear disaster wasn't the only harbinger of extinction fueling the mid-twentieth century's vertical imagination, however. As early as 1956, paleontologists hypothesized that one of the most iconic and debated extinction events in planetary history—the Cretaceous-Paleogene event, responsible for the eradication of nearly seventy-five percent of life on earth, including the dinosaurs—may have been the result of a meteor.[30] Suddenly confronted with the possibility of impacts originating from beyond our atmosphere, scientists wrestled with the prospect of geological catastrophism, a paradigm long rejected by adherents of Charles Lyell's gradualist uniformitarianism.[31] In the late 1970s, geologist Walter Alvarez and his father, Luis, discovered evidence beneath the Yucatán Peninsula of an impact event marking the boundary between the Cretaceous and Paleogene. The discovery is accompanied by a historical irony: an experimental physicist, Luis Alvarez had observed the bombing of Hiroshima from a plane following the Enola Gay.[32] A new vertical threat now loomed alongside nuclear war: that the planet floats in a vortex of so-called kill curves, orbital arcs of meteors coursing through the earth's gravity well. "Astronomical observations of earth-crossing comets and asteroids of various sizes can be used to estimate the expected average times between collisions of large or small objects with earth," writes geologist Michael Rampino; "Geologists must look up as well as down to unlock the story of our changing planet."[33] At roughly the same time that science introduces new vertical frameworks for thinking about the planet, the threat of extinction assumes a major role in cultural discourse.

Today, new challenges have been added to the list of pending global accidents. Climate change and disease outbreaks pose distinct threats to the security of peoples, communities, and countries. Our refusal to learn from these events in any long-term fashion speaks to our general inability to organize them narratively, to understand what is being written. Like Freud's traumatized soldiers, our apparent failure to anticipate and internalize the markers of slow extinction leads to neurotic repetition at institutional levels. Historical recollections are insufficient to prepare ourselves; what we need, in Rob Nixon's words, are "stories of anticipation."[34] Such stories recast the present as a stage upon which the future is prefigured, permutated, and authored. The prospect of extinction reintroduces the concept of the archive as a space that not only logs the past but outlines the future. As Claire Colebrook writes, extinction both fuels and compromises the archival impulse: "There can only be a human archive if the human body couples itself with various systems (inscriptive, technological, agricultural, scientific, moral, political, familial), but these same tendencies toward order are also generative of *disorder*" (italics in original).[35] For Colebrook, the logic of inscription itself is intimately tied to the necessity of extinction. The pharmacological dynamic of deconstruction—the coexistence of the medicinal and the malign—describes the counterintuitive insight of humankind's relationship to extinction: that we understand our current ecological predicament precisely through the very technologies that produced it. In the twenty-first century, the archival impulse bears a troubled relationship to extinction. With the expansion of new digital technologies and server farms, our extinction is being presciently archived in more ways than one: in the documentation of scientific knowledge but also in the planetary scars left by ballooning energy consumption.

Archival methods connote more than mere documentation, however; they tell us stories. Practices of archival identification, inclusion, and description reveal judgments that correspond to a particular vision of history. What can such practices tell us of the ways we understand our extinction, the very foreclosure of archivist activity? Where is the human in the context of endangerment? Where—and what—is the archive of an ongoing process? If, as Mark Bould suggests, the Anthropocene constitutes "the unconscious of 'the art and literature of our time,'" then the archive undergoes a radical recontextualization.[36] Planetary scale displaces categories once considered foundational, including those that oppose the legibility of the past to the obscurity of the future. The prospect of extinction broadens the relation between time and the archive. History is no longer restricted to the domain of that which has already happened, that which can be narrated in retrospect. The ecological depth of our industrial endeavors and the extent of their impact on the biosphere have extruded history into that which, counterintuitively, has not happened. Anthropocene temporality sets in motion narrative feedback loops that reveal archives of untold stories.

Our extinction is one such untold story. If humankind's extinction has been augured by industrial activity, beginning with a historical state of affairs in which capital accumulation shifted from the earth's surface to its subterranean mineral reserves, then we can think of human extinction as being vertically inscribed into the geophysical matter of the earth.[37] The planetary present and future make up a geological script, one that is hardly linear; just as our industrial past determines our present and future, our postwar understanding of climate crisis conditions our perception of the past. In an illuminating reading of Anthropocene logic, Colebrook upends the linear understanding of humankind's impact: that through its industrial modernity, our species disrupted a stable ecology. By contrast, she insists, it is the Anthropocene itself that produces the exceptionalist dream of a return to nature, of humankind engineering itself back to ecological stability.[38] In a similar sense, extinction is not the result of a loss of nature or deviation from the natural; rather, it is the reality of extinction itself that produces the ideal of nature and valorizes the ideology of survival. Colebrook elsewhere describes the framework for this outlook, quite fittingly, as extinct theory, or the acknowledgment that theoretical discourse itself evolves from the precondition of extinction: "if theory after theory has any meaning, should it not refer to a hyperbolic *and* minimal theoretical condition in which we consider not simply the formal absence of a population but an actual disappearance?" (italics in original).[39] Colebrook's wager is not proposed lightly. How are humanists to make sense of a future not for humans? What do fiction and theory have to offer this dark imagination? How can we reconceive the archive in an age of extinction?

Much like DeLillo's counter-archaeologists, Anthropocene archivists turn not to libraries, private documents, and other institutional collections, but to the "curatorial spaces," in Kathryn Yusoff's words, that compose our geophysical verticality: landfills, boreholes, orbital arcs, nuclear debris and fallout, and the dispossessed and buried remains of colonial genocide.[40] These spaces provide a documentation of the past as well as a strong intimation of our planetary future. Here we encounter not, as Jacques Derrida once suggested, "a total and remainderless destruction of the archive," but a redescription of the archive as geological material.[41] As observers of these Anthropocene archives, we perceive ourselves in new relations with other species and earth systems, our behaviors installing themselves in the long consequences of geological and atmospheric temporalities. In such archives, the distinctions between human and nonhuman traces blur, but not in a way that diminishes the value of our stories: "Art and writing are pulsations that are irreducible to the cosmos," Colebrook writes, "but also in vibration with the cosmos—the chaosmos. Those modes of writing [. . .] are responding to the new rhythms of the earth—writing that aims to imagine what it might be to perceive a world without humans."[42] Insofar as the Anthropocene leaves constitutive impressions on the planet, our species courts extinction as an ongoing process and practice of ecological upheaval—an archival geology of cultural production on a planetary scale.

The concept of archival geology troubles familiar distinctions of media and periodization. As the temporal scale expands to include the planetary, classifications between, for example, the Victorian and Cold War eras appear increasingly miniscule. It would be a mistake to lose sight of our archival and disciplinary frameworks altogether, however. Archival geology directs us to consider the differences that characterize media, history, and region with interdisciplinary rigor—to understand the ways that human forms are attuned to their planetary being, conscious of their entanglement with geophysical processes. In archival geology, we bear witness to the excesses and aesthetic interventions of human civilization (particularly in the industrial and postindustrial eras) as well as the liminal spaces where these human forms bleed into the planetary nonhuman. The meaning of something such as Robert Smithson's iconic work of land art, *Spiral Jetty* (1970), for instance, changes with fluctuating water levels of the Great Salt Lake. Novels like Colson Whitehead's *The Underground Railroad* (2016) and Hari Kunzru's *White Tears* (2017) assume new meanings both with the unearthing of mass graves of Black and Indigenous peoples and with our broader understanding of the modern carceral state's impact on local environments. Moreover, archival geology encourages us to look at the ecological meanings not only of aesthetic works but also those of scientific, industrial, and political provenance. Abandoned mines, disused subway systems, dead satellites, landfills, energy infrastructures, and other cultural leftovers transform into ambiguous traces as they drift in obsolescence along planetary pathways. Insofar as the Anthropocene underwrites our continued commitment to humanist study and cultural critique, it expands our network of focus to include the slow (but accelerating) reactions through which cultural objects, including literature, enter the domain of the planet.

Defining and Periodizing Anthropocene Fiction

The incorporation of vertical perspectives in postwar fiction enables its writers to address the planetary domain so central to our modern ecological project, which includes both environmental justice and postcolonial redress, in the harsh light of the Anthropocene. For environmental humanists and ecocritics, this means negotiating the feedback loops that locate regional disruptions within larger global networks, as Ursula K. Heise has lucidly demonstrated.[43] Heise's methodological reframing and emphasis on the role of global risk in ecocritical discourse set in motion much enterprising scholarship that aimed to bring a global, if not planetary, consciousness to bear on local challenges and injustices—from Nixon's "transnational ethics of place" to Dipesh Chakrabarty's call to "connect deep and recorded histories and put geological time and the biological time of evolution in conversation with the time of human history and experience."[44] Embodied in narrative techniques of zooming in and out, floating above and delving beneath, verticality configures a set of metaphorical and rhetorical gestures by which post-1960 fictions mediate our ability to think across local and global scales.

Zooming in and out mobilizes questions of scale by suturing discrete perspectives. Scale is discernible not in the details of given images or representations but in the relations between these details and those of alternative viewpoints. In Joshua DiCaglio's reading of the educational *Powers of Ten* films (1977), which situate the earth in relation to microscopic and macrocosmic orders of magnitude, zoom techniques are crucial to scientific practices that produce "knowledge at the planetary scale by observing differences that are discernible at the level of the planet. It is because these knowledges are so disjointed that we need something to tie these disparate scales of observation together to portray scale itself."[45] In *Powers of Ten*, the shifting magnitude clarifies the ways that scale intervenes in our perception, revealing and concealing various particulars. But how does this specifically visual and spatial effect manifest in literary narrative? In the chapters that follow, I demonstrate that literary verticality yields an aesthetic and critical provocation for readers: in the narrative descriptions and experiences that attend their vertical moments, these fictions introduce temporal impressions in which human existence finds itself possessed by the specter of its own extinction. Put another way, the texts on which I focus deploy vertical perspectives to underscore humankind's sedimentation within broader scales of geological time, both preceding and following the lifespan of our species on the planet.

These literary works engage the Anthropocene through techniques of ekphrastic verticality, geological perspective, and planetary focalization, rather than by plotting human actors in an overdetermined causal relationship with environmental crisis. As Min Hyoung Song argues, narratives of climate fiction frequently fall victim to Edenic dreams of prelapsarian nature, fantasies of human mastery, and other constructs that reintroduce teleological certainty. According to Song, these narrative frameworks are inextricable from the very cultural ideologies that have exacerbated climate change: "Not only are many available forms of storytelling ill equipped to imagine climate change, it would seem, but they replicate the very ways of knowing that have made the problem more possible and that obscure the kinds of literary forms that might emerge from the world as it is."[46] He identifies here a crucial dilemma at the core of environmental narratives—the seeming inability of plot to compensate for the multiplicity of human behaviors and worldly possibilities—and argues that climate fictions might structure themselves around the open-endedness of plot as a means to counter futility.[47] Vertical negotiations of scale offer a means of visualizing such open-endedness by situating potential futures within the material present. The vertical imagination of post-1960 fiction is an aesthetic answer to the challenges of planetary scale and ecological disruption, offering a metaphorical optics through which humans might conjure alternative presents.

For this reason, I refer to the major texts in this book as *Anthropocene fiction* rather than climate fiction—much less postwar or postmodernist fiction, neither of which conveys the planetary scope these texts express. Although suspicious of grand narratives, Anthropocene fiction deviates from postmodernism's narrative iconoclasm in that it affirms a picture of planetwide metamorphosis set in motion by human industry. The Anthropocene may begin with humans, but it likely won't end with us. As an epoch of human-induced environmental upheaval that is initiating a widespread sixth extinction, which may include even humanity's extinction, the Anthropocene has the strong potential to outlast human existence on earth.[48] Anthropocene fictions direct us to intuit the ways that our nonhuman past and future permeate the present, opening onto new planetary vistas as a means of expressing the gulfs of deep time. However, they also reveal the ways that human culture and civilization have infused themselves into the planet, altering its systems and processes, and catalyzing the very disruptions we seek to remedy through our sciences and technologies. In this respect, *Writing Our Extinction* shares some concerns with Adam Trexler's noteworthy *Anthropocene Fictions: The Novel in a Time of Climate Change* (2015); but whereas Trexler argues that "nearly all Anthropocene fiction addresses the historical tension between the existence of catastrophic global warming and the failed obligation to act," I claim that much Anthropocene fiction is not ostensibly about climate change at all.[49] Rather, post-1960 Anthropocene fiction works to focalize vertically the geophysical mesh in which climate change occurs and in which human actors conceptualize the sensitivity of their actions (or inaction).

We are not all of us similarly enmeshed, of course, nor do all humans share equal (or even comparable) responsibility for environmental justice. As a concept, the Anthropocene remains perpetually problematic and pale in color. Binaries of life and death, human and nonhuman, and natural and artificial have often worked to obscure the contours of racial dispossession and exploitation that inform the Anthropocene in many ways. In the last several years, numerous scholars have offered provocative rebrandings such as Capitalocene, Plantationocene, and Chthulucene.[50] These labels speak to various social, racial, and economic inequities as well as the disproportionate distribution of environmental effects in the postindustrial world. They reveal histories and contingencies often overlooked in broad appeals to the Anthropocene, most crucially those pertaining to the forces of capital, racism, and the widespread exploitation of newly discovered planetary resources: "the slave trade consisted of not only the organized deportation of millions of Africans to continents and islands," writes Françoise Vergès, "but also a massive transfer of plants, animals, diseases, soil, techniques, and manufactured goods from Europe."[51] The Anthropocene is not a story of humans, in other words, but of specific humans and systems. It is a story of economically and racially motivated restructuring and extraction, reducing human bodies to instruments of political and industrial power. *Writing Our Extinction* makes these dynamics visible within the unfolding contours of what we often call the Anthropocene, and at various times foregrounds Capitalocene, Plantationocene, and other -cene narratives. Histories of exploitation, dispossession, exclusion, and violence form the bedrock of modernity's material reconstitution of the planet. Only by coordinating these multiply interacting systems can we comprehend the full depth of the Anthropocene's impact.

The interactivity of systems has attracted the attention of literary scholars over the past decade or so, both in ecocriticism and beyond. Critics as varied as Cary Wolfe, Bruce Clarke, Priscilla Wald, Kate Marshall, David Alworth, Caroline Levine, Nathan Hensley, Philip Steer, Anna Kornbluh, Heather Houser, Michael Dango, and Carolyn Lesjak have been drawn to the relationships between system, network, assemblage, and other signifiers of complex arrangements, putting questions of form in conversation with history, culture, and material practice.[52] Lucidly summed up by Levine, many of these systems-oriented analyses reveal "that networks and enclosures are constantly meeting, sometimes sustaining and reinforcing one another, at other times creating threats and obstacles."[53] Such an outlook is useful for reading Anthropocene fiction, which coordinates the historical encounters between human and planetary systems. Forms are unstable but material sites constantly being redetermined by the dynamics of contact playing out within and between them. In Devin Griffiths's helpful reframing, form is "a promiscuous feature of the world," a contingent occurrence within an ecology of material relations.[54] Although not traditionally formalist, such attention to form suggests that certain aesthetic variations of the novel enable authors to elucidate the many manifestations and multidimensional effects of systems in the postwar Anthropocene. Put another way, form matters for the ways authors envision and depict persons, technologies, and other cultural agents within shifting planetary networks.

Insofar as they court the relations between and among social, discursive, and planetary bodies, Anthropocene fictions do not conform to standard genre, modal, or stylistic boundaries. They include works of historical fiction (such as DeLillo's *Underworld* [1997]), magical realism (Karen Tei Yamashita's *Through the Arc of the Rain Forest* [1990]), science fiction (Kim Stanley Robinson's *Red Mars* [1993]), Southern Gothic (Jesmyn Ward's *Sing, Unburied, Sing* [2017]), and other hybrid literary modes. Rather, the term *Anthropocene fiction* triangulates three elements: a technique of ekphrastic verticality, a conceptual engagement with planetary scale, and a post-1960 periodization. As in any attempt at periodization, there are outliers and complications in my categorization of Anthropocene fiction. Noticeably, the novels on which I focus tend to cluster not around the late-1960s and 1970s but in the period after 1980. The reasons for this include escalating ecological and industrial crises, but it is also the case that the Anthropocene as a term did not find voice until the 1980s and wasn't popularized until the 2000s. Furthermore, the extension of speculative narratives into mainstream spheres of cultural production (from Netflix originals to Oprah's Book Club) has led to new literary transformations.[55] Anthropocene fiction emerges and operates within this transformative timeline as a narrative mode that is vertically attuned to humankind's planetary context.

Although climate change is an increasingly urgent component of this planetary context, it is rarely the explicit concern of *Writing Our Extinction*. Even after the publication of Bill McKibben's *The End of Nature* and the meeting of the first Intergovernmental Panel on Climate Change (in 1990), Anthropocene fiction has not become expressly climatological but comprehensively ecological. Landfills and air travel, pollution and boreholes, satellites and nuclear test sites—all are complicit in anthropogenic climate change, constituting a multitude of apertures through which human agency transfers into the realm of the planetary. By drawing on vertical perspectives and impressions from the sciences, Anthropocene fiction uncovers these apertures and casts them as intimately wedded to a post-regional, planetwide geophysics. *Writing Our Extinction* puts landfills in communication with air travel, boreholes in communication with pollution, nuclear test sites in communication with satellites, and reveals the vertical networks that link them together. Through this network, a distinctly post-1960 material culture of the earth emerges.

Another way of putting this is that *Writing Our Extinction* presents these varied scientific and industrial developments as entangled. These entanglements are not merely spatial but extend into the temporal such that past and future become entangled with the present, and disparate temporal scales become ambiguously enmeshed. For instance, the histories of human civilization and industrialization become entangled with the geological past, and the planet's anthropogenically altered future entangles with its present. Traffic jams elicit intimations of prehistoric extinction events (as in DeLillo's *Underworld*); the imagined future colonization and extractive infrastructure of Mars recalls the vast earthmoving and land reclamation projects of the nineteenth and twentieth centuries (as in Robinson's *Red Mars*); and the organizational models of the antebellum plantation and forced labor under Jim Crow dovetail with depictions of the racist and environmentally harmful practices of the postwar carceral state (as in Ward's *Sing, Unburied, Sing*). Through this multitude of overlapping and intersecting temporalities, Anthropocene novels evince a variation of what Nixon calls "slow violence," or the manifestation of injustices over timescales that prevent these injustices from being seen as violent, especially by those who benefit materially from them.[56] Likewise, Anthropocene fiction reframes humankind's relationship to its own extinction, presenting readers with a slow extinction that has already begun even if its culmination remains uncertain: a gradual vanishing "that unravels great tissues of ways of going on in the world for many species, including historically situated people," in Donna Haraway's words.[57] Thinking of extinction not as an event but as a process, an unfolding, an unraveling— less an object than a hyperobject, an entity that pervades imperceptibly large dimensions of space and time—allows us to conceive it as both a geophysical phenomenon and a narrative practice.[58] To the extent that our culture leaves its mark on the planet, it remains as a trace within the "sequence of rocks" that future geologists might read.

From our place on the surface of the planet, with familiar surroundings and the comfort of stable horizons, it is often difficult to intuit the multiple temporalities circumscribed by the Anthropocene; but when we find ourselves suddenly displaced along vertical perspectives, new realities come into focus. By diverting our attention toward the processes taking place above and below us, verticality helps us think of the deep time of geology, the seeping contamination of landfills, the extraction of raw materials, and even the earth system as a whole. It lets us imagine ourselves as microscopic organisms when observed from the distance of an orbital satellite; and it allows us to conceptualize the ground beneath our feet not as a place, a region, or a country, but as a planet. Verticality aids us in navigating the disorientations of scale—in seeing ourselves not only as a culture or civilization but as a planetary force akin to weather, waterfalls, tectonic plates, and global climate. It permits us to see ourselves, as Arnarulunnguaq once did, as extinct—as geo-relics, future fossils. Along with the analogy between industrial intervention and writing, verticality gives rise to another literary analogy, between distant and close reading. This is a messy analogy, and I do not mean to suggest that satellite views correspond to distant reading and examining geological core samples corresponds to close reading. Different scales afford different kinds of information and new patterns of connectivity. Shifting between distant and close reading requires us to recalibrate our scopes, as does shifting between the orbital and the subterranean. The analogy here underscores a negotiation of scale. Just as literary critics adjust their expectations and intuit unique features depending on the scale of their methodology, so too do scientists. As a text, the planet is a body that invites radical modifications of scale.

The major writers found in this study—Don DeLillo, Hari Kunzru, Reza Negarestani, Tim O'Brien, Thomas Pynchon, Kim Stanley Robinson, Jesmyn Ward, Colson Whitehead, and Karen Tei Yamashita—address and render scale to different degrees and from different directions, yet all invoke the aesthetics of verticality. They complement these aesthetics, which draw significantly on the visual culture of a planetary media ecology, with temporal reframings that put human characters in touch with their geological genealogies and fossil futures. Extinction often remains a spectral presence in novels of the Anthropocene, yet one that informs their aesthetic and conceptual maneuvers. Insofar as the Anthropocene names an epoch centered on the industrious power of the human species, it all but guarantees humankind's disappearance. The categorical applicability of the Anthropocene is simultaneously constituted and dissolved by the representational limit of human extinction: "If at some point we vanish," geologist Marcia Bjornerud writes, "it is likely no one else will fret about the definition of the Anthropocene."[59] The Anthropocene will both persist after we're gone and become epistemologically irrelevant. In keeping with this paradoxical feature, Anthropocene fiction deploys aesthetic and perspectival strategies that court indeterminacy, if not impossibility: points of view that permit unlikely details, details that inform incommensurable proclamations of objectivity, and overlapping timelines experienced simultaneously. Readers and characters of Anthropocene fiction face up to the counterintuitive realization that, as Roy Scranton ominously puts it, "this civilization is *already dead*" (italics in original).[60] Confronted with the knowledge that humans have left an inscription in the annals of geological time—one that also imperils our continued existence on this planet—we cannot help but imagine ourselves as somehow already extinct: as, in the words of *Underworld* narrator Nick Shay, "the species factually absent from the scene [. . .]."[61]

The Structure of This Book

Addressing these intersections of extinction, verticality, and narrative, Chapter 1 gives an account of the kind of fiction *Writing Our Extinction* takes as its primary subject, the post-1960 Anthropocene novel. Post-1960 Anthropocene fiction does not denote a specific style or literary mode, but a particular confluence of narrative, cultural, and visual dynamics that engage the issues of scale and representation in the Anthropocene epoch. The chapter examines the interplay of these dynamics and the ways that they illuminate an emerging ecological consciousness in a major work of late-twentieth-century fiction: Don DeLillo's *Underworld* (1997). Often noted for its encyclopedic form and dark perspective on the Cold War United States, *Underworld* is rarely discussed for its environmental themes, which include toxic waste, nuclear testing, and land use. Moreover, DeLillo repeatedly connects these themes to activities of elevation and excavation, making conceptual links to the midcentury vertical sciences. Placing *Underworld* and other DeLillo works in conversation with twentieth-century land artist Robert Smithson, I argue that this author cultivates an aesthetic of planetary realism, illuminating the ecological consciousness of the Anthropocene. Ironically, *Underworld*'s planetary aesthetics also direct us toward the deep complicities between such consciousness and the industries that made it possible, revealing the post–World War II decades as a period of strong Anthropocene emergence that we call the Great Acceleration.

The only chapter to focus on a single writer, Chapter 1 also argues for DeLillo as a writer whose long career—especially from 1976 and *Ratner's Star* to 2010 and *Point Omega*—offers a uniquely sustained literary account of the Anthropocene across multiple novels and writings. Identifying *Underworld* as the apotheosis of this account, I claim that it frames its post–World War II outlook as a retrospective on not the Cold War but rather the Great Acceleration, the postwar and postindustrial phase of the Anthropocene. Despite its specific chronological focus, *Underworld* repeatedly exceeds these temporal limits, indexing a geological time beyond human measure—resulting in what I call the novel's *archival geology*. The representational challenge of archival geology—a concept that includes the industrially driven annihilation of the human species—engenders a paradoxical feeling of proleptic extinction. Over the course of its eight hundred–plus pages, *Underworld* affords readers multiple opportunities to engage the prospect of their own proleptic extinction: the sensation of reading-while-extinct. In its encyclopedic coverage of the latter twentieth century and its serious engagement with the ecological fragility of postindustrial society, *Underworld* (especially when viewed alongside other entries in DeLillo's oeuvre) serves as an exemplar of what Anthropocene fiction is and what its literary effects are.

The remaining chapters of this book move on from establishing the effects of Anthropocene fiction to examining the complex cultural relationship between several literary texts and key scientific, technological, and industrial developments in the vertical sciences. Chapter 2 turns its attention to geological questions in the wake of the IGY, with particular attention to Project Mohole. Proposed as a way to resolve the controversy over continental movement, Project Mohole undertook the unprecedented task (outside of fiction, at least) of drilling to the planet's mantle and taking core samples. In addition to demonstrating the project's ambiguous scientific goals and proximity to the oil industry, this chapter argues that Project Mohole unearthed a geological unconscious in twentieth-century culture that surfaced in multiple works of fiction. I identify this geological unconscious in several moholean texts: Hugh

Walters's *The Mohole Mystery* (1968), DeLillo's *Ratner's Star* (1976), Karen Tei Yamashita's *Through the Arc of the Rainforest* (1990), Kim Stanley Robinson's *Red Mars* (1992), and Reza Negarestani's *Cyclonopedia: Complicity with Anonymous Materials* (2008). This chapter thinks of processes of drilling, excavating, and exhuming as inscriptive practices, etching a story of human industry upon the planet that necessarily includes humankind's extinction. The fictional narratives that I observe in this chapter imagine parallels between writing and undermining, writing as an act of engineering the planet.

Presenting their narratives as analogous expressions of geoengineering, these writers reconceive extinction as a gradual consequence being written by concurrent industrial practices. In each writer's work, Project Mohole's legacy surfaces in different ways and to different degrees. Walters, DeLillo, and Robinson refer to the concept explicitly, whereas Yamashita and Negarestani amplify the cultural anxieties born out of Mohole's speculative efforts. Together, their novels participate in crafting, along with Project Mohole itself, a sense of subterranean uncertainty that I call *speculative geology*. This uncertainty entails not just an epistemological gap but an existential worry: that the ground below our feet might turn out to be hollow, lacking the carboniferous remains that provide us with energy, or even horrifyingly alive, an agent in unforeseen ways.

Chapter 3 continues these subterranean concerns, but pairs them with concerns from above: specifically, issues of satellite surveillance and nuclear damage. Unlike previous studies that have addressed the nuclear threat as visited upon the United States by foreign powers, however, I turn my attention to the nuclear anxieties embodied in the earthmoving fantasies of Project Plowshare and the surveillance network of orbital satellites. Although Plowshare experimented with what it called peaceful nuclear explosions (PNEs), environmental groups saw the potential for vast ecological damage in the controlled detonations—damage that would eventually be realized in nuclear catastrophes such as occurred in the Three Mile Island and Chernobyl reactors. These nuclear anxieties had less to do with the apocalyptic dread of potential annihilation than with unpredictable consequences emanating from the scale of planned explosions. The height of atmospheric elevation provided human observers with a vantage (both physical and metaphorical) from which to comprehend the transformation of the planet's surface by atomic detonations. In this way, even the PNEs of Project Plowshare invited vertical speculations on the future of the earth.

The chapter focuses on three texts of varying length, style, and complexity: Don DeLillo's short story "Human Moments in World War III" (1983), Tim O'Brien's *The Nuclear Age* (1985), and Thomas Pynchon's *Gravity's Rainbow* (1973). DeLillo's and O'Brien's works both invoke the aerial perspectives of orbital technologies; "Human Moments" features two characters in an orbital space station, and the narrator of *The Nuclear Age* entertains perceptual fantasies of circling above the earth. Together, these texts illuminate a perspectival dimension that I call the *orbital field*: a narrative point of view that puts the planet into a new focus. Complementing this orbital space, O'Brien's narrator also digs a fallout shelter in his backyard and concocts a scheme for selling uranium to energy companies, combining the subterranean vector of speculative geology with the atmospheric anxieties of fallout. *The Nuclear Age* features several moments of aerial and geological contemplation, imagining its human narrator as inhabiting not a horizontal landscape but a vertical continuum, providing his satirical narrative with an often unhinged and disorienting tone. Finally, the chapter skips back in time to 1973 and *Gravity's Rainbow*. After the explicitly vertical and planetary perspectives of DeLillo and O'Brien, Pynchon's landmark text reveals itself to be an important genealogical marker—not only of postmodernist fiction but of environmentally concerned Anthropocene writing. This chapter attends to the novel's ecological characteristics and interests, and its framing of them within vertical dimensions implicit in wartime technologies. *Gravity's Rainbow* gives expression to an emergent planetary consciousness in which energy, verticality, and extinction are entangled, producing an experimental form that encourages new points of view.

The fourth chapter vocalizes a question the project's title begs: namely, *whose extinction?* Here, I reframe colonialism's relationship to midcentury science in light of longer racist histories in the United States. This chapter looks at several contemporary works that revolve around the lasting legacies of racism and slavery, and their associations with verticality: Colson Whitehead's *The Intuitionist* (1999) and *The Underground Railroad* (2016), Hari Kunzru's *White Tears* (2017), and Jesmyn Ward's *Sing, Unburied, Sing* (2017). Each of these works telegraphs the convergence of ecological damage and racial injustice, establishing a geophysical link between the land management practices of slavery in the Americas with the large-scale industrialism in the late twentieth century. In particular, these writers highlight the ways in which postindustrial institutions such as the modern carceral state, waste and pollution, policing, and earthmoving projects all emerge from the long history of slavery in the United States. The mid-twentieth-century vertical sciences thereby appear as one stage in the development of American land management, which finds its modern origins in the plantation.

In its focus on the racial dynamics that inform the Anthropocene, Chapter 4 attends to issues of oppression, exploitation, and labor that form a rich theoretical intersection between social and environmental justice. I elaborate this intersection through a concept that I call *fossil labor*, a practice of cyclical exploitation in which Black bodies are managerially forced to work the earth while simultaneously being associated or identified with the earth. This relationship gives rise to a sense of Black planetarity in which writers of color imagine a mode of radical resistance by aligning themselves (and their characters) with a planet that subverts efforts at imperial domination. Drawing on theories of racial geography and geology, I claim that these writers envision Black resistance as rising through geophysical matter, pushing back against White oppression by manifesting as an extinctive force. Just as Western science gives rise to the environmental hazards that invite extinction, White racism gives rise to the social hazards that undermine its institutions.

Writing Our Extinction ends with a short "underview" that considers the idea of resilience in the face of environmental collapse, and the ways in which planetary authorship and the extinction humanities can give us a nuanced sense of recuperative agency. Looking at Octavia E. Butler's *Parable of the Sower* (1993), a work of Black planetarity not previously mentioned, this conclusion reminds readers of the significance that authorship and narrative have for marginalized and dispossessed communities. The destabilizing perspectives that accompany vertical science and planetary authorship reveal new accounts of our ecological place and representative strategies for telling the human story in ways that account for our differences. Planetary experience asks that we acknowledge such differences while working to imagine new modes of communication, empathy, and collective agency. Only through such imaginative work is there hope of writing resilience into the extinction we have authored thus far.

Earthly Language
Don DeLillo and the Novel
of the Anthropocene

Don DeLillo's Planetary Realism

As she flies over the American West, one of *Underworld*'s central characters, the visual artist Klara Sax, wonders at the potential signification that resides in geological features. In a brief passage, the narrator describes the widening earth from Klara's aerial vantage: "From the air, what was it like? The vast swept West, basin and range, you could almost detect the mineral content, the badland shale—it was the kind of immense and unsparing beauty that left you slightly subdued because you didn't know the natural language, the names of formations and mountain folds" (493).[1] The text follows this description with an interjected memory from Klara's youth, in which she remembers her father looking at images of the landscape from a different vantage—the slides of his View-Master stereoscope, with 3-D renderings of "his completely unreachable West" (493–494). Klara's memory segues into a sense of dissociation, her realization of the landscape's distinctly nonhuman quality: "She didn't know the West and she'd never flown above it in weather so clear. It looked young and untouched, it had the strangeness of worlds we'd never seen, it was not ours from up here, it was too flowingly new and strange—we hadn't settled it yet" (494). The final line carries vaguely colonial overtones, implicating the aerial perspective with the totalizing energies of domination. Moreover, Klara's language helpfully pinpoints the land's anachronistic quality when seen from above, its impression as both ancient—*pre*-historic even—and alien, otherworldly, science-fictional. The sequence passes through layers of media and mediation, from airplane window, to youthful nostalgia, to technological reproduction, back to airplane window, and finally to historical decontextualization. The text itself acts as another layer, figuring the West through Klara's point of view. Perceptually evasive, the landscape skirts around the edges of these frames, their limits intimating a massive existence beyond human perception.

The contrast between aerial view and stereoscopic reduction—viewed "in the kitchen because the light was better there" (494)—underscores the varied spatial and temporal scales involved in DeLillo's representation. In the span of several sentences, the narrative frame expands and contracts according to the views afforded by elevation and memory. The function of vertical space in such rhetorical maneuvers is paramount, highlighting the ways in which narrative scale adjusts according to a character's placement within the spatial matrix of the novel. Readers can imagine Klara traveling upward, the panoramic view of America spreading out below her, as though she is a point on graph, her perspective widening as she ascends the y-axis. Yet, it is not only her view of space that expands as she ascends, but her view of time; human history gives way to geological history, revealing the "flowingly new and strange" qualities of an earth prior to civilization. *Underworld* offers its readers multiple embedded scales of perception, mapped out along conditioning cofunctions: time and space on one hand, vertical and horizontal on another. This interplay of human and nonhuman perspectives stages confrontations among the multiple bodies and assemblages that characterize the novel's ecological content.

At over 800 pages, *Underworld* evinces a formal desire to embody history, and the book has long found praise from critics who identify it with a trend of post-Cold War revisionism, including John N. Duvall, Peter Knight, Phillip E. Wegner, and Daniel Grausam.[2] Structured loosely around a narrative of protagonist Nick Shay's life, the novel catalogues a host of associations, conversations, personal histories, and cultural mysteries that give dark shape to the second half of the twentieth century. Sarah Wasserman rightly describes DeLillo as "a writer with curatorial impulses, one whose novels preserve both relic and refuse as they march toward a millennial horizon."[3] *Underworld* is no exception, and its publication in 1997 puts it in the strategic position of diagnosing the social ills that plague the American century. As its title suggests, *Underworld* is about the largely unseen, mostly violent, and almost ubiquitously corrupt systems and practices of American culture after World War II. These systems and practices manifest, much like the novel's experimental perspectives, along a vertical axis: "For every atmospheric blast," thinks DeLillo's comical rendering of J. Edgar Hoover, "every glimpse we get of the bared force of nature, that weird peeled eyeball exploding over the desert—for every one of these he reckons a hundred plots go underground, to spawn and skein"

(51). These lines from the novel's famous prologue, titled "The Triumph of Death" (and previously released as the short novella *Pafko at the Wall* in 1992), set the stage for the remainder of the narrative. The coordination of political complexity and American leisure reveals the broad cultural landscape that *Underworld* takes for its textual playground.

The prologue's targeted associations—between politics and leisure, objects and histories, events and plots—introduce the novel's attention to scale, with respect to both its challenging temporal structure and ecological gestures. Exploring issues of industrialism, commodification, nuclear experimentation, and waste, *Underworld* exhibits concerns toward human culture's impact on the global environment, even if it is not usually described as a work of environmental fiction. In fact, critics have often puzzled over the novel's size and style, unsure whether it falls closer to formal realism or to surreal defamiliarization.[4] I argue that it is in the discrepancies between DeLillo's realism and his sprawling defamiliarization of postindustrial modernity that we can identify the novel's Anthropocene focus: its weaving together of different scales, its uneasy cohesion of perspectives. Throughout the text, the narrative zooms in and out on various characters, casting light on both their intimate experiences and the ecological networks in which they are enmeshed. To achieve this cinematic effect, the novel frequently adopts a vertical perspective, ascending far above the planet's surface and burrowing into its strata. The text also links this strategy of spatial maneuvering to a sense of temporal magnitude and discontinuity, recasting human history within the geological catalogue of deep time. In doing so, *Underworld* reveals the human species' precarious existence on earth, its creation of an archival geology, and the virtual presence of our extinction that already lurks in the foundations of modern society.

These elements inform what I call *Underworld*'s planetary realism: its appeals to strategies of realist and historical fiction set in motion alongside descriptions of a strikingly nonhuman world. According to Amitav Ghosh, such combinations have not come easily to the "mansion of serious fiction," which tends to award its narrative energies to human affairs.[5] This makes sense when we consider the historical context of Ghosh's argument—that the rise of the novel is intimately tied to socioeconomic conditions, and that that association has promoted the genre's formal attention to the details of daily life. In her perceptive reading of Ghosh's *The Great Derangement*, Thangam Ravindranathan notes that, according to Ghosh, the Anthropocene and realism exist in an inverse relation to one another: that as global temperatures warm and sea levels rise, the novel tells a story "of the increasing safety and suitability—read the industrial, capitalist, ever more fuel-intensive securing, use, and development—of earth's spaces for modern human life."[6] Viewed in this way, what we call "realism" in the novel is strikingly counterintuitive, draping a veil of comfort and security over an increasingly insecure and uncomfortable world. Kate Marshall suggests that the literary realism of the Anthropocene is a metacommentary on fictional modes, and that such texts "recast some of these genre questions—questions tied to the reflexive self-understanding of genre itself—in perspectival experiments and novel fictional worlds."[7] In other words, Anthropocene novels ask what becomes of realism when deployed in the service of speculative worlds ravaged by the excesses of late capitalism—worlds whose imagined existence derives from the same history that birthed the eighteenth-century realist novel. It is not only that, within this framework, conventional realist fictions are not up to the task of portraying the Anthropocene, but that the Anthropocene betrays the illusory, if not science-fictional, landscapes of realism.[8]

One reaction to this ostensible representational impasse would be to reject Ghosh's emphasis on "serious fiction" and turn our attention to the purportedly unserious work of genre fiction. Such a move merely preserves the gatekeeping impulse that imposes a categorical distinction between the two, however, and preserves narrow definitions of both realism and what we might generally call *speculative fiction*. If we instead stick with the difficult indeterminacy between realist narrative and the Anthropocene, then we might begin to ask ourselves in what ways the Anthropocene does not simply betray realism as illusory but rather spotlights the ways that realist fiction stages socioecological conflicts between the human and nonhuman, between civilization and the planet at large. This geological or planetary realism wrestles with the simultaneous presentation and imbrication of multiple scales and embedded histories, intuiting future calamity—up to and including human extinction—within the experience of a narrative present.[9] More than simply an element of thematic concern, extinction shapes narrative form. The advent of the Anthropocene promotes new interactions between realism and speculative writing, affording literary critics multiple opportunities to theorize this dynamic.

As a work of planetary realism, *Underworld* constitutes one such particularly salient opportunity. DeLillo's encyclopedic novel begins in 1951 and ends in the early 1990s, covering a period during which attitudes toward, and understandings of, the environment underwent significant changes. Its historical outlook also corresponds to the accelerating industrial and scientific pursuits of the 1960s, and the narrative addresses several of these pursuits directly, including nuclear testing in the American Southwest, the NASA space program, and the manufacturing of household chemicals. These pursuits form a pivotal moment in Anthropocene history, characterized by "exponential expansion in travel, industrial production, and globalization that generate a compounding problem for earth systems today," as Joseph Masco writes.[10] DeLillo incorporates these developments into *Underworld* through the adoption of their vertical perspectives: aerial views of earthworks and dump sites in the Nevada desert, for example, and descriptions of underground facilities and of the *Challenger* space shuttle explosion. Such images not only signal key cultural elements that inform the novel's thematic concerns; they also become narrative strategies for oscillating between scales, temporal and spatial. Through its multiply vertical perspectives, *Underworld* gives its readers glimpses of the imbricated and interlinked sites of human experience and earth systems. It unveils the planet as something written, a work of geological literature.

The example of DeLillo's novel demonstrates that planetary realism emerges as a mode attentive to the enmeshment and decoherence of forms at scales ranging from the humanly personal to the microscopically indiscernible to the geologically vast. It extends its perspectives upward into the stratosphere and downward into the strata, backward into the prehistoric past and forward into the science-fictional future. For literary critics, the concept of the Anthropocene raises crucial questions not only for how we read texts but also how we consider the practice of critique itself. The Anthropocene re-articulates literary history as a process that both reflects upon the world and physically composes it, becoming a portion of its sedimental archive. As an Anthropocene novel, *Underworld* explores what it would look like for a novel to enter the nonhuman scale of the planetary, rather than rescale the planetary to the comfortable level of the human—to engage with what Mark McGurl calls "a deep perplexity surrounding the scale of the human in what we have recently come to call the Anthropocene."[11] In this way, novels of the

Anthropocene engage the problem of communicating knowledge and experience across different scales, and facilitate such communication by invoking strategies found in the vertical sciences.

Scale is one of *Underworld*'s central features, and not one that it incorporates merely thematically but also formally and stylistically. It brings the matter of scale to bear on aesthetic questions, as in the passage describing Klara staring down from her airplane window. The vertical axis of elevation reframes the earth, casting an "immense and unsparing beauty" upon the landscape, which loses the horizon as its vanishing point. This loss of horizon is a crucial element of the novel's scalar readjustment, and its consequences are felt throughout, even when characters remain firmly rooted to the ground. The vertical dimension expresses—conceptually and aesthetically—the displacement of the human in geological time, a development inaugurated by the Anthropocene itself. My primary concern in this chapter lies with what I take to be *Underworld*'s aesthetic strategy as it relates to human existence in the Anthropocene: the text's ability to articulate the decoherence between the scales of human knowledge and vision and those of planetary time and motion. Unlike size, scale is not something we can point to; it does not describe the measurable dimensions of a work, but the relational dynamics that tie those dimensions together. The effort of Anthropocene fiction forges a critical convergence between realist language and the disorienting vortex of scalar disarray, often by depicting characters' realization of expansion and/ or contraction in spatiotemporal perception. In effect, *Underworld* unmasks DeLillo as not merely a quintessential postwar novelist but, further, a writer of planetary realism for the Anthropocene era. When we situate the novel's nonlinear narrative oscillations next to its sweeping depictions of the American landscape and the atmospheric regions of air travel, we perceive its contents in a new light, as well as discerning the ways that its formal structure shifts to accommodate perspectives on different scales, including the nonhuman. One of *Underworld*'s major aesthetic achievements lies in its emphasis on the sensitivity of spatial and temporal representation when dealing with the scale of the Anthropocene. The novel coordinates its characters' experiences of shifting scales through the interaction of vertical and horizontal perspectives, and mobilizes a spatiotemporal dynamic as an aesthetic response to humanity's existence in the Anthropocene.

To bring this dynamic into focus, I draw parallels between DeLillo's strategies of narrative representation and the aesthetic speculations laid out by land artist Robert Smithson—a central figure in the emergence of vertical aesthetics in the 1960s. *Underworld* features its own fictional visual artist in the character of Klara, offering a point of substantive crossover between narrative and visual strategies. Smithson's writings explore the complexities of scale in visual art, particularly postwar minimalism and the artist's own earthworks; and Klara's sprawling art project, set in the Nevada desert, offers a starting point for understanding how land art's appropriation of physical space impacts the expression of literary scale. By refracting the structure and style of DeLillo's text through the prism of Smithson's experimental approach, we can appreciate the complexity of scale in the Anthropocene novel.[12]

Reframing Planetary Landscapes

Aesthetically speaking, the idea of the horizon grounds visual access to an earthbound phenomenological experience. Discussing its role in art history, Hito Steyerl suggests that, until the nineteenth century, the horizon provided "an important tool for the construction of the optical paradigms that came to define modernity, the most important paradigm being that of so-called linear perspective."[13] Verticality disrupts this paradigm, reorienting what Smithson once maligned as the "old landscape of naturalism and realism."[14] Associated with the values and principles of humanism, naturalist and realist aesthetics embody a set of limited techniques from which twentieth-century art needed to break away. In Smithson's case, this meant pursuing the experimental strategies of land art and his concept of the non-site; DeLillo repurposes these strategies for literary aesthetics, exploring what becomes of human perception and experience within the suprahuman scales of the Anthropocene. *Underworld* configures the experimental materialities of postwar visual art and technology within the interplay of vertical and horizontal narrative perspectives to vivify an ecological sense of planetary being, beginning with the image of the airplane. Upon reaching the passages cited at the beginning of this essay, when Klara stares down at the American landscape from an airplane window, it becomes clear for readers that this moment in her life is formative for her eventual career as an artist, to which DeLillo introduces us earlier.

As he drives out to find Klara's mysterious project in the Nevada desert, protagonist Nick Shay notes the starkness of the region: "Heat shimmer rising on the empty flats. A bled-white sky with ticky breezes raking dust across the windshield. And the species factually absent from the scene—except for me, of course, and I was barely there" (63). Unlike Klara's passages later in the text, Nick's are narrated in the first person. DeLillo situates readers with him in the landscape, draws them into the resolutely human perspective of his protagonist driving through the nonhuman dunes. Yet Nick's perspective is a diminished one, "barely there," threatening to vanish on the sands like a mirage. Although told through Nick's perspective, the passage emphasizes the disparity between human subjectivity and the planet: "It was all distance. It was hardpan and sky and a wafer trace of mountain, low and crouched out there, mountain or cloud, cat-shaped, catamount—how human it is to see a thing as something else" (64). Nick anthropomorphizes the landscape, imagining distant mountains as domesticated animals. In a single comment, the novel sweeps from scales too vast for human perception to those contained within our social environment. The first-person narration reduces the landscape even as it acknowledges its nonhuman extent.

The flat panorama of the desert gives way to Klara's ambitious art project involving derelict military aircraft, a scene that unites the horizontal dimension of the desert with the vertical dimension of air travel. Klara identifies the planes as B-52s, connecting the scrap and waste matter of her art with the ruins produced by aerial bombardments during World War II, as well as with the American bombers "that used to carry nuclear bombs, ta-da, ta-da, out across the world" (70). The site of her project overlaps with that of the history of U.S. nuclear rehearsals, coordinating the temporal and spatial immensities of the Nevadan landscape with the global theater of war.[15] Klara's project is spread out not only in space but in time—the time of geology and isotopic decay. It embodies a nexus at which the dimensions of the horizontal and the vertical meet the dimensions of space and time. From this early episode, *Underworld* vacillates along temporal and spatial continuums. Klara effectively sums up this narrative technique when explaining the motivations behind her art project: "This is a landscape painting in which we use the landscape itself. The desert is central to this piece. It's the surround. It's the framing device. It's the four-part horizon" (70). This spatial repositioning happens within the narrative content, but it also signals something occurring at the level of perspective. Klara wants to move beyond the limits of landscape painting, much like Smithson; and much like Smithson, this movement is both temporal and spatial.

DeLillo integrates Klara's art into the narrative of *Underworld* as an expression of the novel's evolved perspective, by which it attempts to render textually something beyond the narrative scale: namely, the spatiotemporal vastness of the Anthropocene and geological time. Her art aesthetically reorganizes itself in space, but it also historically orients itself in relation to the past: "The desert bears the visible signs of all the detonations we set off," she tells Nick; "All the craters and warning signs and no-go areas and burial markers, the sites where debris is buried" (71). The textuality of the landscape marks the feedback loop of human industry and geological change, performing the very entanglement of the Anthropocene and presenting American history as embedded in the geological strata of the American landscape. Klara's project reinforces this entanglement by overlaying a vertical perspective along a horizontal canvas, underscored by Nick's decision to gain an elevated perspective from which to view the planes, appearing "in broad formation across the bleached bottom of the world" (83). Their pattern establishes a monumental vista before the spectator's eye, the vertical demand challenging the scale of human perception: "She wanted us to see a single mass, not a collection of objects," Nick realizes; "She wanted our interest to be evenly spaced. She insisted that our eyes go slowly over the piece. She invited us to see the land dimension, horizonwide, in which the work was set" (83–84). The embedded frame of Klara's project serves as a formal complement to the novel, which employs spatial excess to draw its readers into the temporal flux of the Anthropocene.

The novel renders the vertical orientation of Klara's work explicit when Nick and his wife, Marian, fly over the finished project in a hot air balloon. Looking down from above, in a manner reminiscent of Klara's aerial view from the airplane window, Nick and Marian witness the artwork as part of the earth, a symbiosis of color and rock: "The piece had a great riverine wash, a broad arc of sage green or maybe mustard green with brushy gray disturbances, and it curved from the southeast corner up and across the north edge, touching nearly a third of the massed aircraft, several planes completely covered in the pigment—the work's circulating fluid, naming the pace, holding the surface together" (125). For Nick, the finished work heralds something apocalyptic, "painted to remark the end of an age and the beginning of something so different only a vision such as this might suffice to augur it," while Marian admits that she "can never look at a painting the same way again" (126). The challenge of the work's perspective lies in its subversion of the horizontal landscape, its reorientation of aesthetics on a planetary scale, leading Nick to compare it with "the land art of some lost Andean people" (126). The vertical perspective of Klara's work allows viewers to consider it within geological time—to see it as part of a human history embedded within a larger natural history. *Underworld* presents Klara's work, along with several other textual figures, as strategies for aesthetically and conceptually engaging the Anthropocene, and for bringing its readership into conversation with their geological emplacement.

Expanding on Klara's use of waste in the form of decommissioned aircraft, *Underworld* envisions a veritable infrastructure of perpetual obsolescence. As consumption reached unprecedented levels after World War II, disused commodities found their way to the world's dump sites. In DeLillo's novel, this gives rise to physical landscapes of manufactured and naturally occurring composites, such as the novel's depiction of the Fresh Kills landfill on Staten Island—a magnificent and memorable passage in which Nick's colleague Brian Glassic encounters the landfill after a long and winding drive on the New Jersey Turnpike:

> Three thousand acres of mountained garbage, contoured and road-graded, with bulldozers pushing waves of refuse onto the active face. Brian felt invigorated, looking at the scene. Barges unloading, sweeper boats poking through the kills to pick up stray waste. He saw a maintenance crew working on drainpipes high on the angled setbacks that were designed to control the runoff of rainwater. Other figures in masks and butylene suits were gathered at the base of the structure to inspect isolated material for toxic content. It was science fiction and prehistory, garbage arriving twenty-four hours a day, hundreds of workers, vehicles with metal rollers compacting the trash, bucket augers digging vents for methane gas, the gulls diving and crying, a line of snouted trucks sucking in loose litter. (184)

In this passage, garbage becomes a landscape in its own right, assuming the appearance of mountainside agriculture replete with terraces. DeLillo blends natural and artificial imagery, inflecting the trash heaps of Fresh Kills with a geological dimension; crews of humans excavate the landfill like an archaeological dig, releasing pockets of gas to stabilize the site. This blending of the natural and artificial, geological and human histories, inheres even in the name Fresh Kills: derived from the Dutch *kille*, the name translates into "fresh body of water." Yet the location's eventual transformation into a waste dump, and its tragic historical association with the 9/11 World Trade Center attacks, establish an unsettling connection with the ostensible meaning of the name's modern appearance.[16]

Throughout *Underworld*, waste acts as a connective tissue between human history and terrestrial history, the substance that weighs humanity down into the accumulative layers of the earth. Wasserman argues that DeLillo's geographies of waste highlight "the impoverished environment that the novel's characters inhabit," while Rachele Dini suggests that DeLillo's topographies of waste reveal often unnoticed means of salvage and reuse in postindustrial capitalism.[17] David J. Alworth also notes the centrality of waste in the narrative, going so far as to claim that the garbage dump is "DeLillo's answer to the White Whale, a densely symbolic figure within a Great American Novel."[18] Alworth suggests that although the novel features the dump as a prominent figurative image, it does not formally embody a dump, as do the novels William S. Burroughs wrote using the cut-up method.[19] The point is well made, and I propose that *Underworld* resists approximating a dump formally because it has its sights set on something more expansive: it situates human civilization's production of waste as part of the Anthropocene, embedded within the deep time of geological history. In this respect, its form reflects the very indeterminacy between modernity and prehistory, and between the earth's surface and its geological depths.

The novel's "cosmologists of waste," Nick Shay and his colleagues, comment frequently on the spatiotemporal logic of waste: "I traveled to the coastal lowlands of Texas and watched men in moon suits bury drums of dangerous waste in subterranean salt beds many millions of years old, dried-out remnants of a Mesozoic ocean" (88). As with Klara's aerial perspective on the American West, elevation informs temporal awareness. The prospect of digging and excavation opens onto experiences of the religious occult, as Nick suggests that modern humanity "entomb[s] contaminated waste with a sense of reverence and dread" (88). DeLillo knowingly walks a fine line between the rationalization and mystification of waste, but in a way that critically blurs distinctions between the two. Even if the act of burying waste carries quasi-religious connotations, the experience of being nearer to the earth, or in the earth, produces an awareness of nonhuman scales: "People look at their garbage differently now," Nick muses, "seeing every bottle and crushed carton in a planetary context" (88).

In *Underworld*'s exploration of waste, organic and inorganic do not commingle so much as fuse, embodying an associative mass in which geological time coagulates into an unreal primal scene of human history. The scene is less a return of the repressed than a vivid socialization of the repressed, an introduction of the repressed into the social world. Waste is not hidden in *Underworld*, but routinely seen and discussed, even celebrated: "Bring garbage into the open," says the novel's self-proclaimed waste theorist, Jesse Detwiler; "Let people see it and respect it. Don't hide your waste facilities. Make an architecture of waste" (286). DeLillo achieves this effect by presenting Brian's encounter with Fresh Kills in aestheticized language, even going so far as to invoke a powerful and well-known analogy from art history: sculptor Tony Smith's nighttime drive down the unfinished New Jersey Turnpike, the experience of which manifests for Smith as the "end of art."[20] Famously maligned by Michael Fried in "Art and Objecthood" (1967), Smith's drive became representative of a paradigm shift in aesthetic representation: "What replaces the object—what does the same job of distancing or isolating the beholder, of making him a subject, that the object did in a closed room—is above all the endlessness, or objectlessness, of the approach or onrush of perspective."[21] In *Underworld*, DeLillo stages Brian's encounter with Fresh Kills as the climax of a drive "along turnpikes and skyways," in which the turnpike itself seems to dissipate: "When he went past Newark Airport he realized he'd overshot all the turnoffs and their related options. He looked for a friendly exit, untrucked and rural, and found himself sometime later on a two-lane blacktop that wended uncertainly through cattail mires" (183). The turnpike devolves into a state reminiscent of its incompleteness during Smith's drive. Unlike the abstract "end of art" that Smith experiences, however, *Underworld* offers its readers an aestheticized, otherworldly description of Fresh Kills—a perspective in which human history collapses into the alien expanse of planetary time.

As with the presence of Klara Sax, the novel's incorporation of Fresh Kills offers another productive connection with the history of American art. Broadly speaking, the disagreement between Fried and Smith embodies in miniature the postwar shift in the 1960s to a vertical aesthetic, a perspective through which something like Smith's experience might be formalized. In his 1967 essay "Towards the Development of an Air Terminal Site," Smithson reimagines Smith's road trip as a kind of text that might be read from above: "In a sense, the 'dark pavement' could be considered a 'vast sentence,' and the things perceived along it, 'punctuation marks.'"[22] It is equally revealing that Smithson took issue with Fried's "Art and Objecthood," voicing his objections in *Artforum*. Smithson's language in this response employs the rhetoric of endless temporality, yet this endlessness gives way to an implicit spatiality that redefines the human relationship to time: "Could it be there is a double Michael Fried," he writes, "—the atemporal Fried and the temporal Fried? Consider a subdivided progression of 'Frieds' on millions of stages."[23] For all that Smithson is concerned with time, space is no less important for his aesthetic vision, which posits a warping of chronological time into the disorientations of modern space: "Exterior space gives way to the total vacuity of time," he wrote one year after his *Artforum* piece; "Time as a concrete aspect of mind mixed with things is attenuated into ever greater distances, that leave one fixed in a certain spot."[24] The spacetime dynamic tends toward the infinite for Smithson; space renders time an immeasurable experience, one that sinks into the perpetual cycles of the earth.

Despite Smithson's insistence on time in his writings, the visual element of his work introduces space as a category that invites our attention, and De-Lillo accepts this invitation in *Underworld*. Just as the novel transports its readers from the metropolitan center of New York to the barren swaths of Nevada, Smithson's art and writings reveal the importance of movement and displacement through landscapes—what Jennifer L. Roberts calls his "trademark dialectic between center and periphery."[25] Travel implies both temporal and spatial passage, a narrative transmission that only occurs through shifts in exterior space. These shifts coincide with temporal maneuvers that challenge the progressive linearity of human history, as in DeLillo's *Ratner's Star* (1976), whose coterie of scientists learns that a signal ostensibly received from outer space in fact originated on earth, but from a civilization so ancient that its sophistication was unknown to modern humanity. The temporal absurdity of the novel's revelation is amplified by its spatial (and science-fictional) premise, that of a signal received from a distant star system. This narrative twist reworks spatial distance into temporal vastness and repositions the earth not as an anthropic center but as one planet among countless others: "We come from the stars," the title character tells protagonist Billy Twillig; "Atoms from these stars are in our bones and nervous systems. We're stellar cinders, you and me."[26] The dialectic of center and periphery assumes cosmic proportions in *Ratner's Star*, displacing its human characters from the narrative comfort of their planetary existence.

Whereas *Ratner's Star* plays with deep time in a speculative manner that throws modern scientific notions of the Anthropocene into disarray, *Underworld* deals more seriously with the implications of the Anthropocene for our understanding of the human within time and space. It does not entertain the fantastic possibility of an ancient civilization more sophisticated than modern humanity but suggests that the science-fictional appearance of modernity is on par with the alien strangeness of prehistoric earth. To invoke Smithson once again, "Space Age and Stone Age attitudes overlap to form the Zero-Zero wherin [sic] the spaceman meets the brontosaurus in a Jurassic swamp on Mars."[27] Past, present, and future form a temporal continuum that exceeds the human, and DeLillo presents this extra-human time as one of collapsed spaces, anachronistic objects that occupy the same physical space. Science fiction blends into prehistory in Fresh Kills. Likewise, Nick compares the aircraft of Klara's project to underwater fauna, "finned like bottom creatures" (83), and later associates the oppressive noise and choking emissions of a traffic jam with the Cretaceous-Paleogene extinction event (623). In one sense, the coexistence of distinct spatial regions fulfills a metaphorical purpose; yet, DeLillo's novel also deploys space in a formal manner, as an organizer of narrative perspective—the aerial view experienced by Klara in the plane, and Brian's perspective on Fresh Kills as a kind of earthwork. In both cases, space is more than metaphorical because it organizes how readers experience the contents and temporal moves of the novel. We encounter its spaces not only as conceptual or mimetic figures, but as frames through which we perceive various narrative scales.

Archival Geology and Proleptic Extinction

The overlapping axes of space-time and vertical-horizontal in *Underworld*'s narrative shape the novel's aesthetics of scale and trouble the position of the human on the planet and in history. Subject to the harsh climate of the desert and other environmental pressures, human bodies experience a connectivity to the earth that reveals their embedment within multiple complex systems. *Underworld* extends this connectivity beyond the geological and climatological to the technological; and like the former, which archive human existence within the nonhuman scales of the Anthropocene, the latter marks humanity's existence and extinction as coextensive with the spatiotemporal dimensions of the planet. DeLillo emphasizes this point through the precariousness of aerial technologies, as when Klara's ex-husband, Albert Bronzini, recalls the explosion of the space shuttle *Challenger*: "The vapor stayed intact for some time, the astronauts fallen to sea but also still up there, graved in frozen smoke, and he lay awake in the night and saw that deep Atlantic sky and thought this death was soaring and clean, an exalted thing, a passing of the troubled body into vapor and flame, out above the world, monogrammed, the Y of dying young." Bronzini perceives the astronauts' remains as both descended and somehow textually emblazoned in the sky, the progress of the shuttle's ascent commemorating them in "the high faith of space" (227). Technology intersects with verticality, introducing the element of catastrophic death, humanity's existence and nonexistence archived in patterns of elevation. Like the layers of the earth and sky, *Underworld* serves as a textual repository that shifts depending on its perspective. It conveys the human experience within the Anthropocene through strategies of narrative dilation and contraction, elevation and excavation.

In his essay "Aerial Art," Smithson attributes the vertical axis to contemporary art, dissociating it from the flat perspective of the human. The essay is part of a series of proposals by Smithson and others for new terminal designs at the Dallas–Fort Worth Regional Airport, and Smithson does not downplay the connection between his aesthetic declaration and the technological opportunities afforded by air travel. As science and technology develop and become more complex, so too does humanity's comprehension of its scalar existence: "From the window of an airplane one can see drastic changes of scale, as one ascends and descends. The effect takes one from the dazzling to the monotonous in a short space of time."[28] Smithson does not say span of time, but *space* of time; the emphasis lies on the change in elevation, which occurs in less time due to technological advancements. *Underworld*'s Bronzini makes a similar observation: "How deep is time? How far down into the life of matter do we have to go before we understand what time is?" (222). For Bronzini, the issue of time involves a vertical descent into space, digging down into the matter of things. Such a perspective inevitably impacts the presentation of art, which Smithson argues must adapt to the intervention of new technologies: "There is no reason why one shouldn't look at art through a telescope," he writes.[29] Smithson's comment invokes the cosmic and macroscopic, the large scale that is too distant for human vision, whereas Bronzini's invokes the microscopic, that which is intimately close but infinitesimal in size. Both perspectives are vertically oriented, from the celestial to the terrestrial.

The emergence of the vertical, or aerial, perspective in *Underworld* simultaneously honors and complicates the aesthetic maneuver that Smithson lays out in "Aerial Art" and elsewhere. Klara's elevation above the West, Nick's elevation above Klara's art, the *Challenger* crew in suspended conflagration above the ocean, and Brian's aestheticized dislocation before Fresh Kills all invoke the kinds of scalar reorientation that Smithson pursues. The concatenation of these perspectives introduces a narrative sequentiality lacking from Smithson's primarily visual approach.[30] DeLillo's novel explores what happens when the spatial displacements of earthworks are employed as organizing elements of narrative, and coordinates these displacements at the meeting points of vertical and horizontal perspectives. On one hand, this coordination of the vertical and horizontal reflects what Phillip Wegner calls *Underworld*'s "neo-realis[m]," which maps "the increasing obsolescence during the latter stages of the Cold War period of the older nation-states and system of nation-states and the emergence of a new *global* social and spatial formation" (italics in original).[31] On the other, it recalls DeLillo's own description of the novel as "the last modernist gasp," acknowledging something more like a non-realist style confronting its exhaustive limits. This apparent disparity in how to read *Underworld*—as last-ditch modernism or adventurous neo-realism—speaks to its confusing assemblage of nonhuman spaces and anachronistic details. These topical and stylistic oscillations signal its effort, as an Anthropocene novel, to compose information on different scales. *Underworld* sutures these scales together by performing a concept central to its narrative and familiar to its critics: systemic connectivity.

DeLillo's fascination with systems has long been a topic of critical discussion, going back at least to Tom LeClair's *In the Loop: Don DeLillo and the Systems Novel* (1987), while DeLillo has more recently opined that it is the responsibility of writers to "oppose systems."[32] I am less concerned in this chapter with the systems readings of DeLillo's fiction than with *Underworld*'s aestheticized expressions of scalar complexity—expressions that draw upon the concepts and models of systems thinking. One of the novel's most consistent figures of systemic complexity is that of the think tank where Nick's brother, Matt, works:

> There were people here who weren't sure whether they were doing weapons work. They were involved in exploratory research and didn't know exactly what happened to their findings, their simulations, the results they discovered or predicted. This is one of the underlying themes of systems business, where all the work connects at levels and geographic points far removed from the desk toil and lab projects of the researchers. (401)

The novel never makes clear exactly what the mission of the think tank is, but it has something to do with nuclear weapons research, as the narrator later clarifies. The premise of weapons testing is not only an example of systems operations within the novel but also reminds readers of Klara's work in the Nevada desert, her aestheticization of aircraft bombers. The narrator in this section of the novel also draws readers' attentions to the interplay of culture and geology, situating the human within a planetary scale, "the dune fields, the alkali flats, the whiteness, the whole white sea-bottomed world, the lines of white haze in the distance" (402). Dug into the ground, the think tank is part of the novel's index of Anthropocene space. Named "the Pocket" after a subterranean gopher, it literally occupies the geological strata of the earth (402).[33]

The Pocket's vertical dimension—its location not along the landscape, but beneath it—also inheres in its clandestine operations, which include taking satellite photographs of the earth's surface. Although likely for surveillance purposes, the photos draw Matt's attention to the geographical and geological aspects of the planet, recalling Smithson's proposal for an aerial aesthetic: "The pictures were false-color composites that revealed signs of soil erosion, geological fracture and a hundred other events and features. They showed stress and drift and industrial ravage" (415). The narrator's description explicitly invokes the concept of the Anthropocene, detailing the impact of humanity's expanse upon the earth. As Matt continues to look at the images, he intuits "hidden meanings" in the planet's contours: "a secondary beauty in the world, ordinarily unseen, some hallucinatory fuse of exactitude and rapture" (415). These hidden meanings aren't conceptual, but somehow expressive and aesthetic, implicit in the large-scale patterns of the earth's surface. For characters like Matt, the earth exhibits its own kind of language, one reminiscent of Smithson's artwork *A Heap of Language* (1966)—that is, language as "printed matter."[34]

The notion of a geological or earthly language in *Underworld* represents an evolution in DeLillo's fiction that begins at least with *Great Jones Street* (1973), continues through *Ratner's Star*, *The Names* (1982), and "Human Moments in World War III" (1983), and beyond *Underworld*, in *Point Omega* (2010). In *Great Jones Street*, DeLillo toys with such notions as "latent history [. . .] like the action of bacteria or the rising and falling of mountain ranges."[35] DeLillo magnifies the connection between signification and geological matter in *Ratner's Star*, which satirically explores mathematics as a form of primordial language, a symbolic system that might unveil "the name of names,"[36] while *The Names* makes the fantasy of a primordial language its central premise. "Human Moments in World War III" applies the practice of naming to planetary features, as it depicts the routines and conversations of two astronauts in an orbital satellite who make a game of identifying geographical details. With the publication of *Underworld*, DeLillo brings this orbital fascination partially back down to earth, embedding his characters firmly in the deserts of the American West and the metropolitan concrete, and meditating on the collapse of human form and thought into the sedimentary matter of the planet.[37]

I characterize this evolution in DeLillo's fiction as a gradual means of lyrical and stylistic experimentation by which he aims to recover something like Smithson's *A Heap of Language* for the aesthetic purposes of literary art. If there remains a banal realism to DeLillo's prose, an accessibility that mimics ordinary language, the author complicates this through repeated excursions into the material impact of language: "Not what people mean but what they say," one character explains in *The Names*; "Intended meaning is beside the point. The word is all that matters."[38] The word matters not only because it means, but because it *is* matter, *is* material. By the time we get to *Underworld*, these expressions of language's physicality—of its sound and shape— metastasize into a planetary substance, the natural language of a landscape. Language detaches itself from the human scale, entering a phase of existence reminiscent of geological strata, an underworld of words. The novel presents its readers with the challenge of encountering words, at the level of narrative, as both temporal and spatial phenomena. They compose both a sequence of events and an assemblage of layers. *Underworld* fashions its readers as time travelers as well as geologists and archaeologists, actively burying themselves in what Jussi Parikka calls the "mixed semiotics" of the earth's signifying power.[39]

In this respect, *Underworld* excavates not only the dark histories of postwar America's corrupted corporate underbelly but also a history of scale itself: the emergent technological, geopolitical, and climatological systems that make themselves widely known in the second half of the twentieth century. The sense of language sinking into the earth, becoming a part of the earth, stages a spatial rendering of linguistic experience. If it continues to organize our temporal perceptions of the world, it does so only by occupying space in the world. DeLillo underscores this spatial element through the alignment of language with geological processes, but also through the edification of code in the late 1980s and 1990s, shortly before *Underworld* was published. In the novel's unsettling final section, the character Sister Edgar, who taught Matt and Nick when they were young, is immersed into a different kind of landscape than is imagined earlier in the novel: that of digital data.

The novel's memorable final pages are littered with references to code, connections, and cyberspace, to the point that its conclusion reads as a post hoc preface to the imagined future of William Gibson's seminal cyberpunk novel, *Neuromancer* (1984). DeLillo's simultaneously excessive and exciting depiction of virtual data linkage corresponds, however, to *Underworld*'s overarching concern with planetary scale. There emerges an analogy between data and strata, between the abundance of cultural codes and the accumulation of geological layers: "it's true that geography has moved inward and smallward," one of the characters muses in the novel's final section (788). Sister Edgar's death completes this insinuation, as the narrator describes her passing as an immortalization through code—a process in which all data are de-differentiated from one another through encryption. The novel culminates in an involution of code and geology, as DeLillo associates the codification of all language on the web with linguistic archaeology: "You can examine the word with a click, tracing its origins, development, earliest known use, its passage between languages, and you can summon the word in Sanskrit, Greek, Latin, and Arabic, in a thousand languages and dialects living and dead, and locate literary citations, and follow the word through the tunneled underworld of its ancestral roots" (826).

In these final paragraphs, readers of *Underworld* grapple with its final scalar conceit, the planetary mediation of language itself. Despite a brief period of speculative excitement when the advent of cybernetic media reinvigorated the old Cartesian fantasy of the virtual mind, theorists quickly realized that, if anything, digital media in fact blurred the boundary between mind and body more radically than previously comprehended.[40] This collapse introduced the problem of scale into the heart of human experience. No longer able to associate experience with the immediate presence of mind, humanists were forced to consider the body as a medium: the connective tissue between mind and body, like the planetary tissues running through *Underworld*, exposes subjective experience to new orders of magnitude. The mind is not a hermetic theater, the sealed sanctum of the human, but a porous screen that assembles the human.

As the English novel emerged historically, with what critics have come to know as its formal realism, it evolved to accommodate the scaled perceptions of human experience: or as McGurl puts it, "the limits of the novel are defined by the limits of the human."[41] In modifying the raw material of the world to fit the expectations of their audience, novels asked readers to ignore their bodies—the printed matter of their pages, their formal arrangement—in favor of their minds, of the meanings they contained. What *Underworld* discovers in the concept of the Anthropocene is both a figuration and performance of the breakdown between mind and body, analogous to the breakdown between human and natural history. Language and history blend into the rocks and soil of the planet; human experience finds itself immersed in the nonhuman processes of geological time, erosion, extinction, continental drift. Readers encounter themselves as agents of both human and natural history—as a species of global change, and a species absent from the scene, virtually extinct.

By "virtually extinct," I mean two things: first, that humans still exist in DeLillo's novel; and second, that the novel's human characters encounter their extinction in the visual and encrypted archives of virtual media. An illicit viewing of the leaked Zapruder film causes Klara "to wonder if this home movie was some crude living likeness of the mind's own technology, the sort of death plot that runs in the mind, because it seemed so familiar, the footage did—it seemed a thing we might see, not see but know, a model of the nights when we are intimate with our own dying" (496). The humans in *Underworld* may be extant, alive, but they are also already, proleptically extinct; they inhabit an extinction already taking place. DeLillo creates this impression by imposing anticipations of futurity onto the cultural images and materials of the present. As schoolchildren, for example, Nick and Matt wear dog tags as a means to identify their corpses in the wake of a nuclear strike (717). In 1965, as Nick wanders the shadowed city streets during that year's failure of the Northeast power grid, he contemplates the mass cultural anxiety that occupies those trapped in subways and elevators: "The always seeping suspicion, paralysis, the thing implicit in the push-button city, that it will stop cold, leaving us helpless in the rat-eye dark, and then we begin to wonder, as I did, how the whole thing works anyway" (635). Death, extinction, and cultural obsolescence affirm themselves in the text of the novel, which entwines with the material structure of the planet, the "ancestral roots" of life and language. The earth becomes a receptacle for humanity's entry into the deep time of geological history, an event registered by intimations of extinction played out across the novel's material culture.

In *Imagining Extinction*, Ursula K. Heise points out that, in the twenty-first century, the Anthropocene itself emerges as a form of speculative fiction in which the present of our contemporary global age appears "as an already if incompletely materialized future."[42] Heise argues that we can view anthropogenic climate change as a real-world corollary to the fictive trope of terraforming, the artificial alteration of planetary atmosphere, and points to Bill McKibben's *Eaarth* (2011) and Naomi Oreskes and Erik Conway's *The Collapse of Western Civilization* (2014) as examples of recent texts that make this generic connection.[43] Yet there is another sense in which the Anthropocene may be viewed as a kind of speculative fiction—one that *Underworld* implies in its description of Fresh Kills as "science fiction and prehistory." Specifically, the Anthropocene is a speculative account that pits itself against the diminished scale of formal realism in the sense that the earth emerges as a record of human activity on the planet, as something on which the history of humans as geological agents can be seen and read. It is precisely through such speculative valences, counterintuitively, that *Underworld* achieves a kind of planetary realism. The text negotiates the representational ravine between narrative prose and unrelenting geology by reimagining geology as an archive.

Underworld's archival geology embeds the figure of the database within the earth, combining the commemorative impulse of elegy and history with the ineluctable accumulation of matter. As more elements and events fall into the geological record, they redistribute their impact on a relative basis. One major extinction event comes to look less important when viewed along a continuum of extinction events. The effect of the novel's deep-time database is to estrange the moment of the present, to reimagine the present not as the culmination of historical progress but as a contingent situation of geological processes. Deep time presents an accumulation of material in the manner of a database, yet this doesn't make that database free of ideological structure. To the contrary, databases function according to "the question of what can and cannot be remembered," as Geoffrey Bowker argues.[44] *Underworld* intervenes in this determining structure by configuring the earth as an archive so as to reveal what is usually forgotten—waste, ruin, noise. It narrates the disorienting relationship of humanity's, and human history's, relationship to the planet through the lens of the Anthropocene.

In DeLillo's planetary realism, speculation serves less as a generic or stylistic template than it does a signifier of the already alien present. In one of *Underworld*'s most explicit nods to the referential power of science fiction, Klara and others attend the screening of a fictional Sergei Eisenstein film, *Unterwelt*. If the eponym were not enough, DeLillo describes the film's strange contents:

> It seems you are watching a movie about a mad scientist. He sweeps through the frame, dressed in well-defined black and white, in layered robes, wielding an atomic ray gun. Figures move through crude rooms in some underground space. They are victims or prisoners, perhaps experimental subjects. A glimpse of a prisoner's face shows he is badly deformed and it is less shocking than funny. He has the sloped head, shallow jaw and protuberant lips of an earthworm—" (429)

The passage pairs a second-person perspective with commentary on Eisenstein's notoriously jarring camera angles—"In Eisenstein you note that the camera angle is a kind of dialectic" (429)—momentarily inviting readers to occupy Klara's place. To this perspectival twist, DeLillo adds a description of a film taking place underground, recalling the subterranean test sites for nuclear detonations, and connects the film to the science fiction genre: "Klara thought of the radiation monsters in Japanese science-fiction movies and looked down the aisle at Miles [Lightman], who was a scholar of the form" (430). The confluence of details in this passage—science fiction, verticality, nuclear testing, and cinematic form—signals *Underworld*'s self-conscious formal interrogation. DeLillo's novel does not amount to science fiction, at least not in terms of the latter's historical market appeal; but it acknowledges what we might call the science-fictional effects of its prose. DeLillo asks readers to consider the ways that a thematic or conceptual understanding of science fiction might be used to describe the narrative dynamics at work in *Underworld*.

This notion of science fiction as a kind of signifying term or conceptual category, rather than generic description, has gained traction recently among critics, some of whom seek to move away from science fiction per se and toward a sense of what Rebecca Evans calls *science fictionality*, a term she associates explicitly with the Anthropocene.[45] We find a similar mode of expression in Smithson's writings, which aren't science fiction per se but rather employ a science-fictional rhetoric in order to move, in Lytle Shaw's words, "from genre as binding horizon of discursive validity to a sequence of generic quotations as shifting siting mechanisms for arguments."[46] *Underworld* picks up this tradition in order to navigate its unstable generic modality, oscillating between scaled representations typical of realist fiction and radically rescaled expressions of vertical, planetary perspective, which the novel delivers via direct and indirect engagements with land art, postwar technology, industrial waste, and other cultural developments. DeLillo combines the confusing effects of Smithson's work with a speculative narrative consciousness, depicting human experience within the Anthropocene through a sustained awareness of scalar dynamics.

Underworld's modal oscillation complements its narrative attention to history, particularly its established chronological bookends, so to speak: 1951 and 1992. These years encompass the period not only of the Great Acceleration, as many scientists define it, but also the period of several revolutionary findings in climate science—from Roger Revelle and Hans Suess's groundbreaking 1957 paper on greenhouse gases and oceans, to the 1965 President's Science Advisory Committee report, to James Hansen's 1988 testimony before Congress, to the first synthesis report by the Intergovernmental Panel on Climate Change in 1990. Just as the novel oscillates between realism and nonrealism, it also oscillates along a temporal continuum roughly concomitant with cultural awareness of the Anthropocene. In the episodes I have examined, many of which revolve around horizontal and vertical spatial perspectives, the narrative temporality breaches its presumably contained historical scope. It performs a transhistorical operation whereby the anthropocentric vision of Cold War history gives way to the deeper impressions of geological time. The dominant geopolitical anxiety of nuclear war dovetails with the nonhuman timescale of isotopic decay, posing a challenge to the premises of narrative realism and speculation through the prospect of a cancelled future.

This relationship to the future transforms, however, when the futurity we encounter is that not only of annihilation but also of the deep time that surpasses annihilation. In this temporal flux, the past merges with the future, and the expanse of deep time rears its head from the geological impact of modern human civilization: "The landfill across the road is closed now," Nick reveals in his final narrated moments, "jammed to capacity, but gas keeps rising from the great earthen berm, methane, and it produces a wavering across the land and sky that deepens the aura of sacred work. It is like a fable in the writhing air of some ghost civilization, a shimmer of desert ruin" (809–810). Such moments intuit the future of humankind's extinction but perceive it as already taking place—as implicit in the very manifestations of industrial progress. In this late passage, as in Brian Glassic's encounter at Fresh Kills and Klara Sax's art project in the Nevada desert, *Underworld* reminds its readers of the ways in which they are intractably and ecologically bound to the planet.

Plot Holes
Anthropocene Fiction
After Project Mohole

Writing in the Moholean Anthropocene

Returning to Don DeLillo's 1976 novel *Ratner's Star*, we find a group of scientists in an underground think tank struggling to decipher a cryptic message received from outer space. One of the novel's eccentric cast of characters, Orang Mohole, eventually discovers that the message has not originated from space at all, but from an earthly civilization so ancient that history bears no record of it. It turns out the planet has drifted into a "value-dark dimension" that Orang narcissistically calls a "mohole," in which information is trapped and played back upon itself, giving rise to exponentially unpredictable outcomes and unknowable realities (180).[1] The ancient message only appears to arrive from deep space; in fact, it arrives from deep time. Despite its astrophysical and quantum characteristics, which resemble a black hole without the gravity, DeLillo's mohole inspires geological fetishes among the scientists on earth, particularly insofar as they realize the ancient civilization's remains are below their feet. One of the characters, archaeologist Maurice Wu, discovers that at a certain geological depth, ancient artifacts actually begin to grow more complex: "Man more advanced the deeper we dig" (321).

Orang Mohole's name invites comparisons between DeLillo and his postmodernist godfather, Thomas Pynchon, whose characters' names run the gamut from mildly amusing to riotously ludicrous; and like many of the inventive names in Pynchon's fiction, "Mohole" isn't unique to DeLillo's novel. It appears fifteen years earlier as the name for a scientific project carried out by the American Miscellaneous Society (AMSOC). In 1961, Project Mohole officially began when the drilling barge *CUSS I* took the first steps in removing sedimental layers from the seafloor in an initiative that today still sounds less like science than science fiction. The team aboard the ship sought to retrieve rock samples from the earth's mantle to determine more precisely the geological makeup of the planet's interior. Covering the expedition for *Life* magazine, John Steinbeck documented its progress: "This is the opening move in a long-term plan of exploration of the unknown two thirds of our planet that lies under the sea. We know less about this area than we do about the moon. Therefore this log will concern itself with men and events rather than with scientific conclusions."[2] The novelist's account of Project Mohole is rarely mentioned by literary scholars today, yet it represents a telling moment in which elements from the scientific imagination crossed over into the literary—a cultural intersection that produced apt comparisons with another vertical pursuit of the 1960s, the space race: "We spend treasures daily on fantastical sky rockets aimed feebly toward space," Steinbeck goes on to say: "Our lustful eyes turn to the moon, not as the Queen of the Night but as real estate. We spend and devise and dream toward the nearest star unreachable in a lifetime of travel. And meanwhile we know practically nothing of far the greater part of our home planet covered by the sea."[3] The allusion to Cold War tensions between the United States and the Soviet Union isn't unwarranted. In 1970, the Soviet Union began its own drilling project; since 1989, the Kola Superdeep Borehole in Russia is the deepest artificial point on the planet.[4]

The full history of Project Mohole goes back to 1957, when a team of geologists and engineers, with funding from the American Miscellaneous Society, proposed to investigate the cause of the Mohorovičić Discontinuity (named after Croatian geologist Andrija Mohorovičić), or Moho: a hypothesized change in material composition between the earth's crust and its mantle. Behind the ambitious enterprise of Project Mohole lay an institutional division between so-called fixists, who subscribed to a primarily static earth (aside from minor up-and-down shifts), and mobilists, who subscribed to Alfred Wegener's notion of continental drift, which would eventually inform the dominant theory of plate tectonics.[5] The scientists responsible for the project, who included geologist Harry Hess and oceanographer Roger Revelle, hoped that acquiring samples from the earth's mantle would put an end to debates between fixists and mobilists. The controversy was more than a minor squabble, heralding a paradigm shift in the history of geology. Project Mohole offered one potential resolution—a monumental, if ultimately unrealized, vision of scientific intervention and exploration.[6]

Today, the efforts of Project Mohole look like a strange fabulation, and have inspired at least a few science-fictional renderings, including *Ratner's Star* itself.[7] Eight years before DeLillo's novel, British author Hugh Walters published *The Mohole Mystery* (1968) as part of his *Chris Godfrey of U.N.E.X.A.* series, a *Hardy Boys*-esque sci-fi series about a group of young astronauts. Released as *The Mohole Menace* in the United States, the novel concerns a successful drilling effort that reveals a vast subterranean cavern within the planet's mantle, and is the only installment in the series in which the protagonists venture underground rather than into space. Kim Stanley Robinson invoked the project in his 1992 science fiction work *Red Mars*, as human colonizers drill moholes to release geothermal energy and warm the Martian atmosphere. *Ratner's Star* presents a more fanciful but no less relevant extrapolation of the project, imagining its planned terrestrial hole as bored through the fabric of the universe. The information it unearths rises from deep space (both outer space and the subterranean depths) and from deep time.

Although ostensibly a spatial undertaking, Project Mohole's dig was also an exploration of geological evolution. It aspired to a comprehensive understanding of the earth's makeup and history, the story of its formation. This chapter argues that Project Mohole is a salient historical figure of geological anxieties and contradictions that begin to materialize in the twentieth century, and serves as a theatrical instance of the subterranean uncertainties that characterize a burgeoning geological imagination in post-moholean literature—what I call *speculative geologies*.[8] The following section unpacks the theoretical implications of these speculative geologies as they manifest in writings surrounding the project, including Steinbeck's documentation, Walters's novel, and comments by scientists involved in the project, particularly geologist Hollis Hedberg. The remainder of the chapter traces fictional samplings of speculative geology in post-moholean fiction: Robinson's *Red Mars*, Reza Negarestani's *Cyclonopedia: Complicity with Anonymous Materials* (2008), and Karen Tei Yamashita's *Through the Arc of the Rain Forest* (1990). Despite their significant formal differences, these novels offer accounts of modernity's geological unconscious after Project Mohole. Published across a range of decades, they afford us a critical and historical distance through which we can trace the continuing cultural import of the project—its understated effects on the literary imagination, but also its association with the fossil fuel industry and postwar energy concerns.

These novels also catalogue the postindustrial dynamics of the Great Acceleration, which names both the quantitative and qualitative shift in market growth and production after World War II. Although scholars continue to debate the origins of the Anthropocene, the post-World War II moment is agreed by many to be the beginning of, in Masco's words, "an emergent, petrochemical-based American society" that yielded ramifications across the globe.[9] In addition to the accumulation of waste in an era of baked-in obsolescence, the Great Acceleration also saw the postwar frenzy of oil extraction and refinement, methods for which evolved out of engineering feats such as Project Mohole. For this reason, I refer in this chapter to the period of the Great Acceleration as the Moholean Anthropocene. What we discover in works of literature from this period is not the explicit (or much less realist) depiction of methods like drilling or fracking, but the fictive rendering of resource extraction's speculative premise: the unknown underground. In Negarestani's and Yamashita's works, this premise emerges as the agency of the planet itself—of the waste and dead matter that gets pressed down, reassembled, and then resurfaces in imaginatively imposing ways. The Anthropocene designates an epoch in which humans have become geological agents, but the Moholean Anthropocene reclaims agency for the planet. It expresses a sense in which the planet expresses back.

Project Mohole serves as my point of access for understanding these fictions of speculative geology because it marks a historical moment in which humanity considered the uncertainty beneath its feet, and pursued the fanciful heights (or, more appropriately, depths) that science dreams of reaching. *Ratner's Star* provides an appropriately weird entry into this conversation in its presentation of a mohole not as a tunnel dug into the earth, but as a warping of the cosmos. By contrast, Robinson's *Red Mars* reclaims Project Mohole's original geological significance, but transplants it to a different planet. Its speculative geology manifests through a vision of geological practice in an alien context. Drilled for the purpose of geothermal energy, *Red Mars*'s moholes are an extension of the twentieth-century energy industry on earth. Delivered in a scientifically realist prose style, Robinson's novel nonetheless emphasizes the estrangement of the Moholean Anthropocene by reimagining it in an extraterrestrial landscape. Negarestani's and Yamashita's novels depart from *Red Mars*'s scientific realism to pursue this connection even further through their stylized depictions of moholean exhumations of the planet, featuring ironic if also unsettling images of ways that geology itself strikes back at human exploration. *Cyclonopedia* engages this uncertainty in its coordination of geological science's complicity with the fossil fuel industry, and renders this complicity through its strange vision of Middle Eastern oil as part of a sentient terrestrial entity that parasites Western capitalism for its own ends. The figure of the Matacão in Yamashita's *Through the Arc of the Rain Forest* presents a different twist on moholean imagery, surfacing (literally) as a speculative stratigraphic layer made up of materials refined from petroleum.

In Negarestani's and Yamashita's novels, extraction assumes uncanny forms: as a conspiratorial network of conflict production in *Cyclonopedia*, and the return of repressed waste matter in *Through the Arc of the Rain Forest*. These images configure the unintended consequences of industrialism's *longue durée* as strong agential forces; they bestow these consequences with, if not quite intention, then what Karen Barad describes as "an ongoing flow of agency through which part of the world makes itself differentially intelligible to another part."[10] The irony is that, in making themselves "differentially intelligible," these consequences reveal themselves to be of human creation. They appear different, yet weirdly familiar. This sense of the purportedly inanimate world looping back to greet humankind is a fitting complement to Timothy Morton's description of the ecological uncanny: that "human being disturbs Earth and its lifeforms in its desperate and disturbing attempt to rid itself of disturbance."[11] Through their various speculative geologies, Negarestani and Yamashita trouble humankind's status in the Anthropocene; in response to the capitalist and imperialist drives to access and own the underground, the underground confronts humankind with the incalculable threat of extinction.

By invoking the Anthropocene, I frame these texts not merely as part of a moholean history, but as part of a post-1980s cultural awareness of environmental crisis wrought by human industry. Their intense focus on geological agency, planetary complexity, and the ineluctability of extinction augured by the fossil economy aligns them with a variegated tradition of Anthropocene writing that also includes physicist James Hansen's 1988 Senate testimony on increased carbon dioxide in the atmosphere, Bill McKibben's *The End of Nature* (1989), and the First Assessment Report from the Intergovernmental Panel on Climate Change (1990). Taken together, their anticipatory and speculative tones express what Stephanie Wakefield calls the "Anthropocene back loop," a period of experimental and unpredictable reorganization among geophysical systems.[12] I argue that these novels extrapolate from the moholean

1960s a sense of speculative geology informed and complicated by an evolving ecological tradition. Attentive to the social, political, and economic disparities that plague global capitalism, their works illustrate the asymmetrical manifestation of the Anthropocene on local and planetary scales and express the geological unconscious of postindustrial modernity. They reimagine the earth not as an antecedent ground on which humanity has built its culture, but as the artificial cultural ground that humanity has built. By literalizing the underground's incompleteness—both as physical hollowness and perpetual reconfiguration—they make explicit the extinctive tendency of Anthropocene existence.

Project Mohole and Geoengineering Extinction

Fantasies of the underground aren't unique to the post–World War II period, first becoming widespread in the nineteenth century—a host of imaginative works that "foretell the arrival of the extractive industries in all their gargantuan force," Robert MacFarlane writes.[13] Others, such as the nineteenth-century German writer Novalis, contemplated the potential vivacity of the underground and whether it was "possible that beneath our feet a world of its own is stirring in a great life."[14] Edgar Allan Poe, Jules Verne, and Willa Cather all ruminated on underground spaces throughout the nineteenth and early twentieth centuries; and in 1928, Arthur Conan Doyle's "When the World Screamed" envisioned a layer of the earth that seems to be alive, and cries out when breached. Jussi Parikka identifies these fictive explorations of the underground as part of an emergent cultural consciousness toward the planet, driven by increasing market demands for raw materials and minerals: "Theories of the Hollow Earth might not have persisted except in popular fiction, but the idea of the underground artificial infinity—now as a seemingly infinite resource too—gained ground."[15] Beyond the spheres of genre fiction and the Gothic, the underworld has found life everywhere from modernist prose to memoirs, suggesting powerful creative threads between the Anthropocene, literary tradition, and cultural history. As science and technology developed throughout the twentieth and twenty-first centuries, so too did attitudes toward the underground, shifting from fanciful presentations of vibrant worlds to speculative meditations on the geologies of human social life.

Tendrils of this subterranean imagination continue to creep into the cultural consciousness of the present. A recent inventive use of the hollow earth trope occurs in Negarestani's *Cyclonopedia*, in which the narrator offers an analogy between hollow portions of the earth and textuality, particularly Hidden Writing: "In books of Hidden Writing, the textual subtopia consists of plots, narrations and autonomous author-drones populating the ( ) hole complex of Hidden Writing" (62).[16] In Negarestani's novel, steganography figures as a kind of planetary inscription, adapting secretive discourses to geological timescales. Meanwhile, Yamashita's *Through the Arc of the Rain Forest* imagines the history of industrialized capitalism as a compressed layer beneath the earth's surface called the Matacão—a layer comprising petroleum by-products including postwar media technologies. As she weaves together her characters' plot threads, Yamashita reveals the ways that global media, finance, and the energy industry combine to form a narrative of planetary transformation. This geological genealogy from Project Mohole to *Cyclonopedia* reveals a framework that Mark McGurl has dubbed "cultural geology," in which human cultural codes (from global capital to hidden writing) find themselves repositioned within "a long now, a now whose duration is hard to measure but which is unquestionably eventful."[17] Cultural geology affords McGurl a method of reconceptualizing twentieth-century writing, particularly the always-shifting boundaries of modernism, postmodernism, and post-postmodernism. Subsumed under this new category, the fictions of Negarestani, Yamashita, and Robinson take on a common cultural gravity. They index a planetwide coming-to-consciousness of humanity as a geological agent.

These speculative geologies of contemporary fiction collectively express an uncertainty toward the ground, a suspicion that what we take to be solid is actually fluid, if not hollow: "I'll never feel safe now," one of the characters from *The Mohole Mystery* admits, "knowing that there's such a big hole under our feet" (37).[18] This anxiety toward a physical discontinuity translates into a philosophical suspicion toward *grounding*: that all postulated metaphysical truths are "the result of a process whose own ground is another, antecedent process extending backward in time."[19] The interminability of metaphysical grounding assumes a strikingly literal form in the earth sciences, in which the earth's fluidity and porosity threatens its legibility for human observers.[20] The precarity and unpredictability that accompany geological events such as earthquakes pose risks to practices of cultural organization. Yet there exists a feedback loop between geophysical stability and modern postindustrial society, as Lucy R. Lippard insists in her discussion of undermining: "pits and shafts that reflect culture, alter irreplaceable ecosystems, and generate new structures; undermining's physical consequences, its scars on the human body politic; undermining as what we are doing to our continent and to the planet when greed and inequity triumph."[21] Histories of land displacement and redistribution reveal the ground beneath our feet to be a porous and precarious admixture shot through by capital and industry. In a strong sense, these complex subterranean networks influence and even produce the land on which we walk.

Compared with the variegated and sometimes violent histories of North American resource extraction, the story of Project Mohole appears politically quaint. Having made barely a dent in the ocean floor, the project justifiably fails to win the attention of historians and critics engaged with the power dynamics and injustices involved in Indigenous land rights. By 1964, "Mohole had become No Hole," as oceanographer Walter Munk quips.[22] Yet its funding and organization betray a complicity with ongoing efforts in deep-sea oil drilling, as Steinbeck intimates in his piece for *Life*:

> If, as seems probable, the greatest part of the world's material wealth is under the sea, there will have to be a re-examination of international spheres of ownership and control. Twelve miles off almost any coast now belongs to anyone who can get there. The only reason the seas have been free is because no one wanted them except for transportation and defense. Available riches may change all that.[23]

He wasn't the only one to anticipate mineral wealth in the ocean floor; *CUSS I*, the barge designed for the purpose of drilling underwater, was named for the oil companies that funded its construction.[24] The moon might be desirable as "real estate," in Steinbeck's words, but the ocean floor promised to yield more accessible raw materials for the world's growing energy demands.

The oil industry's financial interests also made themselves known in other ways. Papers and presentations on Project Mohole were regularly hosted by the American Association of Petroleum Geologists; and in 1961 Hollis Hedberg, a professor of petroleum geology at Princeton (and stratigrapher for Gulf Oil), became chairman of the American Miscellaneous Society, overseeing the developments and feasibility of the project. Ten years later, Hedberg delivered "Petroleum and Progress in Geology" (1971) at the William Smith Lecture Series for the Geological Society of London, a clarion call in which he announced that humanity had entered "the Petroleum Age."[25] Focusing on petroleum's fluid consistency, he laid out an argument for the mineral's importance in the history of geological discovery. In particular, his paper notes that the financial incentives of the petroleum industry intersected with exploratory enterprises in science, insofar as the uncertain location of subterranean oil deposits resulted in "the geological investigation and study of many areas which would never have been looked at, had it been possible to determine more certainly, in advance, the presence or absence of commercial petroleum."[26] Hedberg credits the fossil fuel economy with making feasible geological expeditions in places where they might otherwise not have occurred; even when oil goes undiscovered, the potential financial boon justifies countless wayward digs. What's more, Hedberg goes on, these digs haven't been inconsequential for science, even if they were for the oil industry: "On what unsteady ground would rest so many of our geological hypotheses had we not been able to confirm or deny them by the ready and positive evidence of the drill?"[27] The reference to "ground" rings with a sense of dual meaning— explicitly, the conditional grounds of scientific hypothesis and experimentation; but implicitly, the shakiness and uncertainty of the physical ground, its consistency and composition.

Hedberg does not stop here. It is not only that the oil industry is responsible for intellectual windfalls in the scientific community but also that the subfield of petroleum geology (the scientific avatar of the oil industry) might well constitute the sum total of investigations within all geological sciences: "It early became evident that the breadth of petroleum geology was nearly that of all geology itself, that almost any contribution to the geology of a region was a contribution to its petroleum geology also, and that, vice versa, the requirements of petroleum geology called for accurate and detailed information from almost all of the many fields of geological investigation."[28] This discussion leads Hedberg to declare geology's debt to the economics of petroleum consumption—a dynamic relationship in which the emergence of the oil industry, "initially generated through the application of geological principles, carried along with it development and more and more refinement in the mother science which was so vital to its progress."[29] His perceptive if apologetic sentiment anticipates the inseparability of nature and culture now so well-known within theorizations of anthropogenic climate change: that "in times of global warming," as ecologist Andreas Malm declares, the "iron laws of economics and geophysics boost the past from behind."[30]

Malm's "iron laws" bespeak the Gordian knot of science and capital—the ways that achievements in the earth sciences are often inextricable from industrial development, especially in the twentieth century. We can see this inextricability play out in the case of Project Mohole. When AMSOC no longer wished to be involved with daily operations, oversight was transferred to the National Science Foundation, which listed the following objectives: "(1) The conduct of deep ocean surveys; (2) the design and construction of deep drilling equipment; and (3) the drilling of a series of holes in the deep ocean floor, one of which will completely penetrate the earth's crust."[31] Only the third objective speaks directly to the project's original vision; and only one of its holes appears intended to fulfill that vision. Moreover, the NSF contracted the job out, its top choice being the Socony Mobile Oil Company, followed by Global-Aerojet-Shell, the Zapata Off-Shore Company, General Electric, and Brown & Root.[32] It comes as little surprise that Project Mohole yielded no geological samples from the earth's mantle, a Herculean task even today; but it undeniably gave rise to new drilling techniques, and inspired a race between rigs to reach record depths.[33]

As important for my argument as the project's complicity in the extraction of fossil fuels, however, is its pursuit of speculative geology—a venture that realizes the precarious feat of undermining at the lower depths—and the curious associations by which it has crept into the twentieth-century literary landscape. Project Mohole is a real-world dramatization of geological speculation, and its undertaking provided the imaginative materials for a host of literary texts. Walters's *The Mohole Mystery* telegraphs the crucial interplay between speculative geologies and modernity's reliance on fossil fuel consumption. As the novel's primary scientific voice, Sir George Benson, explains to Godfrey and the others, their investigation of the earth's interior may hold consequences for the industrial stability of Western civilization:

> For generations we've exploited underground resources. First it was coal, then oil, then gas. A terrific amount of material has been extracted from subterranean regions. Nothing has been put back. It was inevitable that, sooner or

later, the stability of the earth's crust should be affected. We've reached that stage now. Seismologists have been warning us for years, and now they're in quite a panic. The great increase in the number and violence of earthquakes, they say, is a warning that cannot be ignored. Either we find out much more about the underworld, including our cavern, or we must cease extracting coal, oil and gas at once. (36)

Sir George's acknowledgment of uninhibited resource extraction is hardly environmentalist but carries a tone of reactionary alarmism. The novel's quasi-colonialist cohort explores the underground earth for the sake of continued extraction, and shows little concern for the sentient macrofungi that they encounter within the mantle. First contact with deep subsurface life is merely an expression of another anxiety: that unknown depths mean uncertain energy futures.

Virtually no critical conversation surrounds Walters's novel today, yet its publication marks the decisive advent of a cultural consciousness toward geological science. It opens with a simplified stratigraphic model identifying the Moho (4). Sir George's explanation of the proposal to send a human explorer underground begins with a description of the geological makeup and history of Dudley, in Staffordshire County, where the British government has dug a successful mohole: "The town is built on an outcrop of limestone," he says, "and is surrounded by old mine-workings centuries old. The area is riddled with huge caves, some artificial and many natural" (30). These lines invoke Dudley's coal-mining history, its role in the nascent eighteenth-century Industrial Revolution. Despite Sir George's insistence that the expedition's primary focus is scientific knowledge, he repeatedly frames it in economic and industrious terms: "The rocks and minerals found down below will be of immense interest. Maybe something of commercial importance will emerge. But this mohole and the investigation of the cavern are going to tell us more about the structure of the earth, its origin and history, than anything has ever done before. It will also tell us if we really must go back to horses and carts" (37). *The Mohole Mystery* reminds its readers of the energy-focused concern that plagues its scientific interests, and that lurks in the background as a persistent cultural anxiety.

When Sir George finally sends one of his team (a Russian cosmonaut named Serge) into the mohole, scientific interests take a backseat to the horror of discovering a form of subterranean life. Serge's transport to the mantle crashes, and he finds himself surrounded by several large, egg-shaped organisms moving slug-like toward him. It's never fully revealed what they are, and Serge makes no significant attempt to communicate with them or understand them, instead immediately assuming a hostile intent: "There was something utterly menacing in the slow, deliberate climb of the large oval body," the narrator tells us; "Serge knew at once that the creature of the underworld was, somehow, aware of his presence. It was coming after him" (154). Eventually, Serge's sole concern turns toward self-defense, as he takes to throwing rocks at the slow-moving target: "His only feeling seemed to be interest as to whether or not he could hit the target and what would happen when he did" (159). In this passage, Serge appears oddly like a child tormenting an insect simply for the satisfaction of seeing it suffer; when he eventually strikes one of the organisms, it bursts in a cloud of powder, giving Serge a sense of gratification (159). Ultimately, the strange egg-like creatures amount to little more than a minor irritation and potential allure to popular imagination, with one of the characters remarking that they would be a successful attraction in zoos (192).

The Mohole Mystery's curious disregard for its ostensibly harmless subterranean critters amplifies its understated concern for securing stable energy. Sir George's (and by extension, the novel's) interests appear fueled by what Imre Szeman has called "strategic realism," or the prevention of energy disruptions by establishing access to resources in the most direct way possible.[34] This mode of political and economic realism translates into the realist rationality of Walters's novel, epitomized by its fixation on short-term human survival. The characters' attitudes tend toward the colonial, perceiving the underground as a world to be explored, but also to be exploited, and the lives of species already inhabiting the mantle are dispensable. These attitudes reflect the international focus on fossil fuels in the mid-twentieth century, specifically oil. As innovations in drilling techniques led to the discovery of subterranean oil deposits, wealthy countries raced to secure their shares. The year 1944 had already seen the establishment of the International Petroleum Council, designed to shield oil from the control of the countries in which it was extracted, and thereby guarantee the access of Western nations, primarily Britain and the United States.[35] In this respect, *The Mohole Mystery* is more than a reflection of neocolonialist policies among Western global powers; it's a fantasy of resource discovery on England's home turf, a revitalization of eighteenth- and nineteenth-century industrial expansion.

For Walters, Project Mohole marked a significant historical event. Although subterranean fantasies occupied the minds of nineteenth-century authors, only after World War II could such fantasies be technologically realized. Moreover, it was only after World War II that the extent of humanity's impact on planetary systems became widely known beyond the scientific community, with the publication of Rachel Carson's *Silent Spring* in 1962 and the landmark 1965 report from the President's Science Advisory Committee (PSAC), chaired by oceanographer Roger Revelle: "Through his worldwide industrial civilization," the report concluded, "Man is unwittingly conducting a vast geophysical experiment."[36] A faculty member at the Scripps Institution of Oceanography, Revelle was instrumental in the conceptualization of Project Mohole, and well aware of the ecological upset brought about by deep-sea drilling. Although the committee's statement appears quaint today, it carried revolutionary force when it was first published. The scientific laboratory had long been held as an institutionally separate space from the outside world; but when the boundary between the laboratory and the outer world disappears, the indeterminacy of the experiment increases. The experimenters are no longer able to extricate themselves, instead playing an inevitable role in the production of results.

Today, we look back on the 1960s as the environmental decade, when humanity began to realize that it was conducting, by the very conditions of its existence, an experiment in which the planet itself was the laboratory. This illustration of the entanglement between historical and planetary processes offers a fresh yet disturbing perspective on the broader history of capitalist modernity. What once appeared as the pinnacle of industrial progress now takes the shape of a long extinction event, as Carson warned in her 1962 address at the Scripps Institution. Carson's description of an "artificial environment" recalls the speculative trope of terraforming common to works of science fiction, in which humanity engineers hospitable atmospheres on alien planets; but in contrast to such works, Carson's words don't promise security.[37] Rather, they invoke terraforming as an expression of anthropogenic climate change—the manufacturing of an inhospitable atmosphere. In this framework, terraforming is a science not of salvation but of geoengineered extinction. The end of humanity is a virtual prerequisite for the achievements of industrial capitalism.

The prospect of extinction is one of literature's wicked problems, and a crucial critical takeaway of speculative geology, encapsulated by this question: how can we narrate the conditions in which narration becomes impossible? According to Claire Colebrook, literary scholars must ask what it means for theory to assume extinction as a premise of critique, particularly insofar as extinction invites a reconsideration of what *theory* and *literature* look like: "Imagine a species, after humans, 'reading' our planet and its archive: if they encounter human texts (ranging from books, to machines to fossil records) how might new views or theories open up?"[38] Colebrook rescales the practice of reading for a planetary context, imagining the planet not only as a text but as concomitant with a temporality that gives rise to nonhuman readers. In her account, the existence of humans in the Anthropocene becomes a kind of trace, designating the planet not only as a reservoir of finite resources, but as a record. Fictions of speculative geology explore the processes of planetary inscription by which humanity paradoxically writes itself out of existence.

Project Mohole embodies a profound (and profoundly absurd) moment of such industrial inscription, and the novels in this chapter are not unaware of its cultural resonance. DeLillo's reconceptualization of the Mohole, being a dimension in which information plays back upon itself, recasts the human characters as recurring figures throughout a cosmic feedback loop. In this revelation, his scientific team's receipt and analysis of the communication is simultaneously its transmission. All the characters' redundant conversations and circular reasoning amusingly revisit them in the book's final pages, as they realize the extent to which they have simply been talking to themselves. The entire premise of *Ratner's Star* reveals itself to be of civilization's own making. The desire for a message from beyond, a script that would unlock the secrets of the universe, suffices only to reinforce the impact of humans' presence on the planet. The novel's rendition of the mohole marks an explicit historical connection that realizes, for DeLillo, the simultaneously impotent and destructive processes of global modernity. The historical event of Project Mohole uncannily literalizes the metaphysical conjectures that proliferate in DeLillo's and others' work. The mohole is a significant figure precisely insofar as it was an intellectual failure and an engineering success.

Martian Moholes and the Red Mirror of the Anthropocene

In Kim Stanley Robinson's *Red Mars*, engineering an environment is the explicit narrative rationale, and speculative geology assumes a foregrounded presence. On orders from the United Nations Organization on Mars Affairs (UNOMA), Robinson's colonists pursue a program of terraforming, which includes atmospheric thickening, nuclear detonation, and the drilling of moholes. The decision is not unanimous among the cohort, however, leading to what the narrator calls "the terraforming debate" (168).[39] The two sides of the debate occupy the green and red positions: that humanity has, respectively, the responsibility to promote life, or the responsibility to preserve the Martian environment. Speaking for the Greens, physicist Saxifrage "Sax" Russell professes that "it isn't enough to just hide under ten meters of soil and study the rock. That's science, yes, and needed science too. But science is more than that. Science is part of a larger human enterprise, and that enterprise includes going to the stars, adapting to other planets, adapting them to us. Science is creation" (178). Sax plainly speaks for Western humanism's colonialist mentality, a commitment to the belief that transforming the world to suit humans automatically means transforming the world for the better. Opposing this position are the Reds embodied by geologist Ann Clayborne: "We are not lords of the universe," she says in response to Sax's comments; "We're one small part of it. We may be its consciousness, but being the consciousness of the universe does not mean turning it all into a mirror image of us. It means rather fitting into it as it is, and worshiping it with our attention" (179). Ann and Sax represent a central disagreement in ecopolitics since the mid-twentieth century: namely, whether to pursue a colonialist or convivial conservationism.[40]

Like much of Robinson's fiction, *Red Mars* tests the contours of the novel form. More than a future history of Martian colonization and the establishment of terraforming settlements, it is also an account of the speculative geology of another planet. Although often read for its commentary on historical materialism and utopianism, Robinson's is a deeply scientific novel, concerned as much with the pursuit of scientific knowledge as with the awakening of class consciousness. Elizabeth Leane argues that these two dimensions are inextricable from one another and constitute a critique of colonialist science, while Eric Otto connects Robinson's interests in utopian communities to Aldo Leopold's notion of the land ethic, situating utopia firmly within the boundaries of a green ecology.[41] Building on these approaches, I claim that the novel's speculative geology affords a critique of the cultural ideologies and attitudes that informed mid-twentieth-century geophysical colonialism, as embodied in expeditions such as Project Mohole. Robinson presents Mars as a geological foil to earth's biological hegemony: the trickle-down feature by which life rationalizes itself as the arbiter of the inanimate world. The author's red planet is an uncanny reminder of earth's geological unconscious, just as the corpse is an uncanny reminder of what we might call the bodily unconscious: *"Mineral; not animal, nor vegetable, nor viral. It could have happened but it didn't. There was never any spontaneous generation out of the clays or the sulphuric hot springs; no spore falling out of space, no touch of a god; whatever starts life (for we do not know), it did not happen on Mars. Mars rolled, proof of the otherness of the world, of its stony vitality"* (96; italics in original). Passages such as this fall outside the purview of plot, performing a metanarrative commentary on Mars's significance. The novel's recognition of this "stony vitality" anticipates the cultural consciousness that critics and scientists associate with the climate crisis, which, as Chakrabarty sums up so effectively, "is about waking up to the rude shock of the planet's otherness."[42] The geological earth is not merely a passive, inanimate orb, but a network of interacting systems charged with energy. As Elizabeth Povinelli writes in her theorization of geontopower, "Nonlife has the power [to] self-organize or not, to become Life or not. In this case, a zero-degree form of intention is the source of all intention. The inert is the truth of life, not its horror."[43] In *Red Mars*, the ambiguous distinction between life and nonlife informs the novel's speculative geology and situates it as a narrative figuration of earth in its infancy.

Insofar as earth serves as a scientific precedent for understanding Mars, it does so through an ineluctably industrial lens, as Robinson understands well: "even on Earth the geology of mineral formation was not well understood," the narrator says, "which was why prospecting still had large elements of chance in it" (274). As with earth sciences, the colonists cannot help but see their quest for knowledge as bound up with industrial concerns. It is no coincidence that the careful overlapping of terrestrial and Martian geologies manifests in the section of the novel titled "Falling into History." In these passages, *Red Mars* hypothesizes that old social and political forms come back to haunt humankind: "we see the evidence of our power all around us," protagonist John Boone says at one point, "we almost get run down by it as it goes about its work! And seeing is believing. Even without an imagination you can see what kind of power we have. Maybe that's why things are getting so strange these days, everyone talking about ownership or sovereignty, fighting, making claims" (323). Even contact with an alien planet cannot break humanity from its capitalist ancestry, although these colonists certainly try. As one of the characters says in the novel's sequel, *Green Mars* (1993), the Martian colony "exist[s] for Earth as a model or experiment. A thought experiment for humanity to learn from."[44]

If the Martian colony is a thought experiment in the trilogy's second installment, in the first it is still very much an experiment in the traditional, physical sense. When someone suggests to Sax that his laboratories are getting messy, the physicist replies: "The planet is the lab" (263). The line is a quip, a throwaway, yet it conveys a hard sincerity in the context of Robinson's narrative, echoing the language of the 1965 PSAC report. Sax vocalizes the extent of his species' impact on Martian geophysics, made brutally obvious in the colony's drilling of moholes, one kilometer in diameter, which release subterranean heat to warm the planet's atmosphere. Surveying the bottom of a shaft, John reflects on the perspective from below: "The sheer size of the shaft was hard to grasp; the muted light and vertical lines reminded him of a cathedral, but all the cathedrals ever built would have sat like dollhouses at the bottom of this great hole. The surreal scale made him blink" (237). Robinson draws his reader's attention to the impression of verticality, the disorientation of looking up from below the planar surface—a historically new perspective, to gaze up from depths unheard of on earth (much less Mars).

Rendered in a mostly realist prose style, the novel's perspective in this moment nonetheless estranges its readers—an effect of the science-fictional mindset that Robinson himself has elucidated. In a 2016 interview with Heise, Robinson suggests the earth itself is "becoming a big science fiction novel that we're all co-writing together. In many ways, if you want to do realism that's truly realistic right now, you're driven to science fiction."[45] Viewing *Red Mars* with its author's comment in mind, we discover analogous inscriptive practices happening at once: the act of composing a cultural narrative and the act of physically altering a planet. The novel's moholes constitute the second kind of inscription, words and sentences in the "big science fiction novel" that the colonists are terraforming into existence. This planetary narrative is told through geological time, and the moholes give the characters a glimpse of this temporal scale, as when John ascends the subterranean shaft: "In the last two elevators they ascended through regolith; first the megaregolith, which looked like cracked bedrock, and then the regolith proper, its rock and gravel and ice all hidden behind a concrete retainer, a smooth curved wall that looked like a dam [. . .]" (237). John's tour through Mars's geological past recalls industrial water management projects on earth, connecting the Martian colonization to histories of environmental control. Moholes and dams alike are part of an inscriptive process that rewrites the organization of planetary materials.

As tensions mount between the Martian colonists and UNOMA, the moholes and other infrastructural projects become targets and the red planet itself is weaponized, transformed from manufactory into warship. Geophysical power becomes a tool for annihilation and suppression. In a show of destructive force whose monumentality rivals that of the moholes, the violence damages multiple aquifers and power plants, resulting in a flood. The only recourse the scientists have is to create a landslide, damming the torrent and capping the water plant to prevent all of it from pouring out. The geological scale of events is difficult to fathom, and the characters can only make sense of it by appealing to landmark geohistorical events on earth: "If we don't cap it," one of them says, "it'll look like when the Atlantic first broke through the Straits of Gibraltar and flooded the Mediterranean basin. That was a waterfall that lasted ten thousand years" (480). The comparison is telling. Not only is the scope of time and spatial displacement unimaginable, but the geological upheaval on Mars has been provoked by human behavior. What on earth took place over millennia takes place on Mars in a matter of hours, a temporal compression that hyperbolically mirrors that of the Great Acceleration.

In the wake of the attacks, the devastation can be fully visualized only from above—an aeronautic complement to the geological confusion and demolition. Flying over the planet, two of the characters witness "a big bowl of land shattered like a plate of broken glass; lower down, patches of frosting black-and-white water surged right out of the broken land, ripping at the new blocks and carrying them away even as they watched, in a steaming flood that caused the land it touched to explode" (487). The description evokes ideas of a primordial earth, a planet stewing with elements but not yet balanced for the emergence of complex life. The characters encounter a striking image of this primordialism when they fly over the partially frozen waters from a damaged aquifer that has flooded a nearby mohole: "And there at its center—where, even flying as high as they were, the ice sea still extended to the horizon in every direction—there was an enormous steam cloud, rising thousands of meters into the air" (497). The heat from the depths of the mohole warms the freezing water up through to its surface, producing a steam tower reminiscent of methane vents on a young earth. As an Anthropocene novel, *Red Mars* collapses past and future in a moment of vertical optics, recasting the planet as a scene of all-too-earthly struggle—a "most un-Martian spectacle," as the narrator declares (497).

Ultimately, much of *Red Mars* is an un-Martian spectacle, looking less like science fiction than a rusty reflection of earth's geo-industrial history. Watching a video of Antarctic drilling, Ann laments the Martian colony's role in the dissolution of the Antarctic Treaty System: "They kept mining and oil out of Antarctica for almost a hundred years," she says, "ever since the IGY and the first treaty. But when terraforming began here it all collapses" (251). Ann's references to the International Geophysical Year and the agreement to keep Antarctica free of industrial exploitation establish a history much longer than that of the novel's timeline. Held during escalating Cold War tensions, the IGY darkly foreshadows the politicization of concerted international efforts, as Arkady explains regarding the colony's shift from a scientific to an economic outpost:

> A return is being demanded for our island. We were not doing pure research, you see, but applied research. And with the discovery of strategic metals the application has become clear. And so it all comes back, and we have a return of ownership, and prices, and wages. The whole profit system. The little scientific station is being turned into a mine, with the usual mining attitude toward the land over the treasure. (342)

Arkady's comparison of Mars to a mine is doubly significant, as it underscores the station's economic value as well as its vertical dimension. The colony's excavations, drilling, and other earthmoving practices amount to large-scale undermining, the removal of rock and dirt from beneath the colonists' feet. Scientific and monetary interests converge in the underground, coordinating a nexus of Anthropocene effects that are decidedly vertical (a convergence that Robinson revisits in his 2017 novel, *New York 2140*, which features a company called Marine Moholes).

In its invocations of Project Mohole and earth science, *Red Mars* presents readers with an engaging and expansive future history. Set on Mars in the mid-twenty-first century, it nonetheless establishes itself as part of a longer cultural history, reaching back to the 1950s on earth. This cultural history parallels an even deeper geological one, surfacing in the Martian moholes and recalling terrestrial anxieties concerning the availability of resources. The novel's speculative mode underscores the already speculative element of Project Mohole and its related developments in oil drilling and resource extraction—the boring of tunnels in the earth and raising what lies below—and makes plain the ways in which these practices are a kind of terraforming. In doing so, it offers a refracted yet plausible vision of geological colonization, and a prescient mirror in which we can read the already occurring slow extinction of the Anthropocene. The remainder of this chapter examines two works that stage the dynamics of speculative geology in pronounced ways, despite not including any explicit references to Project Mohole. Reza Negarestani's *Cyclonopedia: Complicity with Anonymous Materials* assembles the genres of obscurantist theory and weird horror to present readers with a vision of a dynamic, oil-filled earth that comes alive under humanity's feet, while Karen Tei Yamashita's *Through the Arc of the Rain Forest* reimagines the moholean quest for the mantle as an inexplicable planetary event in which subterranean strata emerge from underground. Negarestani and Yamashita extrapolate and complicate the global financial vectors that amplify Anthropocene processes, and represent these vectors as concomitant with geological upheaval, exhumation, and exploitation.

Narrating Extinction Through Oil

In Negarestani's novel, speculative geology emerges through what Amitav Ghosh calls the "Oil Encounter," a hybrid mode that marries cultural and economic histories with complex geophysical architectures: "oil smells bad," Ghosh writes; "It reeks of unavoidable overseas entanglements, a worrisome foreign dependency, economic uncertainty, risky and expensive military enterprises; of thousands of dead civilians and children and all the troublesome questions that lie buried in their graves."[46] For someone like Project Mohole's Hollis Hedberg, these "overseas entanglements" activate the resource base for Western economic and industrial development. The financial motivations underlying the thirst for oil have yielded progress for geological science, filling in the subterranean spaces that have eluded researchers for decades. For Negarestani, however, the oil encounter is a literary opportunity for exposing the cultural anxieties and antagonisms that plague the twentieth-century geological unconscious, manifesting as a dense theory-fiction drafted from the bowels of a tunneled and exhumed earth.

Cyclonopedia evades easy description but can be seen as a faux-academic composite text in the tradition of Vladimir Nabokov's *Pale Fire* (1962), Alain Robbe-Grillet's *Djinn* (1982), and Mark Danielewski's *House of Leaves* (2000).[47] In terms of its politics and cultural history, however, *Cyclonopedia* shares some affinity with Saudi Arabian author Abdelrahman Munif's quintet of novels, familiarly known as *Cities of Salt* (1984–1989). Following the arrival of American oil companies in an indeterminate region in the Middle East, Munif's narrative adopts a bird's-eye view of geopolitical and cultural complexities involved in the international oil economy. In particular, Munif attends to cultural mistranslations between the Americans and the Indigenous Bedouins that center on the exploitation of the underground: "Was there another world underground, with gardens, trees and men, all clamoring for water?"[48] In an illuminating reading, Nixon suggests that *Cities of Salt* presents an "otherworlding of American technological practices," and that this otherworlding occurs via technology's infiltration of the underground.[49] Negarestani's narrative intensifies this otherworlding, amplifying the presence of Western military and extractive technologies while also staging their conflict with obscure geophysical forces. Moreover, and like Munif's work, *Cyclonopedia*'s ambiguous formal structure mirrors the challenging geopolitics that inform its content. Imitating a work of scholarship, the novel plunges readers into a perplexing miasma of military-industrial history, international relations, and speculative fiction.

Even its authorship warrants suspicion; the text features an opening frame narrative written by *XYZT* (2019) author and Negarestani's partner, Kristen Alvanson (and in which a woman also named Kristen Alvanson discovers a text also titled "Cyclonopedia" by someone also named Reza Negarestani).

Beyond its frame narrative, *Cyclonopedia* presents as a mostly plotless expo-
sition of the work of Hamid Parsani, a fictional scholar of Middle Eastern
studies. "[T]he bottom line of my texts is in oil," the novel quotes Parsani
as writing, and Negarestani's narrator reinforces this claim: "Books, foods,
religions, numbers, specks of dust—all are linguistically, geologically, politically and mathematically combined into petroleum" (41–42). Critical accounts
of *Cyclonopedia* often note its petropolitical concerns, with Timothy Morton
going so far as to call it "a demonic parody of environmentalist nonfiction."[50]
Melanie Doherty argues that the text critiques geopolitical relations between
Western superpowers and the Middle East, centered on the notion of "oil as
power."[51] Meanwhile, Robin Mackay sees the novel as an exploration of petrol-
provoked geotrauma: "Capitalism appears as a crazed thanatropic machine,
unlocking the earth's resources—in particular, the fossil fuels that were, in
more optimistic times, referred to as 'buried sunlight'—to release them to their
destiny of dissolution, and thus accelerating the consumption of the earth by
the sun."[52] Against this fervor of capitalistic solar consumption, Negarestani
conjures a "Tellurian Insurgency" by which the planet brings forth an eruptive
energy from its core (147).

Cyclonopedia doesn't shy away from the trappings of postmodern paranoia
but revels in them, even concluding with a discussion of "radical paranoia" in
which human language gets recoded into "the arid winds and oily wetness of
the Middle East" (221). In one of its most paranoid passages, presented as an
excerpt from Parsani's writings, the text indulges in a fantasy of oil's agency,
decoding its spectral presence within ancient languages. In a discussion of the
3,333 diseases of Zoroastrianism, readers learn of the demon Akht's decision
to name his city Taft, which, Parsani reveals, means "to be burnt slowly by the
sun," and is linked etymologically and anagrammatically to the word *napht*—
the Arabic word for oil (159). This passage is one of several that reimagine
the scholar's vocation as unveiling a secret, science-fictional war between the
sun and earth. Parsani's unknown status within the text (he has since disap-
peared) and the mysterious provenance of the diegetic "Cyclonopedia" text
(discovered under a hotel bed) are metanarrative techniques to reinforce this
paranoia, teasing that readers themselves might be absorbed into the tellurian
conspiracy. Yet Negarestani's paranoia is neither in the vein of Philip K. Dick's
schizoid sincerity nor even Pynchon's absurdism, but is analogous to a very

real cultural paranoia that *Cyclonopedia* diagnoses and critiques: the suspicion toward, desire to know, and exploitation of what lies below.

The novel realizes this paranoia explicitly in what the narrator calls the "( )hole complex" of the planet, a theoretical concept that unites the text's many cryptic strands: "It unfolds holes as ambiguous entities—oscillating between surface and depth—within solid matrices, fundamentally corrupting the latter's consolidation and wholeness through perforations and terminal porosities" (43). The term originates in Parsani's fictional writings as *Kareez'gar*, a word that "eludes translation," the narrator says, "but might be rendered, with considerable mutilation, as 'hole complex'—or, more accurately, '( )hole complex', since Parsani's original term implies both a destituted Whole (creation, genesis, state, etc.) and a holey-ness" (42). This felicitous mistranslation mirrors the terrestrial boring of the planet that *Cyclonopedia* associates with resource extraction. What people take to be firm and complete reveals itself to be riddled with gaps, giving way to a support system (physical and metaphysical) that is always already undergoing perpetual recombination. Rather than yield solid ground, the earth cracks and quakes:

> The process of degenerating a solid body by corrupting the coherency of its surfaces is called ungrounding. In other words, the process of ungrounding degenerates the whole into an endless hollow body—irreducible to nothingness—and damages the coherency between the surfaces and the solid body in itself. To talk about holey spaces and Earth is to insinuate the Earth as the Unground. (43)

Negarestani's ungrounding is uncanny in that it doesn't intervene from elsewhere—wayward interstellar objects or alien invaders—but emerges spontaneously from inside the planet itself. The ( )hole complex designates "the zone through which the Outside gradually but persistently emerges, creeps in (or out?) from the Inside. A complex of hole agencies and obscure surfaces unground the earth and turn it to the ultimate zone of emergence and uprising against its own passive planetdom" (44). A regenerative combustion engine, the ( )hole complex is a planetary immune response against capitalism's energy infrastructures.

It doesn't take much effort to read Negarestani's ( )hole complex as a metaphor for the coproduction of Jihadi resistance and global petro-capital.[53]

The novel makes this link explicit when it stages Jihad as a defensive strategy against Western incursion into the Middle East. At the center of this conflict, of course, is oil, but Negarestani amplifies the resource's indispensable role. Not only is oil central in terms of globalized realist economics, as a raw material to be commodified; it is ubiquitous in the conflict between the West and the Middle East. Its function echoes that of the ( )hole complex: "If Islamic war machines are dissolved within oil and oil is an omnipresent planetary entity, then Islamic militarization is not local anymore but global and planetary. The rise of oil as a medium for the mobilization of war machines heralds the decline of tactical offense and the dawn of an ubiquitous offense embedded within the seemingly peaceful omnipresence of nature" (70). In *Cyclonopedia*'s narrative of planetary insurrection, Jihad aligns with the spontaneous rupture of forces from within; it doesn't simply oppose Western incursion but is already dispersed throughout and emerges from it.

The novel describes this "Tellurian Insurgency," of which Jihad is an expression, as an upheaval of earth's geology, a shock to the strata in which the underground violently rises and forms "a bottom-up avalanche as if the core is trying to ascend through the Earth's body in a katahuming (exhuming from within) motion" (162). This regenerative violence mirrors not only the logic of Jihadi insurrection, according to the novel, but the slow devastation of the planet by fossil fuel consumption, conceptualized as terrestrial vengeance from below (or within). Drawing on Zoroastrian demonology, *Cyclonopedia* associates petro-capitalism with Az, the demon of solar passion, using language that recalls PSAC's 1965 report and Robinson's notion of Mars as a planetary laboratory: "Az takes the earth as its laboratory, the playground of its experiment—that is, it makes a pact with the Sun. On a planetary level, this pact with the Sun captures the annihilationist ethos of the Sun not as pure extinction, but as a peculiarly tellurian destruction" (175). The Tellurian Insurgency functions as an expressive reaction to the fossil fuel industry's exploitation of the earth, its virtual engineering of extinction by way of resource extraction and consumption. Negarestani's earth responds to this exploitation by literally removing itself from beneath humanity's feet, making explicit the "insecurity" of dependence on foreign oil.[54] This apocalyptic event amounts to "the cancelation, not merely of the technocapitalist chronosphere, but of western Time" (177). It's no surprise, therefore, that *Cyclonopedia*'s narrative chronology is impossible to discern; its form aspires to that of the extinction it intimates.

Rather than offer his readers a coherent chronological plot, Negarestani develops a "theory-fiction" (according to the back of the book jacket) whose central
concept of the ( )hole complex metastasizes into various insurgent acts, from
Jihad to the eruption of geological matter. The text insists that these superficially
disparate effects are aspects of the same long process of planetary inscription,
or what the narrator identifies as Hidden Writing; and oil is the medium of this
writing, the "lube for the divergent lines of terrestrial narration" (19). As Hidden
Writing, the hollow interiors of the ( )hole complex and the organic emergence
of Jihad reappear as plot holes, or "the activities of a sub-surface life," linking
geological and geopolitical dynamics with the traces of Anthropocene existence
(61). In *Cyclonopedia*'s solar hierarchy, human systems and processes read like
elemental materials of a nonhuman narrative—an account that relies significantly on the figure of speculative geology, in which human temporality plays
an insignificant role. By conceptually (rather than chronologically) plotting the
vectors of petro-capital, militarization, Jihad, and other human systems, Negarestani makes a theory-narrative of planetary features.

This sense of geological textuality isn't unique to twenty-first-century
fiction but finds earlier manifestations in the "layers of history analogous to
layers of coal and oil" in Pynchon's 1973 novel *Gravity's Rainbow* (discussed
in Chapter 3) and artist Robert Smithson's 1970 textual-visual work "Strata:
A Geophotographic Fiction," not to mention the fictions of DeLillo discussed
in Chapter 1.[55] Famous among such geo-textual fabulations, and a major influence on *Cyclonopedia*, is Gilles Deleuze and Félix Guattari's "geology of
morals" in *A Thousand Plateaus: Capitalism and Schizophrenia* (1980): "We
are never signifier or signified," they memorably write; "We are stratified."[56]
As Gregory Flaxman explains, for Deleuze and Guattari, "bodies that traverse
the ground, that build on it or reduce it to rubble, are not separable from the
earth but rather constitute the infinite surface movements that will be folded
into its strata."[57] Flaxman suggests that Deleuze and Guattari capture in their
dense treatise the multidimensional movements of tectonic theory: vertical,
horizontal, and temporal. These movements aren't meaningless; at the appropriate scale, they tell a story. Through its discussion of Hidden Writing, ( )hole
complexes, and sub-surface life, *Cyclonopedia* offers one such story: that of
humankind's erasure from the planet.

Terms like "hidden" and "sub-surface" are tempting for literary critics insofar as they overlap with recent conversations about symptomatic reading

and the hermeneutics of suspicion, which operate according to conceptual binaries such as hidden/revealed and depth/surface. *Cyclonopedia* would appear to traffic unapologetically in these practices but for its nigh satirical incorporation of them into what we might call its surface content. Its combination of theoretical obscurantism and science-fictional tropes invites paranoid readings at the same time that it mocks them, going so far as to insist that the "sub-surface life of Hidden Writing is not the object of layers and interpretation; it can only be exhumed by distorting the structure of the book or the surface plot. [. . .] To interact with Hidden Writings, one must persistently continue and contribute to the writing process of the book" (64). The text's emphasis on exhumation—the unearthing of what's below our feet—connotes more than passive reading; it suggests that in order to read the earth we must participate in writing it. The machinery and technology by which we study the underground become available to us only at a time when we have already irreparably altered the planet.

Although Negarestani's novel deploys the binaries of hidden/revealed and surface/depth, its speculative geology encourages readers to reject these binaries. It may be difficult to make sense of *Cyclonopedia*, but this isn't because it contains hidden meanings. The novel's stratigraphic logic reconceives the underground as part of a recombinant information assemblage, always shifting in relation to humans and other actors. Its textual difficulty derives from its near-total disregard for the temporal scales of realist narrative and reliance on imaginative and even poetic analogies between concepts. Surface and depth no longer hold their binary relation, but feed into one another, generating a dynamic new medium. The reader's task isn't one of cracking codes but of producing structures, of building the text—a task that mirrors humanity's production of the Anthropocene.

Slow Extinction from the Mohole to the Matacão

One affordance of speculative geology is that human characters (and readers) intuit a sense of humankind's ecological impact through fictive engagements with the planet. Hedberg's 1971 lecture presents one example of such a reading, albeit an anthropocentric and conservative one: humanity's reliance on oil transfigures into an ode to resilience, rationality, ingenuity, and progress. Project Mohole embodies a more ambiguous reading. Despite all its ambition and technological innovation, humanity can't overcome the immovable obstinance of the planet. We find here a counterintuitive expression in the mohole's speculative geology. On one hand, the earth's interior keeps its secrets by denying humanity access; on the other, human science's proposal was to learn about the earth through a process of ungrounding, of removing subterranean rock. In other words, although speculative geology appears in *Cyclonopedia* as porous undergrounds and ubiquitous oil, Project Mohole's efforts to realize such porosity failed quite miserably, and yielded no buried sunlight. As is often the case, literary imagination makes explicit certain qualities that go unspoken in lived experience, and reality is, in its own way, stranger than fiction.

Like *Cyclonopedia*, Yamashita's *Through the Arc of the Rain Forest* is a composite text. A speculative adaptation of the telenovela format—part magical realism, part science fiction—the novel delivers its narrative as a surreal assemblage of impossible omniscience provoked by a memory of the narrator, who no longer exists at the time of the story's telling. Both texts revel in layers of narrative mediation and a multiplicity of perspectives, all giving the impression of an interconnected planetary system comprising unfolding regional spaces and vectors of subjectivity. As Yamashita writes in an author's note, the Brazilian *novela* "is pervasive, reaching every Brazilian in some form or manner regardless of class, status, education, or profession, excepting perhaps the Indians and the very isolated of the frontiers and rural backlands" (xv).[58] In the postindustrial worlds of *Cyclonopedia* and *Through the Arc of the Rain Forest*, communications technologies intersect and overlap to create a virtual globe of immanent displacement in which discrete locales find themselves extrapolated into an abstract media ecosystem. In Negarestani's novel, this ecosystem materializes through the ubiquity of oil, the deterritorializing medium of terrestrial narration that turns the entire planet into a geophysical media platform, or what Parikka calls "a media geology of minerals, of chemicals, of soil as the resource for the active mobilization of those things constitutive of contemporary media consumer cultures."[59] The physical structure of the earth assumes the role of a media network, but in doing so disrupts the functions of human social systems; it reframes human lines of communication, themselves prone to corporate and state manipulation, as part of a global and starkly nonhuman entity.

Through the Arc of the Rain Forest performs a similar deterritorialization but adds a new dimension to Negarestani's vision. Unlike *Cyclonopedia* and Project Mohole itself, no digging is required in Yamashita's text. Deep time rises from the earth in the form of the Matacão, greeting the novel's bewildered human characters with its magnetic sheen, which Heise reads as a figure for the global interpenetration of mass media: "As the central symbol of the novel, the Matacão signals not only that there is no such thing as pristine wilderness left, but more decisively that there is no local geography that is not already fundamentally shaped by global connectivity."[60] Being a stratigraphic layer formed from waste material from obsolete transportation and communications networks, the Matacão is a geological complement to the deterritorializing effects of global media, themselves embodied in the character Chico Paco's popular Evangelical platform, Radio Chico, which the novel's narrator describes as "expanding in every direction without control" (144). When the station's pledged coverage of pilgrims to the Matacão grows beyond its means, Chico Paco creates a telethon-like service for would-be pilgrims to call in and donate money, and finally comes up with the idea of using pigeons as "votive messengers" (117). Radio Chico's strategies of compression and spread, by which information from across Brazil intersects and resurfaces at the site of the Matacão, mirror the geological processes of compression and spread that produce the Matacão itself. A locally observable phenomenon that is nonetheless composed of materials from around the world, the Matacão reflects postindustrial developments that redistribute locality as part of an emergent global network—what Andrew Rose describes as the "distributed agency" of the novel's planetary, "mixed-community" ecosystem.[61] Although preceding Negarestani's novel by eighteen years (and occupying a notably pre-9/11 world), Yamashita's novel anticipates what the Iranian writer calls the "exhuming from within" motion of the underground. The Matacão is a body of global waste that exhumes the planet from within, pressing into sight that which humanity has buried.

Despite its inexplicable surfacing, the Matacão hardly offers itself welcomingly to would-be diggers, as the novel's Brazilian native Mané da Costa Pena knows too well: "He and others had been telling tales of the impossibility of tapping underground water sources for as long as he could remember," the narrator relates (14). Mané Pena and other inhabitants of the land determined early that something was impeding their success, keeping those on the surface from digging below; they referred to this underground presence as a *matacão*, "or solid plate of rock that always blocked well-diggers" (15). The apparent immovability provokes numerous studies into and experiments on the Matacão, including engineering developments for extracting pieces of it, one of which eventually proves successful and "involved a complicated combination of laser cutting with amino acids and other chemical compounds" (85). Just as the knowledge of subterranean oil prompted industrial feats derived from Project Mohole, the Matacão prompts its own series of technological advances. Yamashita's science-fictional premise registers the speculative quality of resource extraction in general, echoing the increasingly complex and globalized efforts that go into the identification, removal, and transportation of crude oil around the world.

Theories of the Matacão's strange appearance proliferate early in the novel: "that it was the earth's mantle rising to the surface or the injection of a cement layer by a powerful multinational" (15). In a playful callback to *Ratner's Star*, one explanation proffered by the novel is that it "was the creation of a highly sophisticated ancient civilization that inhabited the area thousands of years ago" (84). The material is eventually revealed to be condensed plastic, and the explanation for its appearance is a startling combination of the early theories offered for it:

> The Matacão, scientists asserted, had been formed for the most part within the last century, paralleling the development of the more common forms of plastic, polyurethane, and styrofoam. Enormous landfills of nonbiodegradable material buried under virtually every populated part of the Earth had undergone tremendous pressure, pushed even farther into the lower layers of the Earth's mantle. The liquid deposits of the molten mass had been squeezed through underground veins to virgin areas of the Earth. (177)

In Yamashita's darkly humorous vision, terrestrial processes sync up with Anthropocene excess; the vast output of human industry seeps into the hollows and byways in the crust, and is pushed deeper by geological pressure. The Matacão may not be made of oil per se, but it comprises obsolete petroleum by-products—the oil from Negarestani's sentient Middle East, refined and consumed, discarded and absorbed back into the planet. Human waste becomes an element of geological sedimentation and uplift. Like *Cyclonopedia*, which indexes humanity's harmful obsession with oil in the figure of a vengeful planet, *Through the Arc of the Rain Forest* imagines humanity's fate as sealed by what it has pushed out of sight. Both novels refashion textual narrative as part of a geological timescale that challenges human centrality.

Like Yamashita's novel, the Matacão is also a composite body, formed over time from a mixture of synthetic and geological processes. A configuration of vertically manufactured ground, it announces "the deliberate shift of material by humans through construction, mining, agriculture and the generation and the movement of materials deemed to be waste," in Stephen Graham's words.[62] As these materials combine and intermix with rock and soil, they can form new geological substances, such as plastiglomerate: "melted plastic associated with campfires [that] has bonded beach pebbles and sand to form a rock."[63] Plastiglomerates designate a unique moment in geological history in which petrochemical by-products fuse with nonhuman matter, compressing and sinking to form discernible strata in the earth's crust. Viewing Yamashita's Matacão as a predecessor of such composites, we can see *Through the Arc of the Rain Forest* as an extrapolation of the agency with which Negarestani imbues oil—an extension of *Cyclonopedia*'s "Tellurian Insurgency" throughout the strata, producing an artificial geological layer as the result of oil consumption.[64]

The entanglement between human cultural and geophysical processes informs the environmental dimension of Yamashita's novel. When asked if she sees herself as an environmental writer, Yamashita responded by acknowledging this entanglement:

> All of these shifting things are part of a larger ecology that is not just the environment. It's a human ecology, animal ecology, all of these things. How we are treating the earth, how we're feeding ourselves, how we're feeding the world, all of these things matter. They're all interrelated. So am I an environmentalist? Yes. Do I worry about the earth? Yes. Am I also interested in the cultures or the ethnographies or the anthropology of people and what their lives are? Yes. For me, it's all related.[65]

Yamashita gives no name to the "larger ecology" in which she's interested, but its scope is planetary. As Min Hyoung Song writes, *Through the Arc of the Rain Forest* "imagines less an American globalism and more a planetary becoming, one that involves a keen interest in social relations and the ecological concerns that are increasingly turning into such an important factor in understanding them."[66] In this sense, we can read the Matacão as a figure for McGurl's cultural geology, the imbrication of human civilization within planetary timescales. A fiction of speculative geology, *Through the Arc of the Rain Forest* coordinates the limits of narrative life and the narratability of extinction on a planetary scale, making explicit humanity's impression on the earth in the form of a speculative—and disruptive—geological layer.

The co-productive dynamic of humanity and the planet is evident from the opening pages of *Through the Arc of the Rain Forest*; the narrator—a mysterious orb that hangs in front of protagonist Kazumasa Ishimaru's head—recalls the memory of its own arrival, cast from the ocean by an ambiguous surge of energy and directly into Kazumasa's forehead, where it leaves a bruise (3). As readers eventually learn, the narrator is made of Matacão plastic, being inexplicably drawn toward it—a quality leading to its acquisition by GGG, the multinational profiting off the Matacão. Kazumasa's orb is a perpetual reminder that Anthropocene waste comes back to haunt humanity. The novel confronts its readers with explicit images of expansive waste, such as a massive industrial dumpsite filled with derelict aircraft and automobiles: "The planes and cars had been abandoned for several decades, and the undergrowth and overgrowth of the criss-crossing lianas had completely engulfed everything. On one end of the field, a number of the vehicles seemed to be slipping into a large pit of gray, sticky goop, a major component of which was discovered to be napalm" (87). Although never specified, the pit is likely one point at the earth's surface through which its garbage descends into the geological depths. The site marks an area at which human history and geological history blend together: "The machines found all dated back to the late fifties and early sixties—F-86 Sabres, F-4 Phantoms, Huey Cobras, Lear Jets and Piper Cubs, Cadillacs, Volkswagens, Dodges and an assorted mixture of gas-guzzlers, as well as military jeeps and Red Cross ambulances" (87–88). In these lines, Yamashita invokes a wartime history of industrial overproduction, leading to excess materials including not just vehicles, but weapons and chemical compounds. The postwar world is not one of progress and social order, but globalized disorder and the outsourcing of waste—the terraforming of a gradually hostile environment.

It would be amusing if Yamashita stopped here, but she extrapolates her narrative from its speculative premise, conjuring an all-too-real version of the future in which humanity attempts to profit off its own waste, generating a feedback loop of suffocating intensity. When J. B. Tweep, a representative of GGG, visits Brazil to conduct research and development on the Matacão, he explains the material's use value: "We've discovered that the stuff that the Matacão is made of is a sort of, well, sort of miracle plastic—Matacão plastic, if you will. We've discovered that it is extremely resistant stuff; we're the ones that have cracked the code in drilling and extracting the stuff, and now we're on the verge of controlling it" (99). As examination of the Matacão continues, GGG discovers more uses for it, including magnetized credit cards, reconstructive surgeries, infrastructure, and even artificial foods (125–127). With this cornucopia of commodification, *Through the Arc of the Rain Forest* imagines a new scene of geological and cultural ungrounding. The novel reveals the Matacão to be not an externality of limitless potential, but a finite resource produced by humanity itself.

Parallels between the Matacão and petroleum haven't gone unnoticed, and the text offers ample evidence for such a comparison.[67] The degree to which Matacão plastic comes to form the basis of postindustrial society echoes the craze of peak oil in the 1970s, and the means of its extraction lead to environmental abnormalities: "The chemical runoff from GGG's secret technique had been collected and analyzed and found to cause genetic mutations in rats after five generations," the narrator cautions (141–142). In a moment of ironic humor, GGG's response to public concern perpetuates the feedback cycles of capital accumulation: "All runoff from Matacão mining is collected, encapsulated in stainless steel containers, and sealed at strategic disposal locations," the official writeup declares (142). If the vague storage procedures of Matacão runoff weren't disturbing enough, GGG doubles down: "Additionally, research and development is proceeding to find methods to extract and employ the currently known benefits from runoff" (142). The environmental hazards of Matacão mining recall the horrors of oil and chemical spills, not to mention private industry's lukewarm pledges to improve their methods. Furthermore, as GGG realizes the implications of future scarcity, it sends Kazumasa and the narrator on missions to locate more Matacão deposits, echoing the work of hydrocarbon exploration: "J.B. had plans to send us to Greenland, central Australia, and Antarctica, not to mention every pocket of virgin tropical forest within twenty degrees latitude of the equator" (132). In its effort to squeeze every last ounce of profit from the Matacão, GGG constructs a world composed of human waste: "After all," the narrator tells us, "Matacão plastic had been molded into everything imaginable, both lifesize and likelike. An entire world could be created from it" (147).

As it draws to a close, *Through the Arc of the Rain Forest* explicitly links the speculative geological figure of the Matacão and its ubiquity in the fabric of built social life to an Anthropocene narrative of deep time. In its concluding pages, everything made of Matacão plastic begins disintegrating, consumed by a plastic-eating bacterium spread in part by Radio Chico's messenger pigeons:

> Buildings were condemned. Entire roads and bridges were blocked off. Innocent people were caught unaware—killed or injured by falling chunks of the stuff. People who stepped out in the most elegant finery made of Matacão plastic were horrified to find themselves naked at cocktail parties, undressed at presidential receptions. Cars crumbled at stop lights. Computer monitors sagged into their CPUs. The credit card industry went into a panic. Worst of all, people with facial rebuilds and those who had additional breasts and the like were privy to grotesque scenes thought only to be possible in horror movies. And there was no telling what might happen to people who had, on a daily basis, eaten Matacão plastic hamburgers and French fries. (180–181)

In the sudden shutdown and collapse of civilization, Yamashita reframes the Matacão, augmenting the text's narrative scale. Not only has the Matacão been a factor in capitalist exploitation of the so-called Global South and globalized practices of resource extraction and distribution; it is also an embodiment of the slow extinction that accompanies this exploitation. Whereas disasters such as those involving *Deepwater Horizon* and Chernobyl appear as distinct, localizable, and identifiable events, the Matacão is the effect of gradual and often unseen processes. It is a twofold sign of Anthropocene excess: it both signifies the relentless consumption of industrialized nations and commands the attention of industrialized nations through its market applications, thereby perpetuating consumption. The novel's final pages reveal that human society has resorbed its own waste material, the fossilized body of its pollution.

With this revelation, the Matacão gives out, realizing in an instant a global version of the previously localized and regional slow violence visited upon resource-rich nations by the Global North. In a final chilling scene, the narrator describes an apocalyptic vista of crumbling buildings and infrastructures lost to wilderness, devoid of humans: "The old forest has returned once again, secreting its digestive juices, slowly breaking everything into edible absorptive components, pursuing the lost perfection of an organism in which digestion and excretion were once one and the same" (185). In contrast to the slow violence that once fed the engines of global capitalism, this old forest possesses a regenerative symmetry. Humanity recedes into a cyclical geology, its existence unveiled as a fleeting element of planetary time.

Fictions of speculative geology underscore the immanence of extinction within narratives of historical progress—extinction becomes in fact a condition of narrative possibility. Such fictions engage, in one way or another, the readability of humanity's presence on the planet, whether through evidence of existence or anticipations of extinction. This readability constitutes a fictive version of what Colebrook has called the "geological sublime": "the challenge of looking at the entire archive of the earth—including human script—as one might look at the marks left on buildings by the forces of weathering."[68] Colebrook's provocation reconfigures the geological archive as an ultimately *unreadable* resource because it necessarily speaks to a world in which there are no readers, a world for whose inhabitants there is no such thing as meaning.

For literary critics, the prospect of unreadability poses a challenge; and whatever we call this challenge—the "geological sublime," "extinct theory," or "cultural geology"—it invites an initiative to conceptualize narrative as organized by dynamic forces that exceed human thought: "theory," Colebrook writes,

> if it takes on the impossibility that is its twenty-first century potential, might be imagined as a radical de-contextualization. Let us not fall too readily into assuming the human, or assuming "our" intentional presence behind texts; let us short-circuit "man's" continuing readability of himself in the context of texts and his reflexive mode of judgment whereby he sees marks drawn in the sand and immediately recognizes his own inescapable will.[69]

Colebrook's "radical de-contextualization" entails the erasure of humanism; or more specifically, it entails the displacement of humanism *as a context* and its reimagining as an episode within the nonhuman context of planetary time.[70] It asks that we open our "geological eye."[71] In many ways, theory is (and has always been) about confronting the spaces where our humanism turns inside out, where cultural codes slip through the fissures of the social surface and find themselves in the subterranean hollows. Fictions of speculative geology offer creative complements to the underworlds of theory: narratives that disrupt the linearity of human social life and dissolve the scalar parameters that render our existence legible. By emphasizing extinction as an ineluctable element of narrative cohesion, speculative geologies expose the Moholean Anthropocene that we mistakenly take to be the solid, natural ground of culture.

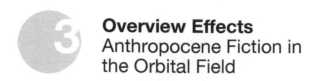

Overview Effects
Anthropocene Fiction in the Orbital Field

Nuclear Infrastructure and the Orbital Field

Whereas for Robinson, Negarestani, and Yamashita, the underworld is a place of gaps and fissures, excavations and shifting associations, for the protagonist of Tim O'Brien's *The Nuclear Age* (1985), it is a source of certainty: "*Terra firma*, I'd think. Back to the elements. A hard thing to explain, but for me geology represented a model for how the world could be, and should be. Rock—the world itself was solid" (68).[1] There is no ( )hole complex in *The Nuclear Age*, and no cataclysmic Matacão; rather, narrator William Cowling insists on the stability of the earth, its presence as a grounding force. "Calm and stable, crystal locked to crystal, there was a hard, enduring dignity in even the most modest piece of granite," he tells us; "Rocks lasted. Rocks could be trusted" (68). There is a conservative thrust to William's language, a sense that geology permits a return to something simpler. His words assume an increasingly ironic, if not absurd, tone, however, as he describes his fondness for a piece of uranium: "I'd put my tongue against it, tasting, thinking about Ping-Pong and Chuck Adamson and collapsing stars, thinking doom, but the uranium was a friend. It had staying power. Man was goofy but the earth was tolerant. In geology, there was always time" (69). The novel presents uranium as a fetishized object, something that transcends inert matter. William interacts with it as one would a friend or lover. It even encodes memories.

The dual nature of uranium—as cold rock and warm companion—mirrors a secondary duality, implicit in these lines from *The Nuclear Age*: uranium as both a component of nuclear reactivity and a sign of the earth's age. The irony of William's description derives from the interplay of these dualities. On one hand, he finds more comfort in rocks than in people: "You can't *talk* to rocks," his father tells him; "Human contact, William, it's important" (36; italics in original). On the other hand, he finds comfort specifically in the time afforded by geology—despite the fact that this same time guarantees human extinction, a fate that William regularly fantasizes in *The Nuclear Age*. As the narrative develops, William's anxiety ebbs and flows, eventually manifesting as his compulsion to dig a fallout shelter in his backyard, a practice that counteracts the safety in geology that he found earlier: "I'm alert to the possibility of a cave-in," he explains; "Carefully, I check the four granite walls for signs of stress, those hairline fractures that can cause conclusion. You never know. Two weeks ago I was fortunate to be topside when a quarter-ton boulder sheared off along the north wall. It taught me a lesson: You can die saving yourself" (198). The underground might provide protection from fallout, but it weakens the solidity in which William takes comfort. As he begins removing ground from beneath his feet, the speculative geologies discussed in Chapter 2 of this volume come into view once again.

Yet *The Nuclear Age* pairs its geological angle with another distinctly vertical framework: the intervention of the view from above, the atmospheric and astrophysical territory of spacecraft and satellites. As it comes into focus in novels such as O'Brien's, the view from above occupies a vertical territory that I call the *orbital field*. This territory affords a perspective on the planet that is neither fixed nor stable, but in constant motion, highlighting both the passage of time and gravitational relation between the earth and the orbital subject. At such elevation, the earth is no longer a fixed ground beneath our feet but another displaced orbital body in a circular dance with its satellites. What emerges in the orbital field is, in other words, a new planetary aesthetic rooted in the technologies of displacement that coincide with the vertical sciences: "I was in orbit," William says in *The Nuclear Age*. "The eye of a satellite. A space walk, and I was tumbling at the end of my tether" (150). More than simply an appeal to the world picture afforded by orbital surveillance technologies, the orbital field in post-1960 fiction brings into focus the extinctive temporality of the nuclear age written on the earth's surface.

This chapter pairs three texts that navigate the entanglement of ecological consciousness, verticality, and the nuclear regime: Don DeLillo's "Human Moments in World War III" (1983), Tim O'Brien's *The Nuclear Age*, and Thomas Pynchon's *Gravity's Rainbow* (1973). In these narratives, vertical elevation coincides with fantasies and anxieties of observation—and, by extension, of objectivity. In "Human Moments," DeLillo's unnamed narrator calls objectivity the "privileged vista" of orbital flight: "It makes a man feel *universal*, floating over the continents, seeing the rim of the world, a line as clear as a compass arc, knowing it is just a turning of the bend to Atlantic twilight, to sediment plumes and kelp beds, an island chain glowing in the dusky sea" (326, italics in original).[2] The story's astronauts experience a simultaneously alienating and absorptive sensation, removed from the planet yet also attuned to features that are unobservable from its surface. Like O'Brien's novel, DeLillo's story explores conflicting attitudes about the earth as a planet, about its existence as both a gravitational foundation and a foundationless, fragile piece of matter. Whereas speculative geology implies the possibility of grounding if only we could know the underworld, the orbital field troubles this possibility by revealing that any such grounding would still be part of a celestial body spinning through a vacuum, itself an object in orbit.

Literary and cultural criticism has had much to say about the impact of atomic energy and the nuclear regime, particularly over the last two decades. Scholars such as Jessica Hurley, Joseph Masco, Daniel Grausam, and Daniel Cordle have illustrated the ways that nuclear anxiety and infrastructure find their way into narrative form, plotting, visual culture, and the rhetorics of power that shape race and gender relations.[3] The vertical aspect of nuclear narratives remains relatively undiscussed, however, as well as the dynamic between verticality, nuclearity, and the Anthropocene concerns of these texts. In this chapter, I focus on the ways that DeLillo, O'Brien, and Pynchon deploy vertical perspectives downward upon the planet, which they also connect with the emergence of global nuclear and energy regimes. Intensely imagined by all three writers, these fictive orbital views constitute efforts at planetary narration that complement the speculative geologies of Chapter 2. Furthermore, they offer a new framework for discussing the vicissitudes of nuclear anxiety that are so prominent in postwar and postmodern fiction.

The orbital perspective revitalizes and adapts the nuclear paranoia often associated with postmodernist literature, wedding both postmodernism and paranoia to the technoscientific investment in seeing the planet: what Fredric Jameson has called "the problem of the view from above."[4] For Jameson, the ubiquity of the planetary media ecosystem becomes visualizable only from an impossible vertical perspective—impossible because, in order to account for itself as another medium within the world system, it must somehow achieve a perspective on itself. This paranoid momentum pushes toward that which lies beyond the borders of vision. Narratives that incorporate this kind of paranoia feature characters who are "menaced from without, haunted by cryptic characters, at once ubiquitous and maddeningly elusive, sinister shadows which the hero can't quite figure, or finger," as Jerry Aline Flieger posits.[5] Verticality indexes the paranoid effort to expand one's scopes, to encapsulate a greater amount of information; yet this effort entails a troubling contradiction for the paranoid subject, as the greater the objectifying distance the more difficult it becomes to perceive particulars. Distance and surveillance unexpectedly counteract each other. The challenge and simultaneous affordance of paranoid thinking becomes the task of visualizing the subject within the world system, developing what Jameson has influentially called a "cognitive map" of global postmodernity.[6]

In contrast to the outward momentum of paranoia described above, Emily Apter elucidates a visual program of global paranoia that encircles subjects within the curvatures of terrestrial spacetime. Terming this program "one-worldedness," Apter argues that it "locks the mind into a loop of intersubjective projection that brooks no outside world."[7] This framework places an emphasis not on what the world system leaves out, but on the entanglement of all worldly elements: with the result that the system leaves out nothing, that "everything is connected," as the narrator of *Gravity's Rainbow* evinces (717).[8] These dual paranoic poles of oneworldedness and the view from above introduce distinct yet related meanings of paranoia: that of totality (everything is part of the same conspiracy) and that of incompleteness (certain things are always unobservable), respectively. By no coincidence, these dual poles also correspond to the planetary perspective that Dipesh Chakrabarty outlines—that the inter-reliance of earth systems gives rise to a sense of both total connectivity and elusiveness.[9] Within these frameworks of planetarity and paranoia, verticality becomes a rhetorical instrument for negotiating discrete scales of information, from the granularity of a single text to the big data of the archive.

Although the figurative rhetoric of verticality undoubtedly plays a role in the works of DeLillo, O'Brien, and Pynchon, I want in this chapter to offer another historical dimension of verticality: specifically, the exploration of the upper atmosphere—the orbital field—and the impact of this exploration on planetary consciousness. The satellites and spacecraft that drift through the orbital field move not only up and down but around; they are circumplanetary bodies forming an atmospheric media network. The analogy to draw here is not to any other technological media but to the medium of the atmosphere itself: the climatological medium, which entertains not only satellites but pollutants, contaminants, greenhouse gas emissions, and other agents of global climate change. In the case of both information networks and atmospheric pollutants, the orbital field mediates an ongoing feedback between local disturbance and global crisis and suspends its subjects between two competing tendencies: toward *grounding* (the totality of the world system) and toward *groundlessness* (the incompleteness of the view from above).

An emergent historical space, the orbital field is bound up with Cold War hostilities. As Fred Kaplan discusses in *The Wizards of Armageddon* (1983), these hostilities became sharper in the United States with the launch of the *Discoverer* satellite in 1960, which allowed image analysts to "identify objects as small as thirty-six inches."[10] The advent of aerial reconnaissance circled (and circulated) fears of nuclear proliferation, both at home and abroad. While the nuclear bomb informed concerns of foreign assault, it also very quickly informed equally pressing concerns about civilian safety within U.S. borders. "The bomb was supposed to be a weapon that could be directed against an enemy," Rebecca Solnit writes, "but it proved to be a plague that touched everything."[11] On top of concerns about radioactivity, experimental programs like Project Plowshare, an Atomic Energy Commission (AEC) effort, introduced the potential for increased nuclear explosions on the home front, as a means of land exploitation and reconstruction. Presented to the public under the deceptive guise of "peaceful nuclear explosions" (PNEs), Project Plowshare attempted to institute nuclear detonation as a regular infrastructural practice.

The case of Project Plowshare underscores the value that nuclear power held for U.S. economic concerns. The Test Ban Treaty of 1963 may have prohibited detonations in the atmosphere and underwater, but it left open the possibility of subterranean testing—which, as it turned out, was where the United States directed its focus and funding. Writing in his lengthy 1962 defense of Project Plowshare for the federal government, political scientist Ralph Sanders makes the connection between these economic concerns and worries about U.S. access to raw materials: "It is well known that the United States has ceased to be a materials surplus nation and has become a materials deficit nation."[12] Like Project Mohole, PNEs were viewed as a gambit in the country's nascent energy crisis. Although nuclear power plants had been in use since the 1950s, they did not answer needs for particular minerals and alloys the United States required to support its domestic markets. Instead, scientists and engineers shifted their attention to the power of underground nuclear detonations to dislodge inaccessible resources: "Plowshare techniques for exploiting oil from tar sands and shale may provide a solution to the long-term petroleum problem," Sanders writes; "Nuclear techniques could remedy problems of steel production by allowing the mining of large deposits of hard taconite (very low grade iron ore) which presently must remain largely unused."[13] Sanders notably refers to "techniques" rather than explosions or detonations, a rhetorical maneuver that reinforces the project's appeal to peace, prosperity, and scientific rationality. Viewed this way, Plowshare is Cold War science through the looking glass: the suspicious warping of violent technologies for "peaceful" ends, and the pursuit of geopolitical supremacy through an energy regime rather than outright war.

Given this turn to underground experiments and earthmoving initiatives, it might seem odd to focus on the orbital field, the space above and around the planet's surface. Project Plowshare shares a subterranean fixation with Project Mohole, an interest in the composition and mineral contents of the strata, and this chapter does not intend to ignore the underground (it is a major concern in texts such as *Gravity's Rainbow* and *The Nuclear Age*), but rather to put it in conversation with the overhead: to view it, in Masco's word, as "networked" to systems of measurement and surveillance.[14] As urban geographers and architectural theorists have argued for some time, the vertical boom of the postindustrial city emerged out of a series of horizontal relationships to the urban grid.[15] Likewise, the earthward gaze of orbital satellites is tied to an epistemological urgency to know the planet—its geophysical systems and geographical patterns. The vertical continuum produces varying scales of perception, from orbital networks to geological excavations, all of which tie together within the midcentury pursuits of the vertical sciences. Moreover, although nuclear science reaches its tendrils into the orbital arena of atmospherics and satellite surveillance, its consequences are dreadfully earthbound, clinging to rocks and minerals for centuries.

For the three texts at the heart of this chapter, nuclear initiatives and orbital perspectives are inextricable from humankind's planetary agency. These
narratives make explicit connections between nuclear armament and vertical infrastructure and acknowledge the presence of military satellites and
aerial imagery as constitutive elements of the Cold War. DeLillo's "Human
Moments" appeared in *Esquire* magazine in July 1983, a mere three months
after Ronald Reagan announced his Strategic Defense Initiative to protect the
United States from nuclear strikes. In DeLillo's story, two astronauts in an
orbital station gather information presumably for national security purposes:
"We swing out into high wide trajectories," the narrator explains, "the whole
earth as our psychic light, to inspect unmanned and possibly hostile satellites.
We orbit tightly, snugly, take intimate looks at surface activities in untraveled
places" (325). The ovoid orbit of DeLillo's astronauts allows them literally to
zoom in and out, to occupy different spatial orientations toward the planet.
O'Brien's *The Nuclear Age* finds a similar effect in vertical perspectives, meditating on the ostensible unity afforded by high-altitude aerial views. Unlike
DeLillo's astronauts, however, O'Brien's narrator, William, also enjoys the ostensible firmness of solid ground, negotiating various states of comfort and
anxiety that direct readers both skyward and earthward. Published in 1973,
a decade or more before DeLillo's and O'Brien's works, Pynchon's massive
Gravity's Rainbow manages to express a planetary-scale rendering of postwar
vertical science, which it depicts as enmeshed with geophysical systems and
nonhuman agencies, echoing the revelations of Rachel Carson's *Silent Spring*
(1962) and environmental developments of the 1960s.[16]

The arc of this chapter is nonchronological, beginning with DeLillo's short
story, which offers an explicit and sustained depiction of human observers in
orbit, and ending with Pynchon's novel, which features no characters in orbit.
The point of this development is not to trace literal examples, however, but
to illustrate a complexity of vertical expression; although *Gravity's Rainbow*
contains no depictions of orbital satellites or spacecraft, Pynchon nonetheless
builds the anticipation of such technologies into the plot and structure of the
text. All three works in this chapter are orbital narratives, albeit in different
ways and to differing degrees. "Human Moments in World War III" depicts
the literal experiences of astronauts in orbit, restricting its narrative possibilities to what they observe from above. *The Nuclear Age* expands on this

effect, at times imagining the planet from above but also giving readers a temporally unmoored first-person narrator who cycles through the second half of the twentieth century. For O'Brien, orbital narration also means temporal orbiting. In *Gravity's Rainbow*, we find an impression of orbital narration in the figure of a seemingly omniscient third-person voice that orbits both temporally and spatially within the text. Pynchon's orbital narrator reflects the vertical pursuits and nuclear infrastructure that emerge in midcentury science, and which are already implicit in the wartime technologies of *Gravity's Rainbow*.

I end this chapter with Pynchon's 1973 novel not only because it presents a sophisticated and nuanced portrayal of planetary perspective, but also to underscore its place in a literary genealogy other than postmodernism. In addition to being a precursor of "Human Moments" and *The Nuclear Age*, *Gravity's Rainbow* is also often seen as an ancestor to works such as Yamashita's *Through the Arc of the Rainforest*, DeLillo's *Underworld*, and Negarestani's *Cyclonopedia*. By reading backward from these later novels to *Gravity's Rainbow*, I aim to complicate the novel's oft-mentioned status as the watershed publication of postmodernism.[17] This is to say that we should situate *Gravity's Rainbow* not only as a preeminent (if not the foremost) text in the history of postmodernist literature but also as a progenitor of a longer, ongoing tradition of post-1960 Anthropocene fiction. Through its engagement with postwar science and technology, the emergence of a global energy regime, and the planetary perspectives afforded by these developments, *Gravity's Rainbow* sets the stage for a postmodernist tradition whose experimentalism is intimately wedded to the history of the Anthropocene.

Through their disparate but comparable approaches to vertical perspective and nuclear concerns, the texts in this chapter suggest that postwar scientific developments produce new orientations toward the planet, and that these developments carry serious ecological repercussions. For these writers, nuclear initiatives pose an existential threat not simply through the gratuitous spectacle of nuclear detonation but also through the consequential factor of fallout, which permeates the atmosphere across countries and continents. Of these two nuclear initiatives, the former has more often been associated with verticality. As Stephen Graham has shown, practices of postwar censorship ensured that when it came to cultural representations of World War II bombers, museums and patrons preferred elevation: "the view from the plane; the God's-eye view of before-and-after maps and aerial or satellite pictures; the almost sublime view of the flaming or exploding city below."[18] There is an unmistakable politics to such representations, which erase granular violence with the cohesion of the ethereal overview. The panorama of the view from above conceals the chaos below, and the view from underground was no better. Civil defense programs offered little corrective to such sanitized visions, but rather promoted shelters as utopian enclaves of technological mastery that nuclear disaster couldn't penetrate.[19] Finally, nuclear fallout offers a more diffuse notion of verticality than the solitary missile's view from above or the bunker's view from below. Unlike the bomb or shelter, which can be plotted along singular spaces and trajectories, fallout is a distributed agent—it "exceeds any existing map."[20] Fallout spreads, occupying a greater portion of the orbital field than individual bombs. This spread is not merely analogous to information media but is in fact a kind of information, as scientists used radioactive signatures to document weather patterns and ecosystem dynamics.[21]

Insofar as DeLillo's, O'Brien's, and Pynchon's texts register the overlap between nuclear fallout, media ecologies, and orbital perspective, they signal a key development in theories of the Anthropocene: the increased presence of radioactive elements distributed across the planet. Moreover, they acknowledge the interconnected histories of these overlapping concepts. The orbital field describes the space in which nuclear science and military strategy coalesce with climatology in a dynamic global network. The unexpected affordance of environmental thought in a postwar nuclear context is that it presents us with the ecological dimension of the built world itself, the anthropogenic world that includes houses, highways, skyscrapers, jet engines, ocean acidification, contaminants in groundwater, and carbon emissions. In McKenzie Wark's words, the "Anthropocene calls attention not to the psychic unconscious or the political unconscious but to the *infrastructural unconscious*," in which social and cultural bodies are no longer distinguishable from those of the nonhuman world (italics in original).[22] The Anthropocene fiction in this chapter amplifies this indistinction by narrating its manifestation in the orbital field.

The authors addressed in this chapter engage the indeterminacies that emerge through the vertical imagination. Beginning with DeLillo, we find a particular emphasis on orbital figures and nuclear temporalities. "Human Moments in World War III" takes place entirely within a surveillance satellite, and deals with the speculative aftermath of nuclear war. Attending to this orbital perspective, I argue that DeLillo explores the vicissitudes of planetary consciousness as it emerges through the technologies and sciences of verticality. The chapter then turns to *The Nuclear Age*, offering an account of the ways that O'Brien brings the orbital back into conversation with the geological, constructing a prolonged dynamic between these two vertical spaces that foregrounds the extinctive drive of the Anthropocene. The chapter concludes with Pynchon's *Gravity's Rainbow*—a monumental work that has become a touchstone of postwar literature—in which the narrator metastasizes into a full-fledged planetary voice, an observing and inscriptive apparatus that also embodies the entanglement of multiple vertical layers.

Seeing in Scale and the Overview Effect

When Russian cosmonaut Yuri Gagarin commented on his experience as the first human to orbit the earth, his words carried a subtle ambivalence. Ostensibly awed by his perspective from the upper atmosphere, Gagarin nonetheless hinted at a strange feeling of suspension: "Astonishingly bright cold stars could be seen through the windows. They were still far away—oh, so far away—but in orbit they seemed closer than the Earth."[23] Gagarin emphasizes a sense of distance and separation, somehow closer to the stars than to his home planet. Moreover, he switches to the passive voice, suggesting a disconnection from his body—stars could be seen, but by whom? The remark evinces an eerie isolation and chill, an alienation uniquely associated with the experiences of astronauts.

Orbital perspective is a provocation for literary narrative, which until the availability of flight technologies could only fantasize about such views (aside from certain limited perspectives offered by particular elevated locales). The prospect of not only seeing from above but seeing from an artificially produced vantage presented a new dimension to the artifice of fiction, an opportunity to connect the literary imagination with the one being authored by vertical science. It is no coincidence that Hollis Hedberg, upon flying over the United States, imagined a fanciful notion of temporal travel through strata, or that Klara Sax in DeLillo's *Underworld* reveled at the uncanniness of the landscape seen from above. Space historian and cultural critic Frank White adds another element to the mix when reflecting on his cross-country flight experience: "as the plane flew over the deserts and mountains of the western states, the flood of insights continued. I could look down on the network of roads below and actually 'see the future.' I knew that the car on Route 110 would soon meet up with that other car on Route 37, though the two drivers were not yet aware of it."[24] White describes the effect as quasi-prophetic, as opening an optical portal into the future. From his vertical vantage, the future appears inscribed within the activities of the present.

To whose present are we referring, however? White claims to see the future, but this ability is materially tied to the position he occupies, and he admits as much: "mental processes and views of life cannot be separated from physical location. Our 'world view' as a conceptual framework depends quite literally on our view of the world from a physical place in the universe."[25] This comment carries theoretical implications for orbital perspective, especially insofar as the concept of the overview has been coopted as a metonymic figure of surveillance and even objectivity, or what Donna Haraway calls the "conquering gaze from nowhere."[26] White's view from the airplane does not actually give him a view of *the* future, an objectifying notion that renders time linear and deterministic; rather, it narrows the possible futures toward which the present is trending, much as the history of industrial civilization has narrowed the possible futures toward which it develops. The aerial, or orbital, perspective complements the planetary consciousness of the Anthropocene in that it elucidates the entanglements between past, present, and future. Both set in respective future scenarios (DeLillo's at an indeterminate date and O'Brien's in 1995, told through flashbacks), the first two works discussed in this chapter negotiate the temporal effects of verticality and its implications for a narrative point of view.

DeLillo's "Human Moments in World War III" opens with an optical figure, but not that of a satellite looking at earth: "A note about Vollmer," the unnamed narrator says of his orbital companion; "He no longer describes the earth as a library globe or a map that has come alive, as a cosmic eye staring into deep space" (325). In the narrator's description, his crewmate sees (or once saw) the planet as an observing agent, resulting in some curious ambiguities—a living map, something seeing but intended to be seen. The shift in

Vollmer's perception is the result of a war that has "changed the way he sees the earth" (325). Already in the opening sentences, visual vectors permeate the orbital space around the earth, establishing observation and surveillance as central themes: "Our spacecraft is designed primarily to gather intelligence" (325). DeLillo is less concerned with painting the specifics of his vaguely near-future scenario than he is with expressing its atmosphere (literally and figuratively). The characters' perspectives register the material infrastructure of scientific development during the Cold War, but also the surreal valence of human life in a world cascading toward collapse.

Published mere months after Reagan announced the Strategic Defense Initiative, DeLillo's story is inextricable from anxieties about safety and security that plagued U.S. citizens during the Cold War; yet it remains a curiously undiscussed text. As its two characters observe the earth, distant and abstracted below them, they struggle to maintain a sense of humanness, thinking back on the fondness of lazy Sundays and suburban leisure. These "human moments" of the story's title channel a reactionary temporality in which the United States can imagine itself as perpetually superior and safe. As Jessica Hurley points out, Reagan's SDI was a "fictional technology," a fantasy of technological and global mastery that nonetheless generated a cultural energy, bringing with it "all of the phantasmic benefits of other large-scale infrastructure projects that function to give humans a sense of mastery over time."[27] DeLillo's fiction both participates in and troubles this mastery. It envisions the vertical perspective, the overview, promised by the SDI, but disenchants it from the experience of ground control. As the story develops, Vollmer and the narrator seem to transform, becoming more like functions in a virtual program than living people. Suspended in perpetual orbit, they begin to see the planet as something other than an object of mastery.

Within this context of defense systems and global war, one of the story's most striking passages comes when the narrator provides a lengthy account of what he sees happening on the planet below them:

> There is a seaward bulge of stratocumulus. Sunglint and littoral drift. I see blooms of plankton in a blue of such Persian richness it seems an animal rapture, a color-change to express some form of intuitive delight. As the surface features unfurl, I list them aloud by name. It is the only game I play in space, reciting the earth-names, the nomenclature of contour and structure. Glacial

scour, moraine debris. Shatter-coning at the edge of a multi-ring impact site. A resurgent caldera, a mass of castellated rimrock. Over the sand seas now. Parabolic dunes, star dunes, straight dunes with radial crests. The emptier the land, the more luminous and precise the names for its features. Vollmer says the thing science does best is name the features of the world. (331)

On first glance, the passage appears to describe details and effects of geological time, the visible markers of long-term displacement and uplift. Yet the passage is also invested in the intervention of human knowledge in the phenomena of planetary change; by naming geological and geographical features, science gains traction on it. The narrator associates the accumulation of knowledge with appearances of vacancy—that science fills out the world's ostensible emptiness by assigning categories to it. The orbital field introduces an imaginary perspectival dimension, incorporating scales that range from the atmospherically broad to the geologically precise. The literal possibilities of optical physics translate, in the story, into conceptual meditations on planetary experience. In another passage, the narrator relates Vollmer's concern with human existence on a planetary scale: "'It's almost unbelievable when you think of it, how they live there in all that ice and sand and mountainous wilderness. Look at it,' he says. 'Huge barren deserts, huge oceans. How do they endure all those terrible things? The floods alone. The earthquakes alone [. . .]'" (335). Vollmer's words simultaneously register his alienation from the human condition and from the planet. He cannot fathom how people on earth can reconcile their precarious existence with the likelihood of catastrophic geophysical events. The being of the planet does not correlate or cater to that of human life.

For DeLillo, the orbital field's verticality underscores the planet's otherness, which remains ostensibly tamable when scaled to the horizontal plane of humanist thought. As the narrator and Vollmer spend more time in orbit, however, they begin to question their previously held humanist attitudes: "Vollmer is on the verge of deciding that our planet is alone in harboring intelligent life. We are an accident and we happened only once" (337). The narrator attributes this realization to Vollmer, but it is noteworthy that he says Vollmer is "on the verge" of it, suggesting that the thought is, in fact, the narrator's. On one hand, the comment is exceptionalist—that there is no intelligent life in the universe *except* humans. On the other, the narrator calls human life an accident, not an ordained creation or even evolutionarily likely, speaking implicitly to the paradox of extraterrestrial life proposed by physicist Enrico Fermi: "After all, [Vollmer] says, where are they? If they exist, why has there been no sign, not one, not any, not a single indication that serious people might cling to, not a whisper, a radio pulse, a shadow?" (337).[28] The narrator and Vollmer connect their suspicions to the war, but it also appears attached to their verticality, their view of the planet as something nonhuman. Vollmer's account of the unlikelihood of human existence complements his doubt regarding the existence of life across the universe, a kind of cosmic cynicism.

The descriptions of earth in DeLillo's story are stirring in their own right but achieve even greater effect when juxtaposed with the comments of historical astronauts. When John Glenn circled the planet in 1962, he gave an account that anticipates the details of "Human Moments": "While I was reporting in by radio to the Canary Island tracking station, I had my first glimpse of the coast of Africa. The Atlas Mountains were clearly visible through the window. Inland, I could see huge dust storms from brush fires raging along the edge of the desert."[29] Others recount similar experiences, and their words convey the sensations that have come to be associated with the *overview effect*, or sensation of viewing earth from space. In his 1987 book on the concept, which proposes to develop a philosophy of space travel, Frank White theorizes the effect and provides numerous firsthand accounts, being careful to admit that details vary: "If there is a common theme in astronauts' descriptions of changes in spatial perceptions, it is seeing the Earth from orbit and being emotionally unprepared for the experience."[30] White's survey suggests an inability to calibrate oneself preemptively to the spatial and temporal disorientation of spaceflight.

By contrast, DeLillo's story evinces something less like wonder and sublime inexpressibility and more like banal cynicism, a numbness resulting from prolonged exposure to the overview effect. The narrator and Vollmer are no longer absorbed by the planet's beauty but made forcibly aware of beauty's situational effect, a presentation that recalls Michael Fried's criticism of theatricality: "To men at this remove, it is as though things exist in their particular physical form in order to reveal the hidden simplicity of some powerful mathematical truth. The earth reveals to us the simple awesome beauty of day and night. It is there to contain and incorporate these conceptual events" (327). At first glance, these lines might be read as an affirmation of sublimity with their emphasis on beauty; but the narrator describes here the unveiling of what we might call the mechanism of beauty. Displaced from the earthbound human condition, orbital perspective discloses beauty's anthropocentrism. This is not Kant's sublime but what Colebrook calls the "geological sublime": "a sublime that is not that of the world appearing as if in accord with our intentionality, a world that is not that of harmonious order, but that is destructive of the anthropomorphic sense we make of things."[31] Encountering the planet vertically, "Human Moments" mobilizes the sublime as a rescaling device. It makes Vollmer and the narrator feel less at home in their own bodies. The experience stands in contrast to that of astronaut Russell Schweickart, who insisted on the aesthetic ability of the overview effect to generate a sense of humanistic comradery: "If it's, 'They are the enemy and they are over there,' one acts consistently with that perception. If you see it at a higher level, that we are all locked together in a planetary context and are coevolving, that also shapes certain actions."[32] Schweickart thought that planetary consciousness could dissolve the borders between social, cultural, and international disputes, producing a strengthened sense of human cooperation. It could, in other words, dispel war. The overview effect in "Human Moments" generates no such aesthetic appreciation in DeLillo's fictional astronauts; to the contrary, the combination of military escalation and orbital experience dissolves the boundaries of human identity.

Orbiting Speculative Geologies

Whereas DeLillo's story meditates solely on the implications of orbital suspension, O'Brien's *The Nuclear Age* offers a more extensive engagement with the dynamic between the orbital field and grounding, or what I discussed in Chapter 2 as speculative geologies. Near the end of O'Brien's book, William's high school and college love interest, Sarah, reflects on their relationship and involvement in a resistance group, as well as the changing political situation and William's newfound financial prosperity, having discovered an untapped uranium deposit: "You've changed," she tells him; "The uranium, for God's sake. [. . .] Mr. Normal. Ban the bomb to boom the bomb. Denim to sharkskin, plowshares to swords" (272). Sarah is commenting on William's shift from protesting the nuclear regime to profiting off it, but her language is curious for another reason: it flips the words in Isaiah 2:4, "and they shall beat their swords into plowshares," words that also inspired the name of the AEC's Project Plowshare.

The reference is oblique and solitary, yet given the historical association between the biblical verse and the nuclear program, it seems more than co-incidence. The AEC published its handbook *Prospecting for Uranium* in 1949, revising it in 1951 and again in 1957, and providing general instructions on the identification and sale of uranium within the United States.[33] *The Nuclear Age* begins, chronologically, in 1958—one year after the AEC's last revised edition and the same year that physicist Edward Teller proposed "geographical engi-neering" as a pursuit for nuclear testing.[34] Beginning with Dwight D. Eisen-hower's "Atoms for Peace" (1953), the U.S. nuclear program began looking for rhetorically effective ways to spin atomic testing, eventually turning to the alteration of the earth's surface to facilitate trade and transportation: "Plow-share offered a positive image of nuclear detonations in the midst of global nuclear fear," writes Masco, "offering a vision of a world that—if it could just avoid nuclear war or permanently damaging the biosphere and humanity via radioactive fallout—might be a utopia for industry, commerce, and society."[35] Viewed in the context of the U.S. shift toward "peaceful nuclear explosions" and geophysical reengineering, *The Nuclear Age* becomes a commentary not only on the threat of nuclear war, but on what Masco calls "the planetary spec-tacle of the nuclear age itself."[36] O'Brien's novel strives to reflect the full scope of the nuclear regime—its catastrophic vector of aggressive warfare, but also its "peaceful" application, the orchestration of energy for infrastructural pur-poses. It is not surprising, then, that the novel imagines this regime as playing out vertically, in the sky above and the ground below.

In *The Nuclear Age*, the orbital field comes to light in part through O'Brien's liberal use of vertical perspective, which affords narrator William Cowling a glimpse of global goings-on that he cannot possibly achieve. O'Brien strategi-cally deploys orbital optics as an omniscient viewpoint imagined by William, creating an entangled narrative that is, at times, both first and third person. Moreover, the novel suggests that William's perspectival imagination is due in part to a deteriorating mental state, which he repeatedly foists onto the exter-nal world in a move that recalls the textual schizophrenias of William S. Bur-roughs or Philip K. Dick. The indeterminacies of both William's psychology and the vertical perspective he inhabits speak to the novel's Anthropocene consciousness, which encourages its readers to think through the ecological parameters of the nuclear regime.

From its opening pages, *The Nuclear Age* wants its readers to be suspicious of the narrator's tale. "Am I crazy?" William Cowling asks in the novel's opening line, as he secretly ventures into his backyard: "I pick a spot near the tool shed. A crackpot? Maybe, maybe not, but listen. The sound of physics. The soft, breathless whir of Now" (3). The language of physics permeates the text as if through fusion, with such chapter and section titles as "Fission," "Quantum Jumps," and "Chain Reactions." The effect is one of subtle naturalization, as though this language serves as transparent descriptions of the world, but O'Brien offsets even the slightest temptation toward familiarity by calling attention to William's health, as well as to the fact that the hole he digs seems to speak to him:

> "I'm not crazy. Eccentric, maybe. These headaches and cramped bowels. How long since my last decent stool? A full night's sleep? Clogged up and frazzled, a little dizzy, a little scared. But not crazy. Fully sane, in fact.
>
>   *Dig*, the hole says. (7; italics in original)

The absurdity of the scenario occasionally drifts into satire, but it remains the case that the hole effectively serves as a character in the text—and a decidedly vertical one at that. Although their conversations and William's reflections on his physical and mental wellbeing make plain the trope of the unreliable narrator, the hole itself is an inverted material embodiment of William's verticalized perspective.

In many ways, *The Nuclear Age* is about more than its title suggests. Although nuclear destruction is one of its concerns, it is largely interested in the accelerative momentum of the United States after World War II generally speaking: atomic energy, but also geopolitical volatility, capitalist expansion, and civil unrest, as figured in William's participation with an antiwar resistance group modeled on the Weather Underground. Moreover, the novel's focus on the planet establishes another dimension to William's psychological state; not simply a commentary on cultural anxieties during its titular historical period, *The Nuclear Age* stages tropes of fantasy and delusion as metaphors for the industrial exploitation of the nonhuman world, which often manifests along a vertical axis. Vertical dynamics of elevation and depth assume multiple meanings in O'Brien's narrative. The underground is literally the space of nuclear test detonations and fallout shelters, but it also connotes paranoia and secrecy, the clandestine operations of government agents and resistance groups. Likewise, elevation describes the space of military satellites and weapons systems, but it also coordinates the scale of industrial and technological expansion, the urgency with which capitalism reproduces itself and with which its opponents respond: "the critical dynamic of our age," as William says during his time training with the antiwar cell; "It was all escalation" (107). *The Nuclear Age* translates this escalation into vertical energies above and below the planet's surface.

As a novel published in the midst of the Reagan era, *The Nuclear Age* has received attention for its intense focus on Cold War anxieties, and some critics have noted that its thematic framework exceeds that of simply nuclear catastrophe. "The novel's concern is not with the explosion of the Cold War into nuclear heat but with the experience of living with this threat, unresolved, over a long period of time," Daniel Cordle writes, situating the novel alongside psychological diagnostics of Cold War anxiety.[37] Cordle suggests that the novel's attention to the etiologies of nuclear anxiety opens onto broader textual questions of language and lived experience, and he contends that many readings neglect its linguistic ambiguity, cultivated through delightful scientistic metaphors.[38] Daniel Grausam also targets the high-strung anxieties of O'Brien's narrator, but turns his attention to the rhetorics of gaming and simulation as textual strategies for, as he puts it, "represent[ing] one of the ways in which nuclear war was displaced in the American imagination."[39] In Grausam's reading, *The Nuclear Age* is not a paranoid novel but a thoughtfully critical one, pinpointing the ways that a cultural consciousness compartmentalizes the threat of disaster.

Cordle's and Grausam's insightful accounts have much to say about the ways that Cold War anxiety and psychology operate in *The Nuclear Age*, but less about the ways the novel draws on perspectives made available by the orbital field, and what these perspectives afford its planetary imagination. By juxtaposing the psychological trepidations made clear by Cordle and Grausam with O'Brien's vertical propensity, we discover that *The Nuclear Age* aligns these trepidations with epistemologies clearly directed toward the atmosphere and underground. When, as a boy, William attends therapy sessions due to what his parents perceive as antisocial behavior and anxiety, the therapist, Chuck Adamson, tells William that astronomy is depressing: "Doom! End of the world, end of everything! You want a depressing hobby? Try astronomy— *doom!*" (52). O'Brien's satire of psychology borders on the absurd, with Adamson revealing himself to be a wildly incapable analyst and acting more like a patient than a doctor; yet his association of astronomy with annihilation is a formative one for William, who goes on to pursue geology at college: "That was my main love, and from my first day at Peverson I knew I'd be majoring in rocks" (68). It is not only that William loves rocks, however; he also finds a therapeutic consolation in them: "I wasn't crazy. I didn't unravel" (69). Opposed to the apocalyptic and dissipative thrust of astrophysics—the death of stars, ineluctable entropy—rocks provide security for William.

It is unsurprising that precisely what affords William a sense of security should become an object of fetishism. His obsession animates the ground, turns it into a vibrant, talking subject. The irony of this fetish is that the hole's animation countermands its security. It exposes itself as place of both refuge and risk: "*Here's a riddle,*" it asks William: "*What is here but not here, there but not there?* Then a pause. 'You,' I say, and the hole chuckles: *Oh, yeah! I am the absence of presence. I am the presence of absence*" (198; italics in original). This language undermines the hole's purported stability, its existence as a singular, determinate thing. It also pinpoints the ambiguity of hole-ness, recalling Negarestani's ( )hole complex and echoing artist Carl Andre's dictum, "A thing is a hole in a thing it is not."[40] O'Brien undoubtedly has puns in mind, as evidenced by a poem William's wife, Bobbi, writes about his obsession with the hole: "*Here, underground, the flashes / are back, filaments of history / that light the tunnels / beneath the mind / and undermine the softer lights / of love and reason. / Remember this / as though in flashback: / A bomb. / A village burning. / We destroyed this house / to save it*" (198–199; italics in original). Bobbi's poem refers to undermining in a dual sense, as a rhetorical and geological practice. As William displaces the earth in his backyard, the foundations of house and family begin to weaken. Bobbi and William's daughter, Melinda, cannot understand his fixation, leading him to coerce them into the shelter, to force them to participate in his fantasy of earthly solidarity.

Given William's obsession with the hole, it is curious that he appears also to find comfort in the detached experience of air travel. "I put myself on glide, breathing deep," he says while onboard a plane, "imagining I was aboard a one-man spaceship tracking for the stars" (148–149). As this fantasy takes hold—a youthful atmospheric complement to his midlife bomb shelter—William finds himself drawn into a kind of trance: "Far below, the home planet spun on its axis, a pleasing vision, those lovely whites and blues, the fragile continents, and as I sailed away, as the world receded, I felt a curious measure of nostalgia, desire mixed with grief. Here, in space, there was just the smooth suck of inertia" (149). The calm that he finds in this dream of space travel seems to run counter to the comfort afforded by his hole. An explanation for this apparent idiosyncrasy begins to take shape when we contextualize it within O'Brien's larger chain of figurative associations concerning ground and atmosphere. Specifically, his experience in the airplane takes place after he has begun to grow wary of his involvement with an antiwar group that practices violent resistance, which O'Brien models on the Weather Underground in an obvious pun: "So anyhow, welcome to the depths," the character Ollie Winkler tells William; "Depths—underground, get it?" (146). A strange parallel emerges between William's hole-digging—his being literally underground—and his youthful resistance, his metaphorical time underground. For this reason, the hole can never afford William complete psychological comfort; it reminds him too much of the figurative hole he dug earlier in his life.

In *The Nuclear Age*, geology turns out to be a deceptive comfort, at first welcoming and warm but revealing itself as uncanny, ominous, and layered with multifarious experiences. Just as geology archives the age of the planet and all its prior denizens, so does it signify the entirety of William's life, which he unearths upon digging his hole: "When I think back on the summer of 1968, it's as though it all occurred in some other dimension, a mixture of what had happened and what would happen. Like hide-and-go seek—the future curves toward the past, then folds back again, seamlessly, and we are locked forever in the ongoing present. And where am I? Just digging" (121). O'Brien sets up this analogy well before William's time in the resistance group, hinting at it already in one of Bobbi's poems, titled "The Mole in His Hole": "*Down, a digger, blind and bold, / through folds of earth / layered like the centuries, / down / to that brightest treasure. / Fool's gold*" (57; italics in original). The poem telegraphs the spatiotemporal overlap that characterizes earth's strata, their spatial layering and temporal significance. As William digs deeper, he exposes these layers, sending readers on a cyclical narrative through his memory.

The analogy of geological depth with memory maps a humanist narrative onto the scientific premise of "reading" the history of the planet. Stratigraphy corresponds to a kind of psychoanalysis of the earth, or in the context of the postwar energy regime, we might say that extractive methods correspond to memory mining. Appropriately, William's memory mining does not unfold in a linear, easily comprehensible fashion, but repeatedly extends and retracts, expands and compresses. He loses himself, and those around him, in the unspooling petrification of time:

> Folded in forever like fossils. I don't want it but I can see it, as always, the imprints in rock, the wall shadows at Hiroshima, leaves and grass and the Statue of Liberty and Bobbi's diaphragm. Here, she can't leave me. The fossils don't move. Crack open a rock and she'll be curled around me. Her smile will be gold and granite. Immutable, metamorphic, welded forever by the stresses of our age. We will become the planet. We will become the world-as-it-should-be. We will be faithful. We will lace through the mountains like seams of ore, married like the elements [. . .]. (302)

This passage, near the end of the novel, revels in the narrative detours and digressions that have preceded it. O'Brien vividly reimagines William's life both as the evolution of geology and within geology, with William and Bobbi becoming fossils in the far future of deep time. His descriptions invoke the images of nuclear shadows (silhouettes left by the heat of an atomic blast) and preserved bodies embracing in volcanic ruins like those of Pompeii. The pressures and upheavals of matter become "the stresses" of human history. If there is comfort in these lines, it is an inhuman comfort—the serenity of being part of the planet.

Such a serenity brooks no sustainable perspective for O'Brien, however; *The Nuclear Age* cannot fully pursue the collapse of humankind into the planet, since doing so invites a narrative that exceeds the limits of the novel. Instead, the novel situates us in its narrator's vertical experience of planetarity. William encounters a version of the end of the world, but not an apocalyptic one; rather, he discovers extinction as an element of perspective. Through its implicit ubiquity in *The Nuclear Age*, extinction manifests as a hyperobject, its multiple temporalities layered over each other: "the *end of the world* but not an apocalypse," Timothy Morton writes, "not a predictable conclusion" but rather "discovering yourself *inside of something*" (italics in original).[41] O'Brien's novel is partly a meditation on the psychological and social contortions that accompany life in a nuclear regime, but it is also an acknowledgment (and indictment) of the fact that this regime is authoring a story that outlasts the human. William's anxieties are informed by the discovery that his narrative is taking place inside another one.

The vertical spatiality of *The Nuclear Age* is more than a reflection of the orbital technologies and scientific developments happening in the mid-twentieth century; it is a narrative strategy for coordinating the layered temporalities of human and geological history. Viewed in this way, William's accumulation of details he could not possibly know begins to make sense. As he courses above the country in a Trans World Airlines plane, William catalogues what passes beneath him in a surreal planetary menagerie, echoing the descriptive lists of DeLillo's story:

> I could see the lights of Atlantic City, the scalloped edges of Chesapeake Bay, the tidewaters of Virginia. The clarity was amazing. Telescopic breadth and microscopic precision. I could see Baltimore and Richmond and Washington, the glowing dome on the nation's Capitol, the Lincoln Memorial, the dark Carolinas, Cape Hatteras and Cape Fear, the quiet suburbs of Norfolk, the rivers and inlets, the Jersey shore, north to Maine, south to the keys, all of it, the whole profile, the long sleeping silhouette of midnight America. (149)

William's narration encompasses both the plausibly visible and that which tests credibility. Despite his testament to "microscopic precision," what seems more important for him is that his vantage affords him a way of mapping his knowledge of history and geography. The United States appears to him in profile, a sign that what he sees is only half the country (indeed, only the eastern seaboard) but somehow a characteristic portrait too. Even, implausibly, details of architecture and ambient sound somehow make sense when viewed from such a height, William suggests.

As the flight continues, the objects that William sees become more varied and imaginative, submarines in shallow water and lights in the Kremlin, "men in blue uniforms beneath the translucent earth. The men wore silk scarves and black boots" (150). At this point, however, his observations turn ambiguous, as William himself evinces: "They were not real men, of course, for none of it is real, not the blue uniforms and not the boots and not the Titan II missile with its silver nose cone and patriotic markings" (150). These lines cast suspicion on all his observations, but they also direct us to consider what kind of reality William might be talking about. After all, there certainly are submarines in some water and lights in the Kremlin, as well as rockets lathered in U.S. propaganda. Narrating from this removed height, William interrogates what happens to information at different scales of perception. His vertical remove enables a narrative mode that engages, in Timothy Clark's words, "this new reality of elusive agencies and distant or invisible wrongs, happening at counterintuitive scales."[42] Clark advocates for a kind of scalar literacy that navigates across disparate scales and perspectives, and theorizes the ways that new information becomes available. *The Nuclear Age* proffers an opportunity for such literacy through its deployment of vertical perspective, situated in the developments of midcentury science.

In O'Brien's novel, this literacy materializes through a paradox of vision that accompanies vertical perspective: "I could see all of what cannot be seen," William admits, cryptically, "because it's beyond seeing, because we're sane" (150). The reprisal of psychological language once again bridges the divide between information and paranoia, that union so common to canonically postmodernist fiction. Whereas postmodernism's standard paranoid venture is an anxious search for unseen connections, however, *The Nuclear Age* appears to reject such searching in favor of leaving things unseen, merely imagined. In this way, O'Brien adds another layer of complexity to the orbital field. The atmospheric abode of satellites and overview effects invites paranoid thinking, not because it promises a total constellation of facts and data but because it permits the detours of fantasy:

> One by one, all along the length of the eastern seaboard, the great cities twinkled and burned and vanished. A half-dream, I thought. I felt no fear. I buckled my seat belt. I knew what was next, and when it came, I watched with a kind of reverence. There were flashes of red and gold. There were noises, too, and powdery puffs of maroon and orange and royal blue, fungal arrangements in the lower atmosphere, the laws of physics. But it was not real. When it happens, I realized, it will not happen, because it cannot happen. It will not be real. (150)

Air travel enables William's fantasy of nuclear annihilation, but enables it explicitly *as* fantasy. As he describes in vivid detail the colors and patterns of nuclear detonations, he acknowledges its quasi-dreamlike quality; it lingers somewhere between the world O'Brien inhabits and another, speculative world, conjured by the conditions of the first.

We can take William's words to mean that the fantasy of nuclear calamity is unreal in the sense that it is imagined; yet it is also true that the contents of fantasy are real, if not realized in an empirically verifiable sense. Furthermore, William insists that his vision is not real, cannot be real, "because we're sane"; and yet his indulgence in paranoid fantasy and obsession with his backyard hole complicates this stance. I claim that what registers in these passages of *The Nuclear Age* is not, in fact, a meditation on nuclear anxiety, but rather a complex negotiation of the way that nuclear devastation and human extinction infiltrate the time of life in the Anthropocene. This negotiation cannot be expressed logically, as William's repeated paradoxes convey. It surfaces as a series of engagements with the narrative modes of realism and fantasy, and the styles of speculation and paranoia.

The Nuclear Age turns on such engagements, assuming the appearance of a delicate equation, a balancing act between the acknowledged ferocity of industrial exploitation and the willful delusion of progress. Viewed through this framework, William's binary of sane and insane betrays its contradictions. On one hand, insanity for William entails the exploitation and destruction of the earth, which he fantasizes from the Trans World airplane; yet it is precisely this exploitation that has afforded William and his family their life of luxury, having made a fortune off uranium mining. The understated fantasy of *The Nuclear Age* is not that of nuclear annihilation, but that industrial progress and postwar affluence can continue indefinitely: "I will endure," William says, "I will live my life in the conviction that when it finally happens—when we hear that midnight whine, when Kansas burns, when what is done is undone [. . .]—yes, even then I will hold to a steadfast orthodoxy, confident to the end that E will somehow not quite equal mc^2, that it's a cunning metaphor, that the terminal equation will somehow not quite balance" (312). These lines suggest that William will persist in his delusion that human life will continue, a rejection of apocalyptic fantasy. Yet they express a secondary meaning as well: that human civilization and the planet participate in an asymmetrical relationship, that what capitalist modernity takes from the planet does not match what the planet provides.

In O'Brien's narrative, issues of speculation and exploitation sync up in William's capitalizing on uranium deposits that he locates and sells to Texaco (after a bidding war that includes Gulf Oil and BP). William frames this enterprise and desire for stability once again in terms of fantasy: "What I wanted above all was to join the world, which was to live and to go on living with the knowledge that nothing endures, but to endure" (262). After taking the money and starting a family, William prepares for disaster, but none arrives: "The balance held," he says; "It was not a fantasy" (283). Yet the novel also reflects the damage done to the earth, the manufacturing of a new landscape through mining: "I showed [Bobbi] where the mountain had once been. With my hands, I shaped it for her, explaining how we'd followed the clicking trail toward riches, and how, at a spot roughly between Orion and the Little Dipper, in the age of flower children gone sour, we had come across the source, the red-hot dynamics. It was science, I told her" (283–284). Although William's transaction—his disclosing of resources in exchange for wealth—does not seem to accrue any unforeseen costs, the novel prepares its readers for the inevitable calling of debt:

> I know the ending.
>> One day it will happen.
>> One day we will see flashes, all of us. [. . .]
>> I know this, but I believe otherwise. (312)

William's visions of death and ending—which recur throughout the narrative, at times waning but never disappearing—inscribe the reality of extinction within the affairs of the present. *The Nuclear Age* toys with elements of speculation both narratively and thematically, but it also insists that readers perceive these speculative energies in the context of the everyday. The reality of future collapse is already etched into the entanglements of the postindustrial nuclear age.

Orbital Narrative and the Planetary Mission

Published in the 1980s, DeLillo's and O'Brien's works channel a late Cold War zeitgeist in the throes of escalating geopolitical violence (including the early days of U.S. intervention in the Middle East) and, somewhat counterintuitively, the beginnings of a thaw. Urged on by the firebrand liberalist rhetoric of Margaret Thatcher and Ronald Reagan, and emboldened by the U.S.S.R.'s weakening position on the global stage, American attitudes began to embrace a feeling of ascendant triumph—a feeling punctuated by the collapse of the Soviet Union in 1989. This newfound affirmation of liberalism informs what Jessica Hurley calls a "prophylactic time" that "locates safety within a restricting and oppressive closed temporal loop in which the present is rendered safe by returning to a past that was, from the perspective of the 1980s, more secure."[43] Hurley provides an explanation for the seemingly odd return to the idea of the 1950s as a time of safety and prosperity under Reagan (a return that would occur again in the late 2010s under Donald Trump), despite the fact that the United States was engaged in an escalating arms race with the Soviet Union. For Reaganite conservatives, the purported triumph of Western liberal democracy sterilized the decades of the Cold War; any prior uncertainties could be retroactively washed away because, following versions of the "end of history" thesis, victory had been guaranteed all along.[44]

DeLillo and O'Brien are suspicious of such sterilization, and *The Nuclear Age*, with its satirical and deeply unnerving portrayal of suburban America, appears particularly critical of any celebratory nostalgia. Casting their gazes into the 1990s and possibly beyond, both authors paint unappealing pictures of our hypothetical nuclear future. Yet from our perspective in the 2020s, neither DeLillo nor O'Brien can be said to have quite hit the mark, being steeped in the technophilic fantasies of the Strategic Defense Initiative and the apocalyptic imagery that accompanied depictions of nuclear war. This is not to say that nuclear anxieties were unfounded or that they should no longer trouble us today, but that the nuclear imaginary conjured by both writers could not quite capture the realities of energy production and consumption in the twenty-first century.

Put another way, the 1980s promoted cultural fantasies in both directions: the nostalgic longing for a "safe" 1950s, and the paranoid visions of an exponentially radioactive future. Of course, we would be misguided to assume that DeLillo and O'Brien were ever interested in giving readers anything like a realist account of nuclear living in the second half of the twentieth century, and yet questions of historicity persist. Now, in the final part of this chapter, I am rewinding the tape to Thomas Pynchon's 1973 novel, *Gravity's Rainbow*. Despite being set at the immediate end of World War II and not ostensibly interested in nuclear warfare, Pynchon's novel is nonetheless heavily invested in the industrial and infrastructural narratives of military defense, centered on the development of V-2 rockets in Germany. Long a poster child for postmodernist readings (no doubt informed by the foundational work of Fredric Jameson and Brian McHale), and more recently the subject of historically grounded readings (such as those by David Cowart, Luc Herman and Steven Weisenburger, and Paul K. Saint-Amour), *Gravity's Rainbow* remains a frequent object of literary analysis.[45] Drawing elements from both postmodernist and historicist accounts of Pynchon's novel, I argue that *Gravity's Rainbow*—like the works of DeLillo and O'Brien—is a piece of speculative literature charged with the draw (the gravitational pull, we might say) of Anthropocene temporality.

Questions of time and futurity themselves are not new in Pynchon criticism. As Heise notes, the novel's disorienting anachronisms and revisions are less a dismissal of history than a provocation about how to think historically in the postwar world.[46] Even geared toward the future as it is, *Gravity's Rainbow* poses to its readers the problem of history in a rapidly accelerating world, or a world whose future seems to be cascading backward through time, colliding with the present in surreal if not always damaging ways. Technological anachronisms catalyze this effect, such as the narrator's mentioning of a "Cybernetic Tradition" in 1920s Germany, well before Norbert Wiener popularized the word in the late 1940s (241).[47] Even more curious is the narrator's ability to offer statements that border on prophecy, such as the parenthetical quips on the term "critical mass"—"(get it? not too many did in 1945, the Cosmic Bomb was still trembling in its earliness, not yet revealed to the People)" (548)—and references to Ishmael Reed, who did not publish his first writings until well after 1945 (598). Throughout the novel, Pynchon targets this cascading future through vertical narrative maneuvers: specifically, an orbital narrator whose presence encircles (albeit incompletely) the planet, temporally and spatially, and an emergent planetary assemblage in which human practices (mainly war) are cast as geophysical forces. Published prior to the Star Wars frenzy of the 1980s, *Gravity's Rainbow* intuits the enmeshed quality of vertical science, the ways that the orbital field and speculative geologies merge to form a singular (if circuitous) planetary narrative.

The challenge for anyone writing about *Gravity's Rainbow*—whose narrator indulges in temporal and spatial leaps without warning—lies in connecting its many historical tendrils, narrative threads, and philosophical reflections. To put it reductively, the novel tells the story of Tyrone Slothrop's quest to understand the correlation between his casual hookups and V-2 rocket strikes near the end of World War II; but in a less plot-driven sense, it is about the disorienting and largely incomprehensible (at the time) historical shift from a Taylorist machine age to what Hunter Heyck calls the "age of system."[48] The novel's expansive cast of characters includes soldiers, scientists, psychics, actors, politicians, revolutionaries, octopi, lightbulbs, and more, many of whom intersect with one another in ways that mean less for their narrative development than for the intimation of a global system beyond readerly apprehension. Any full map of these intersections is impossible in a single chapter, let alone a section; but we can apprehend the ways that certain details and developments tie together, and the conceptual corridors they form.

Gravity's Rainbow opens famously with a description of Pirate Prentice's apocalyptic dream: the evacuation of London during a missile strike. Already, Pynchon situates his readers not only in a scene of technologically induced devastation, but in an industrially produced history: "certain trestles of blackened wood have moved slowly by overhead, and the smells begun of coal from days far to the past, smells of naphtha winters, of Sundays when no traffic came through, of the coral-like and mysteriously vital growth, around the blind curves and out the lonely spurs, a sour smell of rolling-stock absence, of maturing rust" (4) The passage recalls London's industrialization, its mining of coal and refining of crude oil. Furthermore, within this short space, Pynchon coordinates overlapping scales of local and global; the English mined coal primarily on the home front, whereas oil was piped in from elsewhere. *Gravity's Rainbow* repeatedly performs these involutions of local and global, insinuating that it is neither about London nor the war-torn regions of Europe, but about the postwar world writ large: "No zones but the Zone," as one character tells protagonist Tyrone Slothrop (338). Throughout its pages, the novel illuminates the global energy infrastructure at work in the mid-twentieth-century world of its narrative, and the intersections between war and fossil fuels.

The novel's opening sequence expresses this global infrastructure in another way, however—one that becomes clear when we recall that Pirate's dream of a missile strike on London is a kind of nonlinear completion of the "descent" of the rocket in the novel's final pages. The narrative begins when and where it ends, but only to an extent. Whereas Pirate's dream imagines a missile attack on London, the novel's closing pages transport readers to California, and the final lines leave us with the rocket looming above a Hollywood movie theater, perhaps even merging with the screen to suggest that the entire story has been "all theatre" (3). The narrative link between these two geographical locations implies a broader connectivity in which the entire surface of the earth is incorporated into the singular Zone, mediated by the narrator's effortless orbital surveillance. Pynchon renders this orbital perspective both vaguely omniscient and cinematic, as when the German scientist Webley Silvernail reflects on the mechanics of observation: "From overhead, from a German camera-angle, it occurs to Webley Silvernail, this lab here is also a maze i'n't it now . . . behaviorists run these aisles of tables and consoles just like rats 'n' mice. [. . .] But who watches from above, who notes *their* responses?" (232; italics in original). The narrator's description here implies not only German military surveillance but Expressionist film, and gestures obliquely to unseen observers. Ostensibly these observers are the novel's ominous "Them," the unnamed overlords presumably directing events; but the comment is also self-referential—who watches from above? One answer is: the narrator.

This vertically positioned view is already present in the novel's opening pages, and continues throughout, comprising what Kathryn Hume calls a "perspectival subtext."[49] Hume focuses lucidly on the ways that Pynchon narratively realizes such views, yet it is also the case that he embeds them in less explicit ways. Upon waking from his dream of a rocket strike, Pirate continues to fantasize what such an attack would feel like and look like as he watches distant launches. Seeing the vapor trail of a V-2 rocket—"a short vertical white line"—he contemplates the logic of his vision:

> "Well, the range of these things is supposed to be over 200 miles. You can't see a vapor trail 200 miles, now, can you.
>
> Oh. Oh yes: around the curve of the Earth, farther east, the sun, over there, just risen over in Holland, is striking the rocket's exhaust, drops and crystals, making them blaze clear across the sea. . . ." (6–7)

This vaguely planetary image yields some significant particulars, as Steven Weisenburger helpfully clarifies. Not only is the rainbow from the vapor's refraction orbital instead of arch-shaped (meaning it encircles the earth rather than descending into it), but it would be impossible for Pirate to see unless he were "perched high over the North Sea."[50] The vision in these lines is not simply that of Pirate's imagination; it is inflected with both the technologies of aerial exploration and techniques of narrative experimentation. It is a narrative effect inextricable from the vertical sciences with which Pynchon is centrally concerned. *Gravity's Rainbow* can be described as a literary cataloguing of, and formal meditation on, the propulsive energies that enabled the vertical-orbital perspectives of the postwar Anthropocene.

The novel's opening pages provide a suggestive starting point given that issues of energy, industry, and the planet continue to occupy the text in telling and often overlapping ways. As the narrative unfolds, expands, dissolves and resolves by turns, readers are given an image of a world built upon—and embedded within—crisscrossing vectors of energy: "The War needs coal," the narrator explains; "The War needs electricity. It's a lively game, Electric Monopoly, among the power companies, the Central Electricity Board, and other War agencies, to keep Grid Time synchronized with Greenwich Mean Time" (135–136). In *Gravity's Rainbow*, war and technology intermingle and breed a new geography unbeholden to national borders: "army convoys waiting at the crossings as the train puffs by," the narrator says, describing the war's rerouting of transportation corridors, "never a clear sense of nationality anywhere, nor even of belligerent sides, only the War, a single damaged landscape" (261). The description is jarring; the war is everywhere, yet there are no opposed forces, no pitched combat. Rather, it is being orchestrated by multinationals and global financial markets, institutions like IG Farben and "Shell, with no real country, no side in any war, no specific face or heritage: tapping instead out of that global stratum, most deeply laid, from which all the appearances of corporate ownership really spring" (246). As Pynchon is surely aware, IG Farben played a particularly crucial role in Germany's energy aspirations, being the largest private corporation in Europe at the time and in possession of massive amounts of lignite for creating fuel.[51] The author's futural vision anticipates the increasing complexity of geopolitics after 1945, after World War II fundamentally rewrote the modern world in terms of energy dominance.

Historically speaking, such a view of modernity no longer permits nationalist narratives of victories and losses. Instead, war becomes synonymous

with (or indecipherable from) processes of technoscientific and industrial development that permeate virtually the entire world. *Gravity's Rainbow* has a
name for this entanglement of war, science, technology, and industry: *"the
planetary mission"* (530; italics in original). Incommensurate with standard
narratives of history or fiction, the planetary mission is a reactive, reflexive,
nonlinear network:

> We have to look for power sources here, and distribution networks we were
> never taught, routes of power our teachers never imagined, or were encour-
> aged to avoid . . . we have to find meters whose scales are unknown in the
> world, draw our own schematics, getting feedback, making connections, re-
> ducing the error, trying to learn the real function . . . zeroing in on what in-
> calculable plot? (530)

In these lines, Pynchon anticipates Negarestani's ( )hole complex—an imaginary network of unseen links and exchanges that subvert narrative order—
and the archival geology of later Anthropocene novels. The "incalculable plot"
suggests less the telling of a story than the paranoid assembly of information,
a practice that John Johnston associates with *Gravity's Rainbow* as a whole.[52]
Moreover, this notion of paranoia has come to define not only Pynchon's writing, but the general urgency of postmodernism from 1960 to 1990, roughly
speaking, extending even to the hermeneutic practices of the reading public.
As Friedrich Kittler provocatively puts it, "the critical-paranoid method of the
novel infects its readers. They turn from consumers of a narrative into hackers
of a system."[53] What often escapes readings of the novel's paranoia, however,
are the ways that Pynchon strategically ties his geographical (and horizontal)
remodeling to an emerging geological (and vertical) consciousness.

The vertical dimension of *Gravity's Rainbow* emerges from its intelligent
depiction of the coproduction that occurs between human industry and the
planet itself, figured in the interplay between missile telemetries above the
earth's surface and the energy reserves flowing beneath it. Published the same
year as the first OPEC oil embargo, *Gravity's Rainbow* is deeply attuned to the
avenues of energy that give shape to the globalized postwar world. Describing
the death of the character Tchitcherine's father in the Port Arthur siege of
1904, the narrator imagines "the slowly carbonizing faces of men he thought
he knew, men turning to coal, ancient coal that glistened, [. . .] a conspiracy

of carbon, though he never phrased it as 'carbon,' it was power he walked away from, the feeling of too much meaningless power, flowing wrong . . ." (356). This "conspiracy of carbon" is a recurrent image in the novel, from the energy networks that reroute transportation, to the plastics required to construct the ominous Schwarzgerät (the rocket being built by the Nazi villain Weissmann), to the text's version of the Gaia hypothesis: "that history is Earth's mind, and that there are layers, set very deep, layers of history analogous to layers of coal and oil in Earth's body" (600). The "conspiracy of carbon" unfolds across multiple vertical spheres, resulting in a planetary infrastructure in which geophysical systems are infused within human ones, including the jet propulsion technologies that rely on fossil fuels.

Although set prior to the era of space exploration and orbital networks depicted in DeLillo's and O'Brien's works, *Gravity's Rainbow* nonetheless acknowledges this facet of rocket propulsion technologies. The prospect of exploring the atmospheric heights of the orbital field (if not beyond) occupies the novel's vertical imagination, an implicit acknowledgment that the development of postwar weapons systems was a historical prerequisite to the era of space exploration.[54] In one of the novel's many flashback sequences, Leni Pökler recalls her husband Franz's scientific aspirations in the Society for Space Travel, set in prewar Berlin. The antithesis of Franz's cold rationalism, Leni's creative intuition raises her suspicions about propulsion technology and the hazards it poses to human existence:

> "They're using you to kill people," Leni told him, as clearly as she could. "That's their only job, and you're helping them."
>
> "We'll all use *it*, someday, to leave the earth. To transcend."
>
> She laughed. "Transcend," from Pökler?
>
> "Someday," honestly trying, "they won't have to kill. Borders won't mean anything. We'll have all outer space. . . ." (406; italics in original)

At first glance, Franz's comments appear prophetic, anticipating the use of rockets for space travel; but Leni is the one who intuits the deadly historical connection between warfare and spacefaring. The military demand for missiles gives way to the post-global imagination of a planet in space. Pynchon knowingly casts this spaceward urgency as a new colonialism, or what antagonist Weissmann calls a "new Deathkingdom" (737). The portmanteau carries a dual significance: Weissmann also goes by the moniker Blicero, a Germanic nickname for death.[55] Weissmann's Deathkingdoms are his "my-kingdoms," future territories authored by violence. His words are a chilling echo of Cecil Rhodes's "Will and Testament," in which the architect of South African colonization longs to "annex the planets."[56] *Gravity's Rainbow* illuminates a genealogy of the technologies that make possible such annexation, an infrastructural realization of Rhodes's imperial fantasy. The drive to occupy atmosphere, outer space, the moon, and beyond reveals the vertical dimension of expansionism, a technologically driven compulsion away from the planet's surface.

In Weissmann's description, colonialism enters into conflict with geophysics, primarily the force of gravity itself. The figure from which the novel gets its name—the arc of a rocket after it has spent its fuel and begins its descent—discovers a new form beyond the earth's atmosphere, yet Pynchon reminds us that the orbital field is still beholden to the dynamics of gravity: "passages out there are dangerous," Weissmann muses, "chances of falling so shining and deep. . . . Gravity rules all the way out to the cold sphere, *there is always the danger of falling*" (737; italics in original). The reference to gravity in these lines reveals the text's movement toward not only a planetary consciousness, but an interplanetary one. As Weissmann declares, gravity does not disappear in space, but finds new centers, accumulates around new objects. Like the speculative geologies of Chapter 2 and the orbital fields of DeLillo and O'Brien, the interplanetary perspective implicit in *Gravity's Rainbow* further destabilizes the earth as a foundation, reimagining it as a body at the mercy of gravity—and a template for other celestial bodies, like Robinson's Mars, that humans might go on to colonize.

In making this move to an interplanetary view, Pynchon invites us to see the earth as a body like any other—human, animal, vegetable, mineral. All are prone to the same physical forces. It is through the mediation of a specifically vertical perspective that this interplanetary view comes into focus, and Pynchon presents it to readers as a future-oriented vision: a text set (mostly) in the wartime past, inflected by Pynchon's post-1960s present, and anticipating a future Anthropocene consciousness. In this respect, *Gravity's Rainbow* can be seen not only as the apogee of postmodernist writing, but as an ambitious early entry in the tradition of environmentally concerned Anthropocene fiction—a novel whose experimentations with style and perspective shed light on the planetary imagination that emerges in the second half of the twentieth century. It has been the aim of this chapter to situate this emergent conscious-ness alongside the vertical possibilities that accompany nuclear proliferation and orbital technologies. Incorporating techniques of orbital perspective into their depictions of nuclear anxiety and planetary systems, DeLillo, O'Brien, and Pynchon reveal the ways that verticality informs new ways of thinking about humankind's entanglement with the earth.

Fossil Labor
Anthropocene Fiction and
the Racial Politics of Extinction

Toward a Black Planetarity

Gravity's Rainbow is anything but subtle when it comes to the racial dynamics that underpin its character systems. As readers with even a passing familiarity with German will note, the novel's villain is racially coded: Weissmann, "white man," the text's German Nazi antagonist. Pynchon's knowledge of German colonial history also figures into these dynamics; one of his characters, Enzian, is a Zone-Herero, a descendent of native Africans displaced by the Germans during the colonization of the continent in the late nineteenth and early twentieth centuries. In the imaginary world of *Gravity's Rainbow*, the Herero have been conscripted to fight for the Germans in World War II but have turned against the colonizer. Pynchon frames the Zone-Herero as revolutionaries in a uniquely geological sense:

> They call themselves Otukungurua. Yes, old Africa hands, it *ought* to be "Omakungurua," but they are always careful—perhaps it's less healthy than care—to point out that *oma-* applies only to the living and human. *Otu-* is for the inanimate and the rising, and this is how they imagine themselves. Revolutionaries of the Zero, they mean to carry on what began among the old Hereros after the 1904 rebellion failed. They want a negative birth rate. The program is racial suicide. They would finish the extermination the Germans began in 1904. (321; italics in original)

Although troubling, the Herero program of "racial suicide" establishes a geological vector—a return to inanimate, earthly matter. Their goal is to assume control of their death, to forestall Germany as an agent of extermination. This control manifests as an urgency toward the planet, and specifically toward the subterranean: "Vectors in the night underground," as the narrator says (323). Like O'Brien in *The Nuclear Age*, Pynchon puns on "underground" as both a literal space and a sense of clandestine operations: "underground communities [. . .] known collectively as the Erdschweinhöhle," a German word for the Herero fertility symbol, a woman partially buried in an aardvark hole (320). The Herero not only seek to become the nonliving matter compressed underground, but also feed on energy that comes from the earth, drawn downward for reasons of sustenance and survival.[1]

This association of Blackness and the underground does not originate with Pynchon, but finds purchase in a Black tradition of subterranean resistance, which includes Ralph Ellison's *Invisible Man* (1952), whose narrator tells the story of his exile from his hideout below Harlem:

> That is why I fight my battle with Monopolated Light & Power. The deeper reason, I mean: it allows me to feel my vital aliveness. I also fight them for taking so much of my money before I learned to protect myself. In my hole in the basement there are exactly 1,369 lights. I've wired the entire ceiling, every inch of it. And not with fluorescent bulbs, but with the older, more-expensive-to-operate kind, the filament type. An act of sabotage, you know.[2]

This oft-cited passage from the novel's prologue marks an early instance of subversive Anthropocene writing from an African American author. He has illuminated his underground hole with energy-consuming incandescent bulbs, attaching himself, as Kate Marshall notes, "to the municipal power grid."[3] This attachment marks the narrator's emplacement within systems of energy production, but also his circumvention of those systems; he taps into the system illicitly, a clandestine consumer who receives no electric bill. These actions might not be environmentalist, but they signify a form of minor rebellion against the fossil fuel economy's stranglehold, forcing the company to eat the cost of the power to these particular 1,369 bulbs. Moreover, the narrator waits, hibernates, in what is literally an excavated piece of earth, a space carved out by urban infrastructural development—an industrial script etched into the planet.

Ellison's anonymous narrator is driven underground during an unspecified riot (likely the 1943 Harlem riot), but African American writers have been drawn to the underground for a variety of reasons. Richard Wright's *The Man Who Lived Underground* was written before the publication of Ellison's novel, although not released until 2021, and tells the story of Fred Daniels, a Black man accused of murder who flees into the sewers. For Wright, Daniels's flight telegraphs a vector of escape that still resonates in the twenty-first century, given the systematic targeting of Black men by the police. Meanwhile, and in a manner resembling the clandestine operations of Pynchon's Herero, Chester Himes's *Plan B* (also posthumously published) culminates in revolution across the United States, whose citizens draw on knowledge of their cities' underworlds. Himes even acknowledges the literary tradition that inspires this narrative choice: "[At] first, the favorite underground hiding places, made appealing by black writers, were the sewers and conduits for the various public services, such as electricity, telephones, water, steam, and the like. These places honeycombed the areas beneath the buildings of every large city and were easily reached by numerous manholes."[4] Himes paints a vivid picture of buried industrial apparatuses, tunneled and interlinked below the city surface. In *Plan B*, these apparatuses become a support system for revolution, providing the space necessary for Black resistance. For Ellison, Wright, and Himes, fugitivity encodes itself in subterranean infrastructures, resulting in a racial history of the underground.

Like Ellison, Himes is conscious of the energy infrastructure that underpins and sustains the city, the destruction of which becomes a weapon for the revolutionaries who sabotage it.[5] Pynchon's *Gravity's Rainbow* offers an even more expansive vision of this revolutionary significance, assuming the theoretical entanglement of Black resistance and infrastructural development as part of its narrative foundation.[6] The novel's orbital sensibilities are complemented by its equally crucial subterranean racialism. In seeking to kill themselves and become part of the earth, the Herero intimate that they will join with the fossil matter underground: "some immachination," the narrator says, "whether of journey or of destiny, which is able to gather violent political opposites together in the Erdschweinhöhle as it gathers fuel and oxidizer in its thrust chamber" (323). In these lines, the narrator juxtaposes the Herero with the mysterious Rocket being constructed by Weissmann, which they intend to destroy. A strange and complex dynamic emerges from Pynchon's inanimate casting of the Herero—that in their desire to become nonliving matter, they become part of the material resources required to fuel weapons of war. In a passage describing oil fields in the Middle East and Russia, the narrator reminds readers of the underground's agency: "All the oil money taken out of these fields by the Nobels has gone into Nobel Prizes. New wells are going down elsewhere, between the Volga and the Urals. Time for retrospection here, for refining the recent history that's being pumped up fetid and black from other strata of Earth's mind. . . ." (360). These lines underscore the entanglement of geology and human history, the "recent history" of war and death becoming the object of extraction. In his vision of postwar Europe, Pynchon expresses the feedback between war and industry, and the ways that history bleeds downward into the subterranean layers.

Gravity's Rainbow amplifies the racial politics of strata that we find in works by Ellison, Wright, and Himes, and that are picked up and further amplified by contemporary African American writers. As Nigel Clark points out, human interactions with geological strata (through subsurface contamination, extraction, fracking, and other practices) have been shown to have measurable socioenvironmental effects in an increasingly smaller time scale, such that they now impinge on political concerns.[7] Pynchon represents a unique example of a White writer intuiting the practices of socioecological exploitation that have historically affected (and continue to affect) Black bodies, in this case the Herero. Just as they have been subject to colonial exploitation by Germany, they become subject to environmental exploitation as they merge with the fossil fuels underground. I call this dual sense of exploitation *fossil labor*: a racialized planetary cycle in which exploited subjects serve as both industrious labor and resource matter for future exploitation. In recent years, critics have illustrated a rhetoric of racialized fossilization that often forms a basis for modernist frameworks of progress, in which industrial civilization is privileged over reductive and primitivized images of indigeneity.[8] Such frameworks entail an ideological investment in specifically identifiable and familiar forms of life, namely White maleness, while people of color are viewed as bodily, animalistic, and physical—traits that make them suited, in the eyes of White colonizers, for manual labor, but also situate them closer to the inanimate ground on which they work. To this end, these racialized ideologies draft a *necropolitics* of exploitation, to use Achille Mbembe's term: practices of institutional domination involving not only the legislative and militaristic control over life (such as executions and drone strikes) but the rhetorical and epistemological control over what counts as living.[9]

At first glance, fossil labor calls to mind Marx's famous dictum, in volume one of *Capital*, describing capital as "dead labour, that, vampire-like, only lives by sucking living labour, and lives the more, the more labour it sucks."[10] This oft-cited remark speaks to the extinctive tendency of industrial capitalism but understandably leaves out vertical energies of fossilization and extraction. To supplement this missing element, we might turn to Martín Arboleda's "*bodies of extraction*," which he borrows from Mbembe: "that is, bodies that extract minerals and are also rendered into living deposits for the extraction of value [. . .]" (italics in original).[11] Arboleda's framework captures the verticality of extraction and fossilization but misses the centrality of extinction. Fossil labor entails the convergence of these narrative figurations—race, verticality, and extinctive temporality—in which planetary agency transforms extinction into survival. As the planet resists procedures of capitalist exploitation, subjects of fossil labor discover a means of empowerment through their identification with the planet.

The dynamic between race, verticality, and materiality reveals a distinct valence when situated in the contexts of resource extraction and environmental exploitation, both of which have been driving factors in the history of colonialism. In this chapter, I argue that contemporary writers of color target precisely this valence in their fiction, with the goal of elucidating the machinations of fossil labor that precede and underpin the vertical orientations of mid-twentieth-century science. More specifically, by aligning and vivifying the continuum between Blackness and the planet, these writers suggest that the vertical sciences are racially coded by the exploitative colonial histories that made their pursuits possible. Like the premise of geological time itself, this encoding is a deep one; it illuminates the centuries-long entanglement between colonial subjugation, racism, and the pursuit of mineral resources. For Kathryn Yusoff, this history constitutes an alternative origin story for the Anthropocene, which she associates not with humanist progress but with the inhumanist violence of extraction and labor exploitation.[12] Building on this notion, expressions of fossil labor in contemporary fiction by writers of color insist not only on the temporal and spatial deepness of racial exploitation, but on the capacities of planetary forces to escape, subvert, and resist the industrious and managerial sciences of White colonialism.

Central to the discourse I present in this chapter is the work of Colson Whitehead, who explores the intersections of power and verticality in his novels *The Intuitionist* (1999) and *The Underground Railroad* (2016). These works invoke speculative tropes in ways that animate the cross-sections of race and verticality: *The Intuitionist* through vertical technics of elevation, and *The Underground Railroad* through an alternative history of geological excavation. Together, they represent a thoughtful and vivid engagement with the earth as a repository of inhumanist history. The geological and inhumanist imaginations of Whitehead's novels extend back to the trope of the underground man (so prominent in Ellison's *Invisible Man* and Wright's *The Man Who Lived Underground*) and expand within the works of other twenty-first-century writers such as Hari Kunzru and Jesmyn Ward. These writers display a trend of vertical thinking in African American and multiethnic literature that imagines postwar science as part of the long history of racism in the United States. Concomitant with this fictive vision is the historical measurement of the Anthropocene neither by industrial ascendency in the late eighteenth century nor by its near-total blanketing of the planet by the mid-twentieth, but by the practices of colonial genocide that served as the bedrock of environmental managerialism as early as the seventeenth century.[13]

My argument in this chapter raises some troubling implications for the title of *Writing Our Extinction*: namely, whose extinction. The ubiquitous "our" performs the problematic task of sweeping distinctions of race, gender, disability, class, and other social categories under the rug, promoting a tragic speciesism within which all are culpable. One goal of this chapter is to combat such ostensible ubiquity and challenge the applicability of the "our." For marginalized subjects, including Black Americans and Indigenous populations, extinction is more than an implicit feature of modern life; it has been an ongoing and lived reality for centuries. A second goal aims to reclaim agency for those subjects excluded by what Yusoff calls the "color line of the colonized."[14] Much like the insurrectionist planet of Negarestani's *Cyclonopedia*, race transforms into a geological force. Novelists from Wright to Ward bring to life the concept of fossil labor by conceiving Blackness as a dimension of planetary power, an element of environmental energy that is both an object of exploitation and an agent of resistance. In terms of literary genealogy, fossil labor erects a bridge between traditions of African American and multiethnic writing and Anthropocene fiction. It reveals Anthropocene fiction itself—in its U.S.-centric, Great Acceleration context, specifically—as predicated on, at one and the same time, the revealing of planetary perspective and time that upends the logic of industrial capitalism, and the elision of the fossil labor that inhabits these planetary modes.

Formations of Black planetarity adopt a perspective that does not shy away from extinction's transformative potential. Extinction serves as both a source of horror, insofar as it is has been visited upon Black communities from slavery to the present, and an instrument of violence, insofar as Black subjects align themselves with extinction for the purpose of turning it back around on their oppressors: "it is at this site of division between the organic and inorganic that racial subjugation is constructed as an ontological horror that campaigns on the senses in psychic and planetary terms," Yusoff writes, "coupling fear of a black and fear of an inhuman planet through the category of the inhuman."[15] The irony of this perspective is that, whereas White science inadvertently twists survival into extinction in the form of an uninhabitable industrialized planet, Black planetarity twists extinction into resilience in the form of an animated geology. The literalization of a subterranean railway system in Whitehead's *The Underground Railroad* resembles the practices of mining and resource extraction that have backed humankind into an existential corner. Yet in Whitehead's vision, this earthmoving feat enables Black survival by promoting (figuratively, at least) an escape from the epistemological and industrial order of White modernity. This is a pattern in the expressions of fossil labor that I examine in this chapter: the repeated reversal of White-ordained extinction into modes of racial resilience.

My examination rests upon an extensive discourse concerning the interrelations between race, energy, ecology, and geology, reaching back to the work of Frantz Fanon.[16] This discursive network establishes historical and theoretical links between a rhetoric of materiality and racial experience, on one hand, and contextual frameworks of the plantation, environmental racism, and carceral capitalism on the other. Through these links, colonized and exploited people of color take the form of a geological substrate, memorably worded in Fanon's *The Wretched of the Earth* (1961): "The poverty of the people, national oppression, and the inhibition of culture are one and the same thing. After a century of colonial domination, we find a culture which is rigid in the extreme, or rather what we find are the dregs of culture, its mineral strata."[17] Fanon's geology is metaphorical, yet of prescient significance; he intuits the relegation of colonized people to an inanimate layer. They become cultural fossils. This imagery resonates with what Gavin Arnall has recently described as the "subterranean Fanon," an interpretation of Fanon's work that resists the Marxist allegiance to dialectics and turns instead to an eruptive energetics: "for the subterranean Fanon, *to theorize is to invent*, to bring into existence an entirely new way of thinking corresponding to an entirely new society" (italics in original).[18] Similarly, Yusoff has identified in Fanon's writing an example of "the subterranean theorizing of the black radical tradition," a critical mode invested in the stratigraphic logic of colonial disenfranchisement.[19] Meanwhile, Fred Moten ascribes a subterranean quality to Black studies as a whole, which belongs to what he calls the "undercommons," an "underground, submarine sociality."[20] This critical mode offers a language of underground volatility that resonates deeply with fictive expressions of Black planetarity: "tectonic collisions, mountain ranges thrown up to the sky, volcanic bombast," says the narrator of Whitehead's *The Nickel Boys* (2019), describing a science book the novel's protagonist discovers in a segregated reform school; "All the violence roiling beneath that makes the world above."[21]

If we extend this planetary schema to include not only the metaphor of geology but its physicality, we encounter a colonial zone in which the premise of resource extraction intersects with that of labor exploitation, specifically slavery, and nineteenth-century imperial rhetoric invokes the sciences of biology and energy to rationalize what it sees as its ordained superiority.[22] This Victorian convergence of scientistic ideologies metastasizes in the mid-twentieth century in the horrors of atomic power and the Holocaust, as scientific progress continued to signal the supposed transparency of cultural and national superiority. We can also trace this history back to the days of colonialism in the Americas, however, when early implementations of large-scale land settlement on the plantations were viewed as a sign of Europe's rightful provenance. This view of racial history in the United States perceives the development of slavery into the modern carceral state as inextricable from histories of environmental exploitation that have relied on the availability of "empty" land and free labor.[23] Whereas previous chapters have unearthed the outlines of the Anthropocene in works of fiction by tracking their vertical inclinations alongside those in the sciences, this chapter highlights verticality to illuminate where the Anthropocene elides its racialized elements: the brutal and systemic exploitation of Black bodies that makes possible the narratives of

Western scientific and industrial progress. In this respect, my argument is primarily methodological. Focusing on works by contemporary writers of color, I bring findings and claims from previous chapters into contact with discourses on race, Blackness, and colonialism. Whitehead, Ward, and Kunzru attend to the exploitative dynamics of the vertical sciences, which have subjugated Black and Indigenous bodies as often as they have the earth itself.

Whitehead is a particularly curious figure for critics due to his experimental embrace of genre fiction tropes alongside a rigorous coverage of historical scope, yet his work is rarely read from an ecocritical perspective.[24] Engaging issues of slavery, Jim Crow, and the legacies of racism in the United States, Whitehead has assembled an oeuvre that speaks to the non-realist dimensions of African American experience while also reflecting on the formal and representational frames through which that experience comes to life. The shifts and developments that take place across the range of Whitehead's work are complex and beyond the scope of this chapter to treat faithfully. For my purposes in what follows, it suffices to make some general observations. Whitehead's debut, *The Intuitionist*, plays on the convoluted and paranoid imagination of postmodernist narrative, yet simultaneously carries, as Michael Bérubé notes, a "muted echo" of African American fictions extending back to the nineteenth century.[25] Meanwhile, *The Underground Railroad* foregrounds Black literary tradition, offering a version of the neo-slave narrative that reimagines the method of fugitive slaves as a literal subterranean railroad. Both novels adopt very different speculative atmospheres, yet might be viewed alongside each other as a kind of African American energy-punk: vaguely alternate history-style narratives that imagine racial oppression and resistance as bound to figures of energy. More to the point, both *The Intuitionist* and *The Underground Railroad* render energy as a vertical phenomenon: elevators in the former, and subterranean travel and mining in the latter. Equally relevant, these vertical expressions are racialized. They configure notions of racial mobility in relation to modern technology. By placing fictions by writers of color—fictions that explicitly engage topics of racism, exploitation, and environmentalism—alongside the "subterranean theorizing of the black radical tradition," I illustrate the ways that vertical perspectives and imagery allow these writers to leverage a critique of the fossil labor that grounds White institutions of domination and exploitation.

Having been active for a shorter period of time than Whitehead, Ward and Kunzru have for only the past decade or so found themselves at the center of ongoing literary conversations regarding race in contemporary fiction and culture. Very recently, Ward's novels have found purchase among critics attentive to the interplay between Blackness and ecology, among them Kirsten Dillender, Henry Ivry, Sara Stephens Loomis, and Rebecca Evans, the latter of whom puts Whitehead and Ward in touch with environmental racism under the auspices of what she calls "geomemory," in which the hauntology of history "plays out in the human use and misuse of land and the human organization of space and infrastructure."[26] These critical interventions have addressed issues of race and the environment but have tended not to see this intersection as a response to the verticality of postwar science, and virtually nothing has been written on ecological matters in Kunzru's *White Tears*. Whereas much of the Anthropocene fiction in previous chapters (and Whitehead's in this chapter) has tended to perceive verticality through configurations of digging, exhuming, ascending, and orbiting, the novels of Ward and Kunzru perceive it through practices of contamination, pollution, and exploitation (although oil extraction does feature significantly in *Sing, Unburied, Sing*). Theirs is a verticality of seepage and sinking, in line with notions of ecosickness and contagion such as we find in the work of Heather Houser and Priscilla Wald.[27] This narrative approach telegraphs the emissions and pollutants produced by exploitative industries, and traces this exploitation back to the plantation. *White Tears* and *Sing, Unburied, Sing* may be contemporary in their setting, but they (like the novels of Whitehead) are deeply historical in their outlook.

By coordinating Blackness as an element of ecological complexity that includes systems of colonial domination (primarily the plantation) and ramifications of exploitation—contamination, toxicity, and waste, but also poverty, inequity, exclusion, slavery and other manifestations of racism at various institutional levels—this chapter participates in recent efforts to theorize race in the context of twentieth-century science and the Anthropocene. As Ian Baucom forcefully puts it, the urgency of planetary thinking vivifies an encounter between histories of racism and ongoing environmental crises in the twenty-first-century Anthropocene.[28] As Black subjects find affinity with the planet and nonhuman world, they discover empowering configurations in environmentalist discourse. Focusing on particular narrative patterns of nonhuman imagery, subterranean associations, connections between environmental damage and racialized managerialism, and connections between Black and planetary agency, I demonstrate that contemporary writers of color engage the Anthropocene precisely through the extent to which it establishes itself along racial lines. Insofar as these writers invoke figures of verticality, we can read them both as part of the Anthropocene tradition I outlined in previous chapters, and as critical of the White, scientific history that has tended to shape this tradition.

The chapter begins with the subterranean fugitivity of Whitehead's *The Underground Railroad*, a novel which traces the entanglement of racism and the environment back to the antebellum plantation. We then shift to Hari Kunzru's *White Tears* and Jesmyn Ward's *Sing, Unburied, Sing*, which stage an interplay between racism, ecology, and incarceration through the implied figure of the Vernon C. Bain Correctional Center in Kunzru's book, and the explicit figure of Parchman Farm in Ward's. The chapter ends by returning to the elevators of Whitehead's *The Intuitionist*, which extend vertical energies skyward, illuminating the exploitation of Black labor on which the vertical sciences relied. These networks of fossil labor, from the plantation to the modern penitentiary, embody a long history of the vertical momentum that emerges full-blown in the 1950s and 1960s. In depicting them, the writers examined in this chapter reveal the ways that industrial (and proto-industrial) capitalism mobilizes verticality at the expense of Black agency; emancipatory and fugitive strategies are thereby bound up with the fossil order, entangled with the very energies they seek to escape.

The Racial Anthropocene and the Antebellum Underground

The Underground Railroad begins less with geology than geography—specifically, the so-called slave garden, a tiny plot of land enslaved persons were allowed for their own use. Alone on the Randall farm in Georgia, her mother having fled, the novel's protagonist, Cora, tends fixedly to her small area of soil: "She owned herself for a few hours every week was how she looked at it," the narrator tells us, "to tug weeds, pluck caterpillars, thin out the sour greens, and glare at anyone planning incursions on her territory." For Cora, the plot marks a nexus of historical narratives, a place where her genealogy overlaps with that of proto-industrial capitalism: "The dirt at her feet had a story, the oldest story Cora knew" (12).[29] Notably, Cora's perspective on the plot mirrors that of property under capitalist relations, and she makes the association explicit:

> White men squabbled before judges over claims to this or that tract hundreds of miles away that had been carved up on a map. Slaves fought with equal fervor over their tiny parcels at their feet. The strip between the cabins was a place to tie a goat, build a chicken coop, a spot to grow food to fill your belly on top of the mash doled out by the kitchen every morning. If you got there first. (13)

The notion of the slave plot, a designated piece of land, resonates ambiguously with the landowner's plot, that piece of land authorized by capital and cartography. Cora's language even quietly echoes that of the slavecatcher, Arnold Ridgeway: "Here was the true Great Spirit, the divine thread connecting all human endeavor—if you can keep it, it is yours. Your property, slave or continent. The American imperative" (80). What Ridgeway idealizes as a virtue bestowed by nationhood, however, Cora recognizes as a bloodthirsty dash for power, especially in the paralegal network of the plantation: "Seeing you out there in the evening calm, smiling or humming, might give your neighbor an idea to coerce you from your claim using methods of intimidation, various provocations. Who would hear your appeal? There were no judges here" (13). Whitehead refracts the valences of property, its legal and raw emotional attachments, through the bleak prism of the plantation system.

In its configuration through Cora's garden plot, the plantation appears resolutely horizontal; its persistence throughout her flight north evinces a sense of geographical tenacity, resurfacing in experiences of traumatic horror: "It lived in them. It still lived in all of them, waiting to abuse and taunt when chance presented itself" (105–106). Economically reliant on the cotton industry, the plantation is a ubiquitous spectral zone, geographically present even when not visibly so. Whitehead pairs this horizontal spread with a distinctly vertical dimension, however, as reflected in the novel's eponymous fugitive subway system and other narrative elements, such as its skyscraper in South Carolina. These decidedly anachronistic figures trouble the pretense of verisimilitude readers might expect and complicate the slave narrative's traditional vocation of revealing the horrors experienced by enslaved persons. As Madhu

Dubey notes, *The Underground Railroad* features Whitehead's signature move of "literalizing metaphor," casting an uncanny filter over his imagined worlds through which narrative figures slide between the ideational and the physically mobile.[30] The text foregrounds its language's slipperiness when, near the end of the novel, Ridgeway confesses his suspicions to Cora: "Most people think it's a figure of speech [. . .]. The underground. I always knew better. The secret beneath us, the entire time" (300–301). Ridgeway's lines can be read as the text's acknowledgment of its figurative ambiguity; but on closer inspection, it also signals the novel's multifarious senses of underground—the subterranean railway by which slaves escape northward, but also the soil and rock in which slavery leaves its mark: "That evil soaks into the soil," as one character proclaims; "Some say it steeps and gets stronger" (277). The ground is home not only to the evils of the plantation, however, but also to the resource base that serves the cotton empire. Moreover, it is the implicit repository of the energy required to operate the novel's runaway locomotives: coal.

The thermodynamics of locomotion in the nineteenth century go largely unmentioned in Whitehead's novel, replaced by the distinctive energy of slave labor: "The ruthless engine of cotton required its fuel of African bodies," as the narrator conveys (161). This engine is decidedly split, however, between the labor of the plantation and that of the railway: "How many hands had it required to make this place?" Cora wonders when she arrives at the station in Georgia (68). As her imagination wanders, she distinguishes the labor of the railway system from the labor of the plantation:

> She thought of the picking, how it raced down the furrows at harvest, the African bodies working as one, as fast as their strength permitted. The vast fields burst with hundreds of thousands of white bolls, strung like stars in the sky on the clearest of clear nights. When the slaves finished, they had stripped the fields of their color. It was a magnificent operation, from seed to bale, but not one of them could be prideful of their labor. It had been stolen from them. Bled from them. The tunnel, the tracks, the desperate souls who found salvation in the coordination of its stations and timetables—this was a marvel to be proud of. (68)

This transposing of labor from plantation to railroad intimates the enslaved person's double-relation to the underground. What appears in the former as the forced managerial cultivation of earth transforms in the latter into the literal hollowing out of the earth, the removal of ground that could serve as material for cultivation. Rather, the underground tunnels of the railway cultivate slave fugitivity, clandestinely dismantling the plantation system and promoting a system of escape.

Insofar as escape is a mode of dismantling, or deterritorialization, its systemic structure is difficult to describe. Even the station operator, Lumbly, can only do so in circuitous ways that call to mind the conspiratorial mutterings of the W.A.S.T.E. adherents in Pynchon's *The Crying of Lot 49*: "You understand the difficulties in communicating all the changes in the routes. Locals, expresses, what station's closed down, where they're extending the heading. The problem is that one destination may be more to your liking than another. Stations are discovered, lines discontinued. You won't know what waits above until you pull in" (68). The secrecy and apparent fungibility of the system complement its fugitive impulse; it expands and divides beneath the plantation, disrupting that symbol of oppression. Whitehead's railroad is another version of what Negarestani calls the "( )hole complex," a subterranean network of hollows in what the surface world assumes to be solid and whole. The replacement of coal with the subversive underground labor of escaped slaves embodies a form of resistance to the fossil labor of capitalism: what Shouhei Tanaka calls the novel's "insurgent energy imaginary," the mobilization of agency through an extractive, earthmoving infrastructure.[31] Yet the fact remains that Whitehead's escaped slaves are still beholden to the steam engine. Although coal itself is understated, the novel's trains are coal-powered, as evidenced by the narrator's descriptions of one train's "soot-covered stalk" (69) and one of the conductor's mentioning he has "just enough coal" for a particular journey (150). The persistence of fossil fuels highlights an internal conflict within *The Underground Railroad*, but one that sharpens the novel's critical edge: the confluence of freedom (specifically, abolition) and fossil fuel consumption. Fossil labor appears as an ineluctable by-product within the ideological nexus of energy capitalism and the fossil fuel economy. Even the ethics of the abolitionist imperative, the escape from slavery, cannot escape the enslavement to carbon.

In *The Underground Railroad*, Whitehead reminds us that environmental racism is more than the disproportionate susceptibility to health and safety risks. It also includes—perhaps most importantly—the coerced complicity of Black bodies in the reproduction of what Timothy Mitchell calls "carbon democracy" while it simultaneously excludes them from participatory politics.[32] In contrast to slave plots such as Cora's—small subsistence gardens that promise momentary freedom within the plantation panopticon—the South is a zone of state-sanctioned necropolitical terror. Moreover, the subsistence plots underscore the extreme ecological disruption that occurs widespread under the monocultural logic of the plantation system. As sites of tempered restraint and care, the plots enable a tender mutualism between human and nonhuman environments, whereas the plantation system indulges in exploitative excess.[33] In *The Underground Railroad*, this ecological imbalance literally inflames the landscape of Tennessee, where much of the state has been plunged into wildfires: "scorched and harrowed as far as they could see, a sea of ash and char from the flat planes of the fields up to the hills and mountains. Black trees tilted, stunted black arms pointing as if to a distant place untouched by flame" (200). After passing destroyed towns, Cora and Ridgeway eventually arrive at one currently engulfed, where a shopkeeper informs them that homesteaders started the fire: "Three million acres, the shopkeeper said. The government promised relief but no one could say when it would arrive. The biggest disaster in as long as anyone could remember" (205–206). The shopkeeper's language invokes that of residents in New Orleans and Puerto Rico after Hurricanes Katrina and Maria, respectively—unparalleled disasters of their time with disproportionate responses.

The fire is a violent figure of human incaution toward the environment and a dark intimation of the burns that plague the United States in the twenty-first century. In Whitehead's rendering, the blaze also embodies a form of planetary resistance, as though the environment is striking back at a system of deliberate exploitation. Passing an unburned field and contemplating the distribution of violence, Cora acknowledges the nonhuman world's carelessness for human life: "Plantation justice was mean and constant, but the world was indiscriminate. Out in the world, the wicked escaped comeuppance and the decent stood in their stead at the whipping tree. Tennessee's disasters were the fruit of indifferent nature, without connection to the crimes of the homesteaders. To how the Cherokee had lived their lives" (215–216). Cora expresses a sense of dissociation from the land, or at least from her humanist expectations toward it. The planet spares no one. The fires might evoke reactions during Hurricanes Katrina and Maria; but unlike the latter disasters, which primarily affected the poor and communities of color, the Tennessee fires in *The Underground Railroad* demolish both Black and White homes, an extinctive force that reaches across the color line.

The natural world's indiscriminate volatility speaks to humanity's forced complicity in the fossil fuel economy. If cotton is an engine and slaves its fuel, then we can read the Tennessee wildfires as an effect of accelerated combustion run amok. In their efforts to escape the plantation system via the underground railroad, fugitive slaves must participate in practices of earthmoving and land management. After being discovered in South Carolina, Cora arrives in North Carolina to find the station decommissioned and condemned: "Rusting tools littered the path. Chisels, sledges, and picks—weaponry for battling the mountain. The air was damp. [. . .] A few feet into the level above, she saw why the equipment had been abandoned by the work gangs. A sloping mound of rocks and dirt, floor to ceiling, cut off the tunnel" (150–151). Cora eventually learns that the cave-in was planned as a ruse to conceal the operation of the railway, but that recent changes to the slave laws in North Carolina resulted in the station being shut down. In fact, the station had been dug out beneath an old mica mine, "exhausted long ago by Indians and forgotten by most" (151). Intersecting with the history of mining, Whitehead's railway is another facet of modern humankind's impact on the planet. Dug beneath the remnants of an old mine, and blasted as a method of concealment, the decommissioned North Carolina station is an earthly inscription.

These networks of subterranean subversion and secrecy paint a uniquely post-1945 vision of the antebellum South. A combination of alternative history and meta-slave narrative, *The Underground Railroad* presents an opportunity for recasting the plantation system as a proto-corporate structure that spawns its own conspiratorial musings, much like the Zone of *Gravity's Rainbow*. And also like Pynchon's Zone, the hallucinatory nightmare of Whitehead's antebellum South engenders what we might call a metaphorics of indeterminacy: plantations are both localized yet somehow ubiquitous, the underground is both a figurative network and a literal space. Casting backward from the twenty-first century, *The Underground Railroad* is a calculated repurposing of both the noted ontological indeterminacy in much postmodernist fiction and the traditional slave narrative's appeal to sincerity. What emerges is a twisted myth, an entanglement of sentimentalism and surrealism; but this entanglement mirrors that of another, implicit in the novel's subterranean focus. Just as the text performs the confluence of narrative modes, so too does it perform the confluence of multiscalar histories—of capital and climate, politics and planet.

In this regard, Whitehead's rendering is truly spectacular and spectacularly complex, juxtaposing the historical and realist premise of the plantation—which cultivates the land in a managerial and violently racialized manner—with the mining of minerals. This mining then reveals a decidedly non-realist network of escape tunnels below the surface, skirting beneath the very soil that is being tilled, the cotton being picked. Finally, the fugitive rail system requires coal, a product of the same industrial process—mining—used to disguise the presence of the railway itself. These looped categories express a disorienting synchronicity that links the plantation to the mid-twentieth century: already in this still largely pre-industrial moment in the United States, fossil labor was being harvested. As Anna Kornbluh emphasizes, in Whitehead's novel "the labor of struggle, the work to survive against the work of the nation, is not historical fiction in the past but searingly ongoing reality in the present."[34] The death and destruction of the plantation system, which Whitehead depicts so surreally yet so vividly in *The Underground Railroad*, calls forward in time to the industrial developments that would exploit the labor base of capital and the fossil remains compacted into the ground.

It is worth pausing for a moment to note that the fossil fuel deposits sought by the industrial titans of the twentieth century are composed not of human remains from the antebellum South or even the early days of colonialism, but mostly of plant matter dating back to the earth's Carboniferous period. We should say that what Whitehead mobilizes in *The Underground Railroad* is a fictive expression of the ways that early colonial exploitation mirrors and anticipates that of the fossil fuel industry—and of the ways that later instantiations of the plantation (the debt economy, work farms, and the modern prison) participate in the worsening global climate. It is here that *Sing, Unburied, Sing* and *White Tears* take up the story that Whitehead begins in *The Underground Railroad*. Ward's and Kunzru's novels imagine the perpetuation of U.S. racism through the ghosts of the past: the characters of Richie in *Sing,*

Unburied, Sing and Charlie Shaw in *White Tears*. More than this, they contextualize these ghostly figures, and the racial suffering they embody, within a modern carceral state that marks the lingering legacy of the plantation and the environmental exploitation of postindustrial capitalism.

Fossil Labor, Environmental Racism, and the Carceral State

In Kunzru's *White Tears*, two young, talented, White postgrads, Seth and Carter, ignorant of their entitlement and privilege, capture an audio recording of a mysterious blues melody that rises from the din of a New York neighborhood. Unsure of the recording's source, and figuring the happy circumstance is theirs on which to capitalize, they assign a name to the artist and title to the song—Charlie Shaw, "Graveyard Blues"—and drop the track online. Unfortunately for the hapless protagonists, the song's origin rears its head, spectrally inserting itself into their lives and revealing the ways that the past is never entirely past. Through its supernatural exploration of Jim Crow, incarceration, and American music, *White Tears* composes an imaginative history of industrialized modernity that inscribes itself on the planet, in the geological strata and in the atmosphere: "Guglielmo Marconi, the inventor of radio, believed that sound waves never completely die away," the narrator relates, "that they persist, fainter and fainter, masked by the day-to-day noise of the world" (43).[35] The conceit of the novel is that these waves do persist, and in a more intentional and effectual way than its characters assume. Preserving the sufferings of Black Americans, doubly manifest in White culture's appropriation of blues and other musical genres, sound waves in *White Tears* constitute an audio archive of racial injustice and extinction engraved in planetary media. The earth becomes a cosmic vinyl record, with human actors caught in what Ellison once called "the groove of history."[36]

As a piece of planetary media, these spectral sound waves form a background hum below the more audible industry of commercial music. The irony is that, in *White Tears*, this background hum assumes a hauntological status, a resurgent agency that disrupts the commodification of Black music by White-owned record labels and production companies. We can read *White Tears* as a response to *White Noise*, Don DeLillo's 1985 novel of technologically homogenized and reproducible modernity. Presenting the repetitive banality and managerial processes of postindustrial production as actual (white) noise,

Kunzru salvages a planetary time that reframes modern progress as reliant upon sufferings told through sound. The legacy of fossil labor rises through what at first sounds like the din of history, only to be revealed as the record of oppression inscribed into the planet itself. Published the same year as *White Tears*, Ward's *Sing, Unburied, Sing* presents a complementary vision of racial extinction. The novel tells the story of a young Black mother, Leonie, and her two children—teenage Jojo and the toddler, Michaela—as they drive to the Mississippi State Penitentiary (more notoriously known as Parchman Farm) to pick up Leonie's White boyfriend and father of her children, Michael. Readers learn that Michael worked for BP's *Deepwater Horizon* drilling rig until its infamous explosion in 2010, his ensuing joblessness leading him to drug trafficking and eventually to imprisonment.

Echoing Kunzru's critique of the music industry, Ward's novel juxtaposes commodification—in this case, of fossil fuels—with a form of good use gardening, which finds its origins in the slave plots that Whitehead depicts in *The Underground Railroad* and that Ward associates with the figure of Philomene, Leonie's mother, in *Sing, Unburied, Sing*. Against the disempowerment and exploitation of fossil labor, good use gardening represents a preindustrial and symbiotic relationship with the earth, the knowledge and skill for taking from the earth what one needs.[37] This knowledge resists the calculating rationalism of capital, embracing instead a cooperative and co-productive sentiment between the planet and other living creatures. Leonie describes this sentiment as providing "a map to the world," if one knows how to read it—"a world plotted orderly by divine order, spirit in everything" (105).[38] In *White Tears* and *Sing, Unburied, Sing*, the contexts of recording and extractive industries (respectively) perform parallel functions. Both index an environmentalism that is racially encoded, vertically oriented, and linked to the rise of the modern prison system. Ward's narrative renders the *Deepwater Horizon* disaster inextricable from the fossil labor that informs the history of Parchman Farm, part of a prison complex that emits vast quantities of carbon, not least in its practice of deforestation. Likewise, Kunzru bases a significant event of *White Tears* in the Bronx neighborhood of Hunts Point, notorious for high levels of pollution and policing, and home to the Vernon C. Bain Correctional Center.

Moreover, both authors underscore the role of fossil labor in their novels through their ghostly characters, who signify the cultural persistence of racial exploitation. The historical conditions of slavery and colonialism compose the contours of the racist present, an effect that Katherine McKittrick refers to as "plantation futures": "a conceptualization of time-space that tracks the plantation toward the prison and the impoverished and destroyed city sectors and, consequently, brings into sharp focus the ways the plantation is an ongoing locus of antiblack violence and death that can no longer analytically sustain this violence."[39] Often understood as emblems of the historical past, the ghosts in these novels serve also as gestures of futurity. Through their spectral quality, these ghosts enact a form of planetary agency. Just as environmental exploitation is inseparable from ecological imbalance, racial exploitation is inseparable from social imbalance. Fossil labor brings these valences together, imbuing past extinction and genocide with the potential for future resurgence. Whereas the plantation and carceral state reduce Black bodies to sources of energy on par with fossil fuels, Ward's and Kunzru's novels salvage a spirit of resistance from cycles of exploitation.

In addition to their both being published in 2017, *Sing, Unburied, Sing* and *White Tears* share another curious similarity: they are both road narratives, at least in part. Ward's novel recounts Leonie and Jojo's trip to Parchman, whereas Kunzru's depicts dual and overlapping road trips taking place in different historical moments. In both texts, the road traverses more than space; it enables transactions across time, blurring past and present. Accompanying the rise of U.S. automobility, the road is also an index of increased fossil fuel consumption. It signals both novels' investments in the energy industry's twin legacies of racial subjugation and environmental crisis. The figure of the car becomes what Loomis calls "a 'petro-hold,'" a ghostly echo of the slave ship, in which oil culture imposes a postindustrial mode of captivity.[40] In Ward's fictional town of Bois Sauvage, racial demographics and hostilities overlap with a deeply felt environmental history comprising extensive oil drilling along the Mississippi coast and the aftermath of Hurricane Katrina (which is the focus of Ward's 2011 novel, *Salvage the Bones*). Viewed within the framework of fossil labor, these contexts are inextricable; the environmental damage suffered by Bois Sauvage highlights a set of ecological relations, not just between human characters but between humans and the nonhuman world. In *Sing, Unburied, Sing*, Ward delineates the long history of racial oppression and exploitation in America as integral to the history of environmental managerialism going back to the plantation system—a system in which Black bodies were valued in much the same sense as the ground on which they worked.

Parchman Farm names not the modern institution—the Mississippi State Penitentiary—but the cotton plantation that existed prior to the founding of the prison. *Sing, Unburied, Sing* realizes the camp's first iteration as still very much alive in the present, embodied in the ghost of Richie, a boy who died at Parchman, and in the stories of River, Jojo's grandfather: "*When I first got to Parchman, I worked in the fields, planting and weeding and harvesting crops. Parchman was a working farm right off. You see them open fields we worked in* [. . .]" (22; italics in original). Jojo eventually sees the fields himself in a ghostly sequence, but River's recollection fills in the invisible gaps:

> *You see them open fields we worked in, the way you could look right through that barbed wire, the way you could grab it and get a toehold here, a bloody handhold there, the way they cut them trees flat so that land is empty and open to the ends of the earth, and you think,* I can get out of here if I set my mind to it. I can follow the right stars south and all the way on home. *But the reason you think that is because you don't see the trusty shooters. You don't know the sergeant. You don't know the sergeant come from a long line of men bred to treat you like a plowing horse, like a hunting dog—and bred to think he can make you like it.* (22; italics in original)

In addition to the description of the farm's cruel disciplinary practices, River's lines highlight the coordination of humanitarian and environmental violence. Deforestation was an observational strategy, a way to track inmates visually across acres of land: "*Damn near fifty thousand acres. Parchman the kind of place that fool you into thinking it ain't no prison, ain't going to be so bad when you first see it, because ain't no walls*" (21; italics in original). River's descriptions reveal not only the inhumane treatment of its inmates, but the managerial practices of land management that complemented this treatment.

Deforestation is not uncommon in penal history, occupying a crucial place in the development of modern penitentiaries.[41] Prisons exploited the labor of inmates at the same time they exploited and altered the land on which they were built. Ward coordinates the fossil labor of Parchman alongside the extractive energies of the *Deepwater Horizon* disaster, relegated to the narrative past and background yet looming hauntingly, much like Richie's ghost, in its present. "I'd spent the days after the accident with Jojo in the house watching CNN," Leonie narrates, "watching the oil gush into the ocean, and feeling guilty because that's not what I wanted to see, guilty because I didn't give a shit about those fucking pelicans, guilty because I just wanted to see Michael's face, his shoulders, his fingers, guilty because all I cared about was him" (92). Michael's memories of the rig are tied to his coworkers, specifically those who lost their lives in the explosion: *"I knew those men—all eleven of them. Lived with them,"* Leonie recalls him saying (92; italics in original). Through her perspective, the disaster reverberates through home and family, and through Michael's gradually deteriorating body (92–93). For Leonie, its consequences are not environmental but deeply personal.

The significance of the oil spill is different, however, when told from Jojo's perspective. After returning from Parchman, Jojo recalls a memory when Michael took him fishing and talked to him about working on the oil rig. In Michael's telling (or rather, Jojo's recollection of it) the ecology of the ocean takes center stage, with sharks becoming "like hawks, hunting in the water" (225). The passage reveals a set of vertically entangled ecologies—sea, land, and sky—gesturing to the complex dynamics by which changes in one ecosystem can impact another. The novel builds on these dynamics by attaching racial tones to this ecological image: "[the sharks] struck under the pillars, white in the darkness, like a knife under dark skin. How blood followed them, too. How the dolphins would come after the sharks left, and how they would leap from the water if they knew anyone was watching, chattering. How he cried one day after the spill, when he heard about how all of them was dying off" (225–226). The suggestion of violence illuminates a history of racial tension that flows throughout the text. At first glance this might be seen simply as a coincidence, or an isolated metaphor on Ward's part; but the language appears less coincidental as readers learn that Michael told Jojo about his time on the rig as a preface to something else: that Jojo's uncle, Given, was murdered by one of Michael's cousins.

As a pretext for Michael's confession to Jojo, the *Deepwater Horizon* spill acts as an expression of fossil capital that orders the social relations between characters. Ward wraps the environmental damage into the racial and the familial, as Michael explains his reaction to the spill: *"Some scientists for BP said this didn't have nothing to do with the oil, that sometimes this is what happens to animals: they die for unexpected reasons. Sometimes a lot of them. Sometimes all at once.* And then Michael looked at me and said: *And when that scientist said that, I thought about humans. Because humans is animals"* (226; italics in original). Michael's comments contain the implicit question of whether humanity would be so cavalier if suddenly a large number of humans died all at once. The irony, of course, is that throughout history humanity *has* been cavalier toward human death, often in instances pertaining to the treatment of people of color: the mass execution of Black subjects over the course of slavery, Indigenous genocide, Jim Crow, and the modern police state. The necropolitics of environmental racism adopt an economic rhetoric of externality; the lives of people of color, nonhuman animals, and energy resources of the earth are viewed as immaterial, their exhaustion negligible.

Sing, Unburied, Sing situates Parchman Farm and *Deepwater Horizon* as inextricable from one another. Together, they are avatars of fossil labor, emblems of an institution embedded in strata. Although predating mid-twentieth-century vertical science, fossil labor nonetheless appears in the novel as a precondition for the geophysical concerns that explode after World War II. Ward acknowledges this genealogy by figuring the history of racial oppression as the foundation on which later industrial and postindustrial architectures were built. Time appears here along a vertical plane, orienting readers downward through soil and rock—the implication (made explicit in the novel's title) being that much of what shapes the world we live in remains buried and unsung. Human history takes its place in an environmental framework, affecting modern social relations as much as it affects ecological ones. It is only fitting that *Sing, Unburied, Sing*, with its ghostly characters and references to deforestation, culminates in a tree of ghosts, victims of racism, poverty, and violence, "women and men and boys and girls. Some of them near to babies" (282). A metonymic figure for the forest, standing in stark contrast to the absence of forestry surrounding Parchman, the tree is also a carbon sink; it takes carbon dioxide out of the air and replaces it with oxygen. The violence of the buried past—the murdered dead but also the oil extracted by *Deepwater Horizon*—is embodied in, and assuaged by, the cathartic, environmental image of the tree.[42]

Just as Parchman Farm assumes a spectral quality in *Sing, Unburied, Sing*, its influence reaching across space and time, so too does the labor camp exceed its physical manifestation in Kunzru's *White Tears*. "I play both sides,"

Charlie Shaw, the novel's perpetual ghost, explains to readers; "Sunday picnics and work camps. All the different kinds of camp. Logging camps, levee camps, places where they'll kill a man and step over his body to get to the barrelhead. Ruled by the knife and the whip and the gun. Turpentine in Louisiana and coal in Alabama. Cane on the Brazos River in Texas. It's all the same, the whole country one big camp" (251). As readers learn of Charlie Shaw's fate—that he was imprisoned and tortured in a labor camp run by J.J.W. Wallace Construction, the company founded by White protagonist Carter Wallace's family—we come to discern Kunzru's point. In believing themselves to have made up Charlie Shaw as a name to accompany the ghostly blues song they accidentally record, Carter and the novel's narrator, Seth, unwittingly enact the continued exploitation of Shaw's labor, even after his death. Charlie Shaw's ghost is a trace of past and future oppression, an embodiment of fossil labor's feedback effect. The whole country is "one big camp" because even on their liberal college campus (the pun is hardly a coincidence), the White students cannot help but perpetuate the appropriation and exploitation of the Black artists whose work they adore.

Whereas Ward evokes a narrative of racism and fossil labor from Parchman Farm to the Mississippi State Penitentiary to the oil industry, Kunzru draws a more far-reaching picture of the racial Anthropocene, whose narrative begins (for *White Tears*) in a historically specific place: the Hunts Point neighborhood in the Bronx. Once his protagonists, Seth and Carter, begin to learn the truth about the song that Seth records by chance during a stroll through the streets of New York, they find themselves embroiled in a legacy of exploitation and incarceration neither of them anticipated. After releasing the anonymous song online, they discover the name and story of the not-so-anonymous person behind the music: a Black man named Charlie Shaw who died in a labor camp owned by Carter's family. The Wallace Magnolia Group, the family company, "supplied earthmoving equipment, built freeways, laid pipelines" (10) and, as the narrative reveals, "*is a leading provider of detention, correctional and community reentry services with 58 facilities, approximately 25,500 beds, and 8,000 employees around the globe*" (260; italics in original). Aligning financial motivations behind fossil fuels, automobility, and the prison industrial complex, *White Tears* telescopes the histories of American blues music and Jim Crow incarceration as part of the long history of racial extinction encoded in the displaced earth of prisons and pipelines as well as the grooves of vinyl.[43] This encoding constitutes another manifestation of archival geology, one that imprints genocidal and oppressive practices into earthly matter.

Like *Sing, Unburied, Sing*, Kunzru's novel expresses a sense of exploited labor itself as fossilized, presenting readers with a dark history of appropriation facilitated by the erasure of Black subjects within the carceral system. By introducing the planet as a recording device, however, Kunzru adds another element to the oppressive matrix. Episodes of institutional and racial violence etch themselves into geophysical media, from vinyl to the very atmosphere that conducts sound waves—a form of contamination that Kunzru links to environmental hazards. Pollution makes itself known in *White Tears*, infused into the New York City heat: "Toxic 14th Street," Seth says; "Gum melted into the sidewalk at the crossings, volatile hydrocarbons lacing the air" (82). The pollutants in *White Tears* manifest against the backdrop of energy infrastructures that become visible as Seth cycles through the city: "I freewheeled down into the smell of gasoline and uncollected garbage. Delancey Street in summer: light particulates, the tar spongy at the crosswalks. I turned north and rode through the projects towards the white chimneys of the power station" (67). Kunzru juxtaposes signs of fossil fuel consumption with descriptions of their olfactory effects, depicting an environmental sensorium overflowing with carbon emissions, waste, and contamination.

As any New York City resident knows too well, pollution is an ever-present element of city living; but *White Tears* is precise in its depiction of the polluted landscape, which parallels the demographics of underfunded communities. When Carter is hospitalized after being severely beaten, Seth learns that his friend had gone to the Hunts Point neighborhood, in the Bronx—an area notorious for high levels of policing and pollution.[44] Kunzru's choice of Hunts Point is far from coincidental, and provides a literary map of the novel's concerns precisely through its insistence that the neighborhood is *not* on Seth's cognitive map of New York City: "I'd never even been to Hunts Point," he thinks to himself; "I barely knew where it was" (79). When Seth reveals his naivete about prostitution and drug use among the residents of Hunts Points, Carter's sister, Leonie, rebukes him: "I know you're, like, his sheltered friend, but you have to see how it looks. Why else would he be in Hunts Point? That's, like, beyond the hood. He wouldn't be stupid enough to try to score on the street up there" (80). As she presses him, Leonie's anger boils over into the vernacular racism of White America: "Is this something the two of you do together, drive up to the Point and bang crack whores? Is it, I don't know, part of Carter's black thing? [. . .] Just be honest with me. Do you get up to this ghetto shit with him?" (80). Leonie's racist line of questioning nonetheless illuminates the demographics that make Hunts Point so relevant for Kunzru's novel. In addition to suffering from endemic drug use and high levels of policing, Hunts Point was home to the Spofford Juvenile Detention Center, which closed in 2011.

Hunts Point's history of policing and correctional operations parallels the projects and investments of the Wallace Magnolia Group in *White Tears*. According to Maria Torres-Springer, former president and chief executive of the New York City Economic Development Corporation, Spofford "was not just a symbol of how juvenile justice from a policy point of view was performed throughout the decades, but also the historic, negative stigma and perception of the area that was embodied in that building."[45] After Spofford closed, the city's demand for carceral space was fulfilled by the construction of the Vernon C. Bain Correctional Center, a prison ship built by Avondale Shipyard—a company created in part by Harry Koch, whose son would found Koch Industries. An emblem of persistent racial profiling and policing in New York, the Vernon C. Bain Correctional Center evokes the carceral system's antebellum genealogy, as inmates' comments have testified: "We were in a cargo hold of a slave ship," in Marvin Mayfield's words, "a modern-day slave ship owned by the City of New York."[46] The long and tangled histories of Avondale and Koch Industries, which have accepted contracts for everything from prison construction to petroleum refining, mirror that of the Wallace Magnolia Group in *White Tears*:

> I remembered something Leonie had said, about grandpa somebody or other moving the family up to DC, so the firm could bid for Federal Government contracts. Already big by then, Wallace Construction became a money machine. Then, years later, the DC children took the next step and moved to New York, to convert all that capital into culture. An invisible thread connected Carter and Leonie to Charlie Shaw. I thought of the buildings I had lived in, the expensive things I had handled and consumed. Whose work had paid for them? (248)

In Kunzru's novel, the Wallace conglomerate—like Parchman Farm in *Sing, Unburied, Sing*—is a metonymic figure for institutional racism in the United States, embodying the social and environmental crises precipitated by the oppressive correctional practices visited upon Black Americans by the police state.

The complementary figures of musical and carceral labor embody the dual features of what Jackie Wang calls *"racialized accumulation by dispossession,"* namely exploitation of physical labor and expropriation of property (italics in original).[47] The dynamic of exploitation and expropriation informs the systemic internalization of debt and carceral control and perpetuates a cycle of racialized disenfranchisement. *White Tears* enacts this cycle, but also illuminates a parallel between institutions of racial and environmental violence. In a late scene when Seth confronts Carter's family at a social function, Kunzru reminds his readers of the malicious paternalism that informs American racism after Jim Crow. "It's a post-racial America now," one character, a judge and business accomplice of the Wallace family, tells Seth; "The only thing we care about is supervision" (263). These disturbing lines betray the managerial logic by which the carceral state repackages anti-Black violence as correction. "You don't have to work 'em anymore," the judge goes on; "You don't have to walk the line with a rifle. All you got to do is get them into the system. Don't matter how you do it. Speeding ticket. Public nuisance. Once they're in, your boot is on their neck. Fines, tickets, court fees. And if they can't pay, well. Days or dollars, one or the other. Either way, we get ours and they stay in their rightful place" (263–264). As these comments make manifest, "post-racial" hardly means that the United States has transcended race or moved beyond its racist past. To the contrary, it means that racism has become even more deeply fused with its cultural surroundings—naturalized itself to the point of becoming plausibly deniable. In so-called post-racial America, racism is simply sewn into the social fabric in new ways, becoming as unnoticeable to many as the environmental repercussions of gassing our cars. Like the hydrocarbons lacing the city air, racism in *White Tears* permeates the American ecosystem.

Transcending Extinction

The Underground Railroad, Sing, Unburied, Sing, and *White Tears* illuminate the entangled histories of carceral punishment—from the antebellum plantation to the modern prison—and environmental racism. We can envision this entanglement through the concept of fossil labor, which identifies the parallel exploitation of environmental resources and Black bodies, even wrapping bodies into configurations of earth and geology, producing a notion of Black planetarity: an expression of Black agency as foundationally geological. Insofar as *The Underground Railroad* and the novels of Ward and Kunzru engage the intersection of racism and planetary verticality, they do so largely through appeals to the subterranean—undermining, burying, excavating, and the like. Their vertical dimension is present but nuanced, expressive, and emerges through the ecological ripple effects of colonialism, enslavement, and exploitation. In *The Intuitionist*, however, verticality assumes center stage. It is with Whitehead's debut novel that we encounter an explicit rendering of verticality as an expression of technological development and racial inequities. This is not to say that the horizontal modes of colonialism disappear, but that the novel situates them as part of a technological project that continues into the mid-twentieth century. As with the figurative slipperiness of *The Underground Railroad*, verticality possesses a multivalent significance in *The Intuitionist*, both as a metaphor for progress (the impulse to rise, to ascend) and as a literal example of what the vertical sciences sought to do.

The novels discussed in this chapter so far mobilize Black agency and sovereignty along the lines of what Yusoff calls an "insurgent geology."[48] They conceive resistance, to return to Pynchon, as "inanimate and rising," coming up from below. In *The Intuitionist*, Whitehead maintains the framework of ascendancy but refracts it through a linguistically experimental, Black literary tradition in which the logics of Western science and rationality no longer function. If the midcentury sciences qualify as part of what Nigel Clark and Bronislaw Szerszynski identify as vertical modernity, then Whitehead's idea of Black ascendancy can be seen as a revision of vertical postmodernity, or what *The Intuitionist* names the "second elevation": a repurposing of elevation technology for emancipatory ends.[49] In this respect, the novel's relationship to postmodernity is neither honorary nor dismissive but critically ironic. Whitehead deploys his narrative against canonical standards of postmodernity, which preserve its notable Whiteness, but in doing so he produces an offshoot of literary postmodernism that salvages Black empowerment from its interstices. *"The elevator world will look like Heaven,"* writes the character James Fulton, founder of the Intuitionist school in Whitehead's novel, *"but not the Heaven you have reckoned"* (241; italics in original).[50] In *The Intuitionist*, extinction is a metaphor for the metamorphosis of the world, a speculative adaptation of White science for Black emancipation. Whitehead's Black characters imagine a future made possible by elevation technologies but adapted from them, brought into service for a new form of knowledge.

Even more than *The Underground Railroad*, with its secret network of escape tunnels, *The Intuitionist* exhibits many similarities to *The Crying of Lot 49*, right down to its plot and characterization. The novel's protagonist, Lila Mae Watson, is the only African American woman employed by the city's Elevator Inspectors Guild, and the titular Intuitionist: someone who senses the stability of elevators, in contrast to the Empiricists who rely on observation. Tasked with solving a mystery surrounding an elevator that went into freefall—a supposed impossibility outside of someone tampering with the machine—she finds herself, much like Pynchon's Oedipa Maas, embroiled in a world of corporate espionage and clandestine history. Placing *The Intuitionist* in the context of Black literary postmodernism, Madhu Dubey sees the novel as a salvaging of postmodern contingency in the service of Black history: "Whitehead participates in a postmodern interrogation of the grand narrative of urban modernization, showing that this narrative gains coherence through racial exclusion. But instead of altogether disavowing urban life, Whitehead's novel undertakes a critical excavation, revealing African-Americans [sic] to be the hidden architects of modern cities."[51] I shall have more to say about the opposition between modernization and racial disenfranchisement later, but I want to underscore Dubey's insightful reading of the text's stratigraphic sensibility. In Whitehead's rewriting of postmodernism, he deploys its own maneuvers against it, dismantling the White grand narrative and exhuming the Black labor and voices beneath and within it.

Attention to *The Intuitionist*'s postmodernist revisionism dominates much of the scholarly conversation, and for good reason. As Alexander Manshel notes, this domination stems in large part from the novel's strategically unstable historical setting, which he claims constitutes "an alternative, but no less historically grounded, method of periodization."[52] The text's power derives from its evocation of Black literary agency within a canon that has traditionally been whitewashed. We find here not a reducing of history to aesthetics, which Fredric Jameson has identified as a hallmark of postmodernist writing, but the illumination of an understated or subterranean history. More so even than this language of postmodernism, however, we discover in Whitehead's appeals to verticality an appropriation of the same rhetoric that galvanized a decade of scientific adventurism: the creation and maintenance of what Frank White calls "overview systems."[53] Like White's universalizing overview effect (discussed in the previous chapter), in Whitehead's novel verticality is cast as a compulsion of modern science to achieve a superior image, a more objective sense of things. Skyward is Heavenward, the realm of perfect and all-encompassing vision. In *The Intuitionist*, Black verticality resists this deterministic and dominant narrative, positing a creative means of escape from Western social and scientific structures.

Throughout the novel, the city is offered as the foremost figure of vertical modernity. Made possible by the science of elevation, the urban setting embodies the energies of modern science that push against gravity; in Stephen Graham's words, the elevator "stalks the interface between the banal and the fearful or unknown within the vertical and technological cultures of the contemporary—and the projected—metropolis."[54] Despite their origins in the nineteenth century, elevation technologies serve as a figure of mid-twentieth-century science in *The Intuitionist*: a world in which scientific knowledge has been streamlined into the organizational principles of postwar systems thought. As Hunter Heyck has documented, the postwar years saw the extension of functional systems logic across multiple fields within the social sciences.[55] The geophysical sciences were not spared this homogenizing process, even if its effects didn't take root in quite the same way. As military budgets and government-funded programs elicited new research and development, even sciences as methodologically diverse as stratigraphy and orbital logistics came under rigorous bureaucratic oversight—as in the drilling, spacefaring, and nuclear projects covered in earlier chapters. Under the auspices of a post-Taylorist systems era, the vertical sciences found their way into financially motivated enterprises spread across industries. In *The Intuitionist*, Whitehead emphasizes this globalization of verticality in the multinational figures of

Arbo and United, the elevator manufacturers whose influence proves to be behind much of the narrative's action: "Arbo and United are the guys who make the things," the journalist Ben Urich tells Lila Mae; "That's what really matters. The whole world wants to get vertical, and they're the guys that get them there" (208). Ben's description of the elevator conglomerates echoes the ubiquity of the plantations, labor camps, and carceral state in *The Underground Railroad*, *Sing, Unburied, Sing*, and *White Tears*. With its depiction of vertical modernity, *The Intuitionist* links the legacies of racial subjugation and exploitation with the managerial structures of postwar science.

Seen in this context, Whitehead's unnamed city signifies more than a single metropolis or even the spread of urbanization across the globe. It reminds readers of the modern city's planetary context, situating it in the expansive frame of the Anthropocene: "From the world's side of the tunnel the skyline is a row of broken teeth," the narrator tells us, "an angry serration gnawing at the atmosphere, but there's a lot of other stuff going on, dirty water and more land beyond that dirty water, the humble metropolitan outpost just departed, a crop of weedy smokestacks, lots of stuff [. . .]" (17). The passage describes Lila Mae's view of the city as she approaches from a highway tunnel, the landscape scattershot with vestiges of industrialism and waste, underscoring the links between urbanization, industrialism, and contamination. This evocation of environmental exploitation telegraphs the city's mineral origins. A flashback depicting Lila Mae's father, Marvin Watson, who worked as an elevator operator, links the city's growth to its planetary roots in fossil fuels: "Studied engineering at the colored college downstate, saw North: the big cities he knew were coming, the citadels pushed from the planet's guts like volcanoes and mountains to take the sky" (160–161). In these passages, *The Intuitionist* casts cities as "inverted mines"—a fitting complement to the derelict mines of *The Underground Railroad*—asking readers to imagine, in Arboleda's words, "what sorts of spaces of extraction are behind the fantastically alien skylines [. . .]."[56] Whitehead repeatedly underscores the city as an emblem of modernity through its upward growth, a struggle against gravity: "But who can resist the seductions of elevators these days, those stepping stones to Heaven, which make relentless verticality so alluring? While the architects understand that the future is up, the future is in how high you can go, it is difficult to shake old habits" (16). Small, squat buildings remain—government ones, the narrator clarifies, in a curious distinction between the headquarters of bureaucratic mundanity and the colossi of private enterprise. The draperies of expansion and extraction coat the narrative background, a subtle nod to the energy infrastructure that enables transport systems of elevation: one scene describes the 1853 Exhibition of the Industry of All Nations, where in "one room is arrayed raw materials on velvet, behind glass: minerals, ores in all shapes, coal, copper, stone, marble, crystal, diverse wonders all" (79).

Although thematically and representationally invested in verticality, *The Intuitionist* does not fail to illuminate the horizons of colonialism and imperialism that have extended their many tendrils across the globe, and that make possible the vertical aspirations of the mid-twentieth century. Still depicting the Exhibition, the narrator describes the locomotive steam engine as "this dynamic age distilled, these vehicular times" (79–80). The unnamed city of Whitehead's novel is representative of the modern convergence between the disparate locales of metropolitan centers and global markets. The skyscraping centers of neocolonialism are spatial inversions of the deep frontiers breached in regions peripheral to the Global North. The relationship between the deep frontier and the metropole is not only spatial but historical, as Stephen Graham notes: "The deepening gold mines of the Californian Gold Rush in the 1850s, in particular, provided the sites where the ventilators, multilevel telephones, early electric lighting and high-speed safety elevators that would later be pivotal to construction of the first downtown skyscrapers were first used systematically."[57] Whitehead's focus on the urban center is hardly negligent of the colonial infrastructure that supports it. *The Intuitionist* hints not-so-gently at the supply chain pathways that link cities, the centers of consumption, to their resource-rich extraction sites around the planet.

The novel's vertical imaginary grows out of this implicit colonial geography, the dominated landscapes and peoples that have powered the modern city's development. Being beholden to the racist ideologies inextricable from this history, vertical modernity cannot offer Lila Mae and other Black citizens of the city (and beyond) a path to real freedom but perpetuates a genocidal legacy in which people of color remain caught in cycles of fossilization and exploitation. This narrative impasse introduces the novel's second major mystery, the legendary "black box," or perfect elevator, never built but supposedly designed by James Fulton: "What does the perfect elevator look like, the one that will deliver us from the cities we suffer now, these shunted shacks?," Lila Mae thinks; "We don't know because we can't see inside it, it's something we cannot imagine, like the shape of angels' teeth. It's a black box" (61). As Graham observes, the association between elevators and black boxes is not Whitehead's alone but has been made by others describing the communicative effect of elevation.[58] Critics have pointed out that the black box is, perhaps most importantly, the butt of *The Intuitionist*'s big joke—a McGuffin, in Jeffrey Allen Tucker's words, emblematic of the chicanery behind Fulton's Intuitionism: "He was joking, right?," Lila Mae eventually realizes; "About Intuitionism. It was all a big joke" (232).[59] The black box, it is revealed, was part of Fulton's fun at the expense of science; Intuitionism was derived not from the technics of elevation, but from Fulton's own disorienting experience as a Black man passing for White.

Despite its function as a narrative distraction, however, the black box maintains a kind of uncanny significance, not least in the historical origins of the term, which date to the decade following World War II. Initially a metaphor in the fields of cybernetics and engineering for describing a machine whose inputs and outputs can be observed but whose internal processes remain indiscernible, the term developed over time to apply in situations beyond those of computing and information. In *Science in Action* (1987), Bruno Latour reflects fervently on the uses and misuses of the black box metaphor, including its relevance for comprehending the scientific process itself. Latour adapts the black box metaphor to describe what happens to scientific claims (or "facts") that become undisputed and make their way into other discourses as stable truths. When this happens, Latour suggests, science acts like a black box; it produces outcomes based on how other discourses rely on it, yet no further attention is given to the inner logic of the claim itself.[60] One way to gloss Latour's rendering is that black boxes serve as vessels of translation; they mediate meaning. In Whitehead's novel, Lila Mae gives Intuitionism a similar gloss: "A joke has no purpose if you cannot share it with anyone. Lila Mae thinks, Intuitionism is communication. That simple. Communication with what is not-you" (241). The parallel between the black box of midcentury cybernetics and that of *The Intuitionist* underscores the scientific genealogies that course through the text, but Whitehead pushes beyond the scope of even Latour's framing. The novel's black box is not a claim produced by science, but a prank pulled on science—an expression of science's blind spots.

Whitehead's black box entails a speculative impulse in that it does not translate across disciplines but rather transmits into the future. It is not representational in a positivistic sense (a word that transparently stands for a thing), but creative. It produces a new reality: "he was having a joke on them at first," Fulton's surviving heir tells Lila Mae, "but it wasn't a joke at the end. It became true" (236). The black box is an imaginative figure for escaping the bonds of vertical modernity, for realizing a world unencumbered by structural racism: "that's what *Theoretical Elevators* did," Lila Mae thinks of Fulton's masterwork, "it described a world, and a world needs inhabitants to make it real. The black box is the elevator-citizen for the elevator world" (100; italics in original). Comparing *The Intuitionist* with its postmodern forerunners, we can detect some similarities to other figures of indeterminacy, such as the Schwartzgerät (black device) in *Gravity's Rainbow* and the mohole in *Ratner's Star*. Yet Whitehead's black box stands apart as an acute response to the Whiteness of the indeterminacy paradigm in postmodernist fiction, configuring race as historically and secretively wed to the intricacies of apperception.

For all its irony and intelligent humor, *The Intuitionist*'s aspirations for its black box derive from the struggle for Black agency in a society beset by structures of racial domination. To achieve this goal, the novel suggests, symbols of vertical modernity must be dismantled: "She hadn't considered all the implications of the second elevation," Lila Mae realizes; "They will have to destroy this city once we deliver the black box. The current bones will not accommodate the marrow of the device. They will have to raze the city and cart off the rubble to less popular boroughs and start anew" (198). Whatever the second elevation is, it does not partake of the same industrial energies that characterize the modern metropolis. Rather, it expresses a figurative energy that circumvents the vertical sciences: a racialized postmodernity that reclaims extinction from postwar science's exploitative rationale.

In a fitting return to where this chapter began, we notice that *The Intuitionist* also features a subterranean element, although it is less emphatic than its language of elevation. Echoing Ellison and Himes, Whitehead underscores the proximity between Blackness and the ground: "This space in the garage is what the Department has allowed the colored men—" the narrator explains of the Elevator Inspectors' Headquarters, "it is underground, there are no windows permitting sky" (18). Repeatedly, the spaces deemed appropriate for the novel's people of color are grounded spaces, if not underground spaces. Rather than seek revolution through the heights, *The Intuitionist* pursues an inventive rupture that echoes the subterranean theorizing of Fanon; it weaves a tale of subtle subterfuge, undermining the energies of literal uplift. Lila Mae eventually uncovers traces of this undermining in Fulton's own journals, which she realizes she had previously misread: "*In this dream of uplift, they understand that they are dreaming the contract of the hallowed verticality, and hope to remember the terms on waking. The race never does, and that is our curse.* The human race, she thought formerly" (186; italics in original). Her altered perspective on Fulton's work is part of what the novel calls her "new literacy," her coming to consciousness of the deep structural ties between race and verticality: "In the last few days she has learned how to read, like a slave does, one forbidden word at a time" (230). In *The Intuitionist*, verticality appears ultimately as a White enterprise, promised for White people at the expense of Black mobility. Whitehead's elevators serve as an expression of vertical modernity writ large, from the urban skyscrapers of *The Intuitionist* to the rockets and satellites that orbit postmodernism, while the black box represents the emancipation of technology from its White overlords: "an elevator from the elevator's point of view"—a nonhuman perspective whose vanishing point rebukes the horizons of thought (62). Whereas vertical modernity underwrites the subterranean associations between Black subjectivity and fossilization, Whitehead's second elevation implies a mode of critical undermining. It promises a Black planetarity that reveals and supersedes vertical modernity's historical foundations of exploitation and suffering.

The Intuitionist and other novels of Black planetarity discussed here foreground race and racialized exploitation as elemental materials of Anthropocene narrative. Giving voice to the sufferings figuratively and literally buried by dominant cultural histories of science, industry, and capital, Black Anthropocene fiction salvages race as part of geological and genealogical strata. I call this reconfiguration fossil labor because it expresses a sense in which racial bodies and subjects are fossilized through colonial and industrial practices, and the processes by which fossilized labor is mined for future exploitation.

As it becomes part of the planet, racialized suffering discovers revolutionary potential in environmentalist and ecological narratives of the nonhuman earth, the earth-without-humans, the earth that withstands species extinction. Imagining powerful connections between Black experience and that of the exploited planet, these fictions craft, like Whitehead's black box, narratives of becoming and survival that circumvent the exploitative histories of White science.

UNDERVIEW
Writing Our Resilience

MY DISCUSSION OF BLACK PLANETARITY in Chapter 4 is hardly exhaustive and inevitably calls to mind another towering work of African American fiction, Octavia Butler's *Parable of the Sower* (1993); yet planetarity in Butler's novel introduces a feature not appearing in works by Whitehead, Ward, and Kunzru. Set in an environmentally and socially riven California in the disturbingly close years of 2024 to 2027, the novel tells the story of Lauren Olamina's flight from her besieged community with a following whom she unites under her Earthseed philosophy, a way of being that embraces change and promotes human departure from the planet: "'The Destiny of Earthseed is to take root among the stars,'" Lauren recites; "That's the ultimate Earthseed aim, and the ultimate human change short of death."[1] Aligning human survival with an expansionist momentum, *Parable of the Sower* navigates an ambiguous coloniality. Lauren's Earthseed vision entails a confusing balance of emancipatory flight and nostalgia for conquest: "As far as I'm concerned, space exploration and colonization are among the few things left over from the last century that can help us more than they hurt us," she admits.[2] On the surface, these remarks feel strange, especially given the novel's race and gender politics. A woman of color, Lauren leads a displaced group of migrants to Northern California in search of a safe place to establish an egalitarian society. If anything, the mission of Lauren's Earthseed should demonstrate anticolonial aspirations at odds with her desire to scatter earth's seedlings across the galaxy. Somewhat strikingly, *Parable of the Sower* interweaves themes also raised in the third and fourth chapters of this book, situating a spacefaring optimism uncomfortably close to the devastating repercussions of fossil labor.

Butler centers this contradiction in her 1998 sequel *Parable of the Talents*, in which Lauren's children resist her dream of spacefaring. The sequel ends on an ironic note, as Earthseed members prepare to depart on the spacecraft *Christopher Columbus*—a warning, Shelley Streeby claims, "of the dangers of seeking 'empire' and transposing the tragic history of European colonialism in the Americas into space."[3] Published at nearly the same time as Kim Stanley Robinson's Mars trilogy, Butler's *Parable* novels link the same ecopolitics found in the former with America's imperial legacy. Robinson's red mirror of the Anthropocene becomes, in Butler's telling, a mirror of many colors, reflecting the prismatic multitude that is both victim and inheritor of colonial violence: "Mars is a rock—cold, empty, almost airless, dead," Lauren writes in her journal; "Yet it's heaven in a way. We can see it in the night sky, a whole other world, but too nearby, too close within the reach of the people who've made such a hell of life here on Earth."[4] For Lauren, the red planet's proximity to earth inspires grander visions of extrasolar exploration, but these visions imply that exploration and conquest are not so easily extricated. Emancipatory desires can conceal exploitative dimensions.

Along with the continuum of emancipation and exploitation, Butler's *Parable* books also remind us of the overlap between extinction and resilience. The Earthseed philosophy and mission emerge from the troubled politics of a settler colonial history founded on industrial ravage and environmental terrorism against people of color. This history adds a crucial element to the Anthropocene critique of science: whereas the Anthropocene reveals that scientific progress is presently authoring a potentially species-wide extinction, the racial Anthropocene reveals that genocidal extinction has been the lived reality of Black and Indigenous peoples for generations. The planetary authoring of extinction is itself underwritten by histories of dispossession, death, and erasure. Resilience would seem to be a faint possibility here but for the narrative craft of many writers, critics, and activists of color. Their narratives are an antithesis to the totalizing and dominating tendency (self-undermining though it may be) of vertical science—an underview against the colonial overview. As Nick Estes has shown, Indigenous resistance envisions itself as resilience through settler colonial science, and he quotes one of the authors of the *Kul-Wicasa-Oyate*: "My people were civilized before the white came and we will be civilized and be here after the white man goes away, poisoned by his misuse of the land and eaten up by his own greed and diseases."[5] Extinction appears here in the form of White settler colonialism's consumption of its own foundations while Indigenous culture stands firm in the march of geological time.

How do we imagine resilience in a planetary fashion, as a response to capitalist excess that acknowledges its disparities and inequities? It was as I finished the chapters of *Writing Our Extinction* that I found myself compelled to explain in the Introduction that the book is not promoting an eco-pessimistic view. Thinking and writing about extinction can be emotionally draining, but emotionally drained isn't what I feel after reading the stories I have been discussing here. Rather, I feel invigorated, inspired, enthralled, enchanted, mystified, mollified, and reassured. Although *Through the Arc of the Rain Forest* envisions the literal disintegration of modern society, *The Nuclear Age* dredges up impressions of human fossilization, and *The Underground Railroad* registers a deep complicity between industrialization and emancipatory practices, I sense in these depictions the specter of alterity. It's too easy to read intimations of extinction as signs of apocalyptic closure, a reduction of the world to a singular fate. We should work to read them instead as gestures of profound differences within the world, opportunities to cultivate new ways of being and seeing.

Eco-pessimism protests too much. There is always something to be done, and in ways that don't involve removing humans from the equation, a solution that is resorting to a purist sentimentality—that humans have corrupted a once pristine and perfect planet. Excessive optimism succumbs to the same fallacy, however; philosophies such as ecomodernism insist that humans can effectively cordon off harmful elements of the environment, hermetically sealing humankind in protective biodomes. Ideologies of both protective isolation and destructive cohabitation ignore the generative nuances of interspecies living, or what Anna Lowenhaupt Tsing calls "histories that develop through contamination."[6] The *Parable* narrative's suspicion of planetary departure returns us to planetary messiness, the intermingling of things, the entangled experience of life on earth. We encounter here a provocative distillation of the vertical perspectives I have been tracking. Verticality both brings the scale of planetary complexity into focus and risks alienating us from its felt realities. It enables us to visualize scale yet threatens to inure us from the consequences of visibility. It makes possible the sight of earth as a planet while relying on industrial infrastructures that destabilize the planet. It pitches us, individually and collectively, into precarity while also empowering us to conceptualize that precarity.

We are met today with the temptation to flee, much like Earthseed's view. We wrestle with the resolution of technological salvation, whether ecologically or astronautically. The challenge of vertical perspective lies in resisting this temptation and revisiting the planetary surface with understandings gleaned from above and below, like the wayward terraformers of Robinson's 2015 novel *Aurora*, who return to earth after a failed attempt to settle an alien planet. For all the risks of vertical movement and outlook, there are also crucial benefits; but these will be for naught if our heads remain in the clouds. Likewise, we will make little headway at all if we refuse to acknowledge the opportunities and insights of vertical science, mimicking the flat caricatures of Adam McKay's *Don't Look Up* (2021). Programs of social change require that we move between scales of knowledge and agency, that we employ methods of acting and interacting. History means contamination. Cooperation means getting our hands dirty. When we write our extinction we also, counterintuitively, write our resilience.

Notes

Overview: Reading Our Extinction

1. Edgar Allan Poe, "The Domain of Arnheim" (1847), in *The Complete Tales and Poems of Edgar Allan Poe* (New York: Vintage, 1975), 609.

2. Ibid., 608.

3. Hollis D. Hedberg, "The Stratigraphic Panorama" (1961), in *Study of the Earth: Readings in Geological Science*, ed. J. F. White (Englewood Cliffs: Prentice-Hall, 1962), 189.

4. Qtd. in Knud Rasmussen, *Across Arctic America: Narrative of the Fifth Thule Expedition* (1927; rprt., College: University of Alaska Press, 1999), 387. For more on Arnarulunnguaq's role in Rasmussen's expedition, see Hugh Raffles, *The Book of Unconformities: Speculations on Lost Time* (New York: Pantheon, 2020), 159–242.

5. Ibid., 387.

6. For an outline of the calendrical model, see Jane E. Dmochowski and David A. D. Evans, "Earth's Changing Climate: A Deep-Time Geoscience Perspective," in *Time Scales: Thinking Across Ecological Temporalities*, ed. Bethany Wiggin, Carolyn Fornoff, and Patricia Eunji Kim (Minneapolis: University of Minnesota Press, 2020), 27.

7. See Walter Benjamin, "Theses on the Philosophy of History," in *Illuminations: Essays and Reflections*, trans. Harry Zohn, ed. Hannah Arendt (New York: Schocken Books, 2007), 261–262.

Introduction: The Vertical Anthropocene

1. Although coined in the 1980s, the term *Anthropocene* was popularized by Paul Crutzen in the early 2000s. See Paul J. Crutzen and Eugene Stoermer, "The 'Anthropocene,'" *IGPB Newsletter* 41 (2000): 17–18; and Paul J. Crutzen, "Geology of Mankind," *Nature* 415 (January 2002): 23, http://doi.org/10.1038/415023a. Delineations of the Anthropocene and the Great Acceleration have occupied scholars for the past two decades, prompting numerous interventions and publications. On the development of

the Great Acceleration as a period of the Anthropocene, see Will Steffen, Paul J. Crutzen, and John R. McNeill, "The Anthropocene: Are Humans Now Overwhelming the Great Forces of Nature?," *Ambio* 36, no. 8 (2007): 614–621, https://doi.org/10.1579/0044 -7447(2007)36[614:TAAHNO]2.0.CO;2. Dipesh Chakrabarty's recent work theorizes the implications of the Anthropocene for historiographic work and provides an extensive overview of the relationship between climate science and the humanities. See Dipesh Chakrabarty, *The Climate of History in a Planetary Age* (Chicago: University of Chicago Press, 2021). For more on the relationship between the Great Acceleration and environmental injustice, see Rob Nixon, *Slow Violence and the Environmentalism of the Poor* (Cambridge, MA: Harvard University Press, 2011), 12–14. For a broader overview of Great Acceleration history, see J. R. McNeill and Peter Engelke, *The Great Acceleration: An Environmental History of the Anthropocene since 1945* (Cambridge, MA: Belknap Press of Harvard University Press, 2016).

2. McKenzie Wark has pointed out the irony that our understanding of anthropogenic climate change owes much to wartime technologies that themselves contributed to environmental damage. See McKenzie Wark, *Molecular Red: Theory for the Anthropocene* (London: Verso, 2015), 170–182. For a more extensive overview of the relationship between military technology and emerging climate science, see Paul Edwards, *A Vast Machine: Computer Models, Climate Data, and the Politics of Global Warming* (Cambridge, MA: MIT Press, 2010). Finally, although mining and drilling (not to mention industrial modernity writ large) predate 1945, the postwar era witnessed an explosion in resource extraction as energy demands skyrocketed and profits were funneled through a small number of multinational conglomerates. See Martín Arboleda, *Planetary Mine: Territories of Extraction under Late Capitalism* (London: Verso, 2020), 245–246.

3. Rey Chow, *The Age of the World Target: Self-Referentiality in War, Theory, and Comparative Work* (Durham: Duke University Press, 2006), 31.

4. See Michelle M. Wright, *Physics of Blackness: Beyond the Middle Passage Epistemology* (Minneapolis: University of Minnesota Press, 2015), 92.

5. See Elizabeth S. Anker and Rita Felski, eds., *Critique and Postcritique* (Durham: Duke University Press, 2017).

6. Anna Kornbluh, "Extinct Critique," *South Atlantic Quarterly* 119, no. 4 (2020): 771, https://doi.org/10.1215/00382876-8663675.

7. See Quentin Meillassoux, *After Finitude: An Essay on the Necessity of Contingency* (2006), trans. Ray Brassier (London: Continuum, 2008), 10; and Ray Brassier, *Nihil Unbound: Enlightenment and Extinction* (London: Palgrave, 2010), 230.

8. For more on *Earthrise*'s impact and circulation, see Bruce Clarke, *Gaian Systems: Lynn Margulis, Neocybernetics, and the End of the Anthropocene* (Minneapolis: University of Minnesota Press, 2020), 102–106.

9. "Chasing the Moon Transcript: Part Two," *American Experience*, WGBH Educational Foundation, https://www.pbs.org/wgbh/americanexperience/films/chasing -moon/#transcript. As Clarke notes, the original image was altered and rotated to give the perspectival impression of an earthrise. See Clarke, *Gaian Systems*, 103.

10. Eugene Kennedy, "Earthrise: The Dawning of a New Spiritual Awareness," *New York Times*, April 15, 1979, https://www.nytimes.com/1979/04/15/archives/earthrise -the-dawning-of-a-new-spiritual-awareness.html. Mere months before *Earthrise* was taken, Stewart Brand's *Whole Earth Catalog* released its premier issue, featuring a 1967 composite digital image of earth taken by the ATS-3 satellite. See Stewart Brand, *Whole Earth Catalog: Access to Tools* (Fall 1968), https://archive.org/details/1stWEC -complete/mode/2up. Brand would include *Earthrise* itself on the cover of the 1969 issue of the *Catalog*. For more on Anders's photograph and its cultural implications, see Benjamin Lazier, "Earthrise; or, the Globalization of the World Picture," *American Historical Review* 116, no. 3 (2011): 602–630, http://doi.org/10.1086/ahr.116.3.602.

11. See Nigel Clark and Bronislaw Szerszynski, *Planetary Social Thought: The Anthropocene Challenge to the Social Sciences* (Cambridge, UK: Polity, 2021); and Jan Zalasiewicz, *The Earth After Us: What Legacy Will Humans Leave in the Rocks?* (Oxford: Oxford University Press, 2008). Zalasiewicz's work as a geologist and as Chair of the Anthropocene Working Group has been instrumental in re-envisioning human activity along a vertical axis, particularly insofar as recent science is challenging the conventional divide between human by-products and "natural" rock, as seen for example in the emergence of plastiglomerates. See Jan Zalasiewicz et al., "The Geological Cycle of Plastics and Their Use As a Stratigraphic Indicator," *Anthropocene* 13 (2016): 4–17, http://doi.org/10.1016/j.ancene.2016.01.002. See also Ian Klinke, "On the History of a Subterranean Geopolitics," *Geoforum* 127 (2021): 356–363, http://doi.org/ 10.1016/j.geoforum.2019.10.010.

12. *Final frontier* is a term made famous by the television series *Star Trek* in the 1960s. For more on the *deep frontier*, see Stephen Graham, *Vertical: The City from Satellites to Bunkers* (London: Verso, 2016), 365–387.

13. See Benjamin W. Goossen, "A Benchmark for the Environment: Big Science and 'Artificial' Geophysics in the Global 1950s," *Journal of Global History* 15, no. 1 (2020): 149–168, http://doi.org/10.1017/S1740022819000378. For background on the geopolitical dynamics of the IGY (particularly between the United States and the Soviet Union), see Jon Agar, *Science in the Twentieth Century and Beyond* (Cambridge, UK: Polity, 2012), 343–348.

14. Hannah Arendt, *The Human Condition* (Chicago: University of Chicago Press, 1998), 1; and Alexander Marshack, *The World in Space: The Story of the International Geophysical Year* (New York: Dell, 1958), 171.

15. For more on the rhetorical confluence of liberalism and spaceflight, as well as the lingering specter of colonialism, see Dale Carter, *The Final Frontier: The Rise and Fall of the American Rocket State* (London: Verso, 1988), 200–209.

16. Goossen, "Benchmark," 154. Martín Arboleda underscores the dynamic between verticality and energy extraction in the twentieth century, linking the mining of planetary resources with the rise of the United States to "the status of indisputable superpower during most of the twentieth century," a geopolitical and economic supremacy founded on the exploitation of fossil fuels. See Arboleda, *Planetary*, 12.

17. Marshack, *World*, 13.

18. Martin Heidegger, "'Only a God Can Save Us': *Der Spiegel*'s Interview with Martin Heidegger," in *The Heidegger Controversy: A Critical Reader*, ed. Richard Wolin (Cambridge, MA: MIT Press, 1992), 105–106.

19. Paul Virilio, *Open Sky*, trans. Julie Rose (London: Verso, 2008), 41.

20. See Les U. Knight, "The Voluntary Human Extinction Movement," VHEMT, http://vhemt.org/.

21. Don DeLillo, *Great Jones Street* (New York: Penguin, 1994), 209.

22. Ibid.

23. Sigmund Freud, *Beyond the Pleasure Principle*, trans. James Strachey (New York: W. W. Norton, 1989), 10–12.

24. Joseph Masco, "The Six Extinctions: Visualizing Planetary Ecological Crisis Today," in *After Extinction*, ed. Richard Grusin (Minneapolis: University of Minnesota Press, 2018), 83.

25. Joseph Masco, *The Future of Fallout, and Other Episodes in Radioactive World-Making* (Durham: Duke University Press, 2021), 18.

26. For a helpful treatment of the distinctions between natural disaster and eco-catastrophe, see Kate Rigby, *Dancing with Disaster: Environmental Histories, Narratives, and Ethics for Perilous Times* (Charlottesville: University of Virginia Press, 2015), 16–23.

27. Justin McBrien, "Accumulating Extinction: Planetary Catastrophism in the Necrocene," in *Anthropocene or Capitalocene? Nature, History, and the Crisis of Capitalism*, ed. Jason W. Moore (Oakland, CA: PM Press, 2016), 119.

28. Paul Virilio, *Open Sky*, 69.

29. Ibid., 70.

30. Michael R. Rampino, *Cataclysms: A New Geology for the Twenty-First Century* (New York: Columbia University Press, 2017), 29.

31. Lyell's theory of uniformity and its acceptance by geologists has had a long and complicated history. For more on its influence and the mischaracterizations that often accompanied it, see Stephen Jay Gould, *Time's Arrow, Time's Cycle: Myth and Metaphor in the Discovery of Geological Time* (Cambridge, MA: Harvard University Press, 1987), 115–132.

32. Rampino, *Cataclysms*, 32.

33. Ibid., 60.

34. Nixon, *Slow*, 216.

35. Claire Colebrook, "Extinguishing Ability: How We Became Postextinction Persons," in *Eco-Deconstruction: Derrida and Environmental Philosophy*, ed. Matthias Fritsch, Philippe Lynes, and David Wood (Cambridge: Cambridge University Press, 2018), 268–269.

36. Mark Bould, *The Anthropocene Unconscious: Climate Catastrophe Culture* (London: Verso, 2021), 15.

37. For more on the transition from land-based agricultural forms of capital to forms based on mineral reserves, see Andreas Malm, *Fossil Capital: The Rise of Steam*

Power and the Roots of Global Warming (London: Verso, 2016), 320–326. For a speculative treatment of the broader dynamics unfolding between capitalism and extinction, see Ashley Dawson, *Extinction: A Radical History* (New York: OR Books, 2016).

38. Claire Colebrook, "We Have Always Been Post-Anthropocene: The Anthropocene Counterfactual," in *Anthropocene Feminism*, ed. Richard Grusin (Minneapolis: University of Minnesota Press, 2017), 18–19.

39. Claire Colebrook, *Death of the PostHuman: Essays on Extinction*, vol. 1 (London: Open Humanities Press, 2014), 43.

40. Kathryn Yusoff, "Epochal Aesthetics: Affectual Infrastructures of the Anthropocene," in *Accumulation: The Art, Architecture, and Media of Climate Change*, ed. Nick Axel, Daniel A. Barber, Nikolaus Hirsch, and Anton Vidokle, an *e-flux* Architecture volume (Minneapolis: University of Minnesota Press, 2022), 15.

41. Jacques Derrida, "No Apocalypse, Not Now (Full Speed Ahead, Seven Missiles, Seven Missives)," trans. Catherine Porter and Philip Lewis, *Diacritics* 14, no. 2 (1984): 27, http://doi.org/10.2307/464756.

42. Colebrook, *Death*, 226–227.

43. See Ursula K. Heise, *Sense of Place and Sense of Planet: The Environmental Imagination of the Global* (Oxford: Oxford University Press, 2008), 59.

44. See Nixon, *Slow*, 245; and Chakrabarty, *Climate*, 7.

45. Joshua DiCaglio, *Scale Theory: A Nondisciplinary Inquiry* (Minneapolis: University of Minnesota Press, 2021), 233.

46. Min Hyoung Song, *Climate Lyricism* (Durham: Duke University Press, 2022), 107.

47. Ibid., 116–120.

48. For more on the discourse and concern surrounding a sixth extinction, see Elizabeth Kolbert, *The Sixth Extinction: An Unnatural History* (New York: Henry Holt, 2014). For accounts of humankind's short-lived existence on the planet—and the planet's ability to outlast us—see Adam Frank, "Earth Will Survive. We May Not," *The New York Times*, June 12, 2018, https://www.nytimes.com/2018/06/12/opinion/earth -will-survive-we-may-not.html; and John Greene, "Humanity's Temporal Range," in *The Anthropocene Reviewed* (New York: Dutton, 2021), 13–21.

49. Adam Trexler, *Anthropocene Fictions: The Novel in a Time of Climate Change* (Charlottesville: University of Virginia Press, 2015), 9. For more on the distinctions between the Anthropocene and climate change as descriptive categories, see Julia Adeney Thomas, Mark Williams, and Jan Zalasiewicz, *The Anthropocene: A Multidisciplinary Approach* (Cambridge, UK: Polity, 2020), 69–86.

50. For an entertaining and intelligent treatment of the list of *-cenes*, see Bould, *Anthropocene*, 7–9.

51. Françoise Vergès, "Racial Capitalocene," in *Futures of Black Radicalism*, ed. Gaye Theresa Johnson and Alex Lubin (London: Verso, 2017), chap. 4, ProQuest Ebrary.

52. For early applications of systems theory in literary studies, see Tom LeClair, *In the Loop: Don DeLillo and the Systems Novel* (Champaign: University of Illinois Press, 1987);

and Cary Wolfe, *Critical Environments: Postmodern Theory and the Pragmatics of the "Outside"* (Minneapolis: University of Minnesota Press, 1998). For studies that bring together systemic topics across a range of disciplines, including literary criticism, environmentalism, sociology, history of science, visual media, architecture, and more, see the following: Bruce Clarke, *Posthuman Metamorphosis: Narrative and Systems* (New York: Fordham University Press, 2008); Priscilla Wald, *Contagious: Cultures, Carriers, and the Outbreak Narrative* (Durham: Duke University Press, 2008); Kate Marshall, *Corridor: Media Architectures in American Fiction* (Minneapolis: University of Minnesota Press, 2013); David J. Alworth, *Site Reading: Art, Fiction, Social Form* (Princeton: Princeton University Press, 2015); Caroline Levine, *Forms: Whole, Rhythm, Hierarchy, Network* (Princeton: Princeton University Press, 2015); Nathan K. Hensley and Philip Steer, eds., *Ecological Form: System and Aesthetics in the Age of Empire* (New York: Fordham University Press, 2019); Anna Kornbluh, *The Order of Forms: Realism, Formalism, and Social Science* (Chicago: University of Chicago Press, 2019); Heather Houser, *Infowhelm: Environmental Art and Literature in an Age of Data* (New York: Columbia University Press, 2020); Michael Dango, *Crisis Style: The Aesthetics of Repair* (Stanford: Stanford University Press, 2021); and Carolyn Lesjak, *The Afterlife of Enclosure: British Realism, Character, and the Commons* (Stanford: Stanford University Press, 2021).

53. Levine, *Forms*, 119.

54. Devin Griffiths, "The Ecology of Form," *Critical Inquiry* 48, no. 1 (2021): 71, https://doi.org/10.1086/715980.

55. See the essays in Rachel Greenwald Smith, ed., *American Literature in Transition, 2000–2010* (Cambridge: Cambridge University Press, 2018), especially Lee Konstantinou, "Neorealist Fiction," 109–124; Kate Marshall, "New Wave Fabulism and Hybrid Science Fictions," 76–87; and Matthew Schneider-Mayerson, "Climate Change Fiction," 309–321.

56. See Nixon, *Slow*, 6–10.

57. Donna J. Haraway, *Staying with the Trouble: Making Kin in the Chthulucene* (Durham: Duke University Press, 2016), 38.

58. See Timothy Morton, *Hyperobjects: Philosophy and Ecology After the End of the World* (Minneapolis: University of Minnesota Press, 2013), 1–24.

59. Marcia Bjornerud, *Timefulness: How Thinking Like a Geologist Can Help Save the World* (Princeton: Princeton University Press, 2018), 131.

60. Roy Scranton, "Learning How to Die in the Anthropocene," in *Energy Humanities: An Anthology*, ed. Imre Szeman and Dominic Boyer (Baltimore: Johns Hopkins University Press, 2017), 388.

61. Don DeLillo, *Underworld* (New York: Scribner, 1998), 63.

Chapter One: Earthly Language

An earlier version of Chapter 1 (copyright © 2021 Purdue University) first appeared in *MFS: Modern Fiction Studies*, Volume 67, Issue 4, Winter, 2021, pages 613-636. Published by Johns Hopkins University Press.

1. Don DeLillo, *Underworld* (New York: Scribner, 1998).Page numbers are cited in the text.

2. See John N. Duvall, "Baseball as Aesthetic Ideology: Cold War History, Race, and DeLillo's 'Pafko at the Wall,'" *Modern Fiction Studies* 41, no. 2 (1995): 285–313, http://doi.org/10.1353/mfs.1995.0091; Peter Knight, "Everything Is Connected: *Underworld*'s Secret History of Paranoia," *Modern Fiction Studies* 45, no. 3 (1999): 811–836, http://doi.org/10.1353/mfs.1999.0052; Phillip E. Wegner, *Life Between Two Deaths, 1989–2001: U.S. Culture in the Long Nineties* (Durham: Duke University Press, 2020), 43–59; and Daniel Grausam, *On Endings: American Postmodern Fiction and the Cold War* (Charlottesville: University of Virginia Press, 2011), 139.

3. Sarah Wasserman, *The Death of Things: Ephemera and the American Novel* (Minneapolis: University of Minnesota Press, 2020), 199.

4. For more on *Underworld*'s realism, see Wegner, *Life*, 45–48; and Wasserman, *Death*, 200–201.

5. Amitav Ghosh, *The Great Derangement: Climate Change and the Unthinkable* (Chicago: University of Chicago Press, 2016), 61.

6. Thangam Ravindranathan, "The Rise of the Sea and the Novel," *differences* 30, no. 3 (2019): 7, http://doi.org/10.1215/10407391-7973974.

7. Kate Marshall, "What Are the Novels of the Anthropocene? American Fiction in Geological Time," *American Literary History* 27, no. 3 (2015): 529, http://doi.org/10.1093/alh/ajv032.

8. Recently, critics have pursued this conjunction of realism and speculation even further, proposing that the Anthropocene undermines conventional literary taxonomies of realism and representation: see Rebecca Evans, "Nomenclature, Narrative, and Novum: 'The Anthropocene' and/as Science Fiction," *Science Fiction Studies* 45, no. 3 (2018): 488–492, http://doi.org/10.5621/sciefictstud.45.3.0484; and Gerry Canavan, "Science Fiction and Utopia in the Anthropocene," *American Literature* 93, no. 2 (2021): 255–258, https://doi.org/10.1215/00029831-9003582.

9. For more on the dynamics between time, catastrophe, and realism, see Kathryn Yusoff, "Geologic Realism: On the Beach of Geologic Time," *Social Text* 37, no. 1 (2019): 1–26, https://doi.org/10.1215/01642472-7286240; and Debjani Ganguly, "Catastrophic Form and Planetary Realism," *New Literary History* 51, no. 2 (2020): 419–453, https://doi.org/10.1353/nlh.2020.0025.

10. Joseph Masco, *The Future of Fallout, and Other Episodes in Radioactive World-Making* (Durham: Duke University Press, 2021), 220.

11. Mark McGurl, "Gigantic Realism: The Rise of the Novel and the Comedy of Scale," *Critical Inquiry* 43 (2017): 407–408, https://www.journals.uchicago.edu/doi/full/10.1086/689661.

12. Similarly, Kate Marshall notes the importance of Smithson for Rachel Kushner's *The Flamethrowers* (2013), another Anthropocene novel, whose protagonist "studied Robert Smithson's *Spiral Jetty* (1970) at a large public university in the west in the early 1970s." See Marshall, "What," 524. Although Marshall doesn't discuss *Underworld*,

the influence of land art in both novels is palpable, and informs their meditations on human existence in the Anthropocene.

13. Hito Steyerl, "In Free Fall: A Thought Experiment on Vertical Perspective," *e-flux Journal*, no. 24 (April 2011), https://www.e-flux.com/journal/24/67860/in-free-fall-a-thought-experiment-on-vertical-perspective/.

14. Robert Smithson, "Aerial Art," in *Robert Smithson: The Collected Writings*, ed. Jack Flam (Berkeley: University of California Press, 1996), 116.

15. I borrow the term *rehearsal* from Rebecca Solnit, who insists that *test* doesn't quite do justice to the incalculable and unpredictable material effects of nuclear fallout. See Rebecca Solnit, *Savage Dreams: A Journey into the Hidden Wars of the American West* (Berkeley: University of California Press, 2014), 5.

16. Fresh Kills was officially closed in early 2001 but was forced to reopen later that year for the disposal of debris from the 9/11 attacks. For more on its controversial history, see Lucy R. Lippard, "Coming Clean," *Nonstop Metropolis: A New York City Atlas*, ed. Rebecca Solnit and Joshua Jelly-Schapiro (Berkeley: University of California Press, 2016), 142–146.

17. See Wasserman, *Death*, 204–205; and Rachele Dini, "'What We Excrete Comes Back to Consume Us': Waste and Reclamation in Don DeLillo's *Underworld*," *ISLE: Interdisciplinary Studies in Literature and the Environment* 26, no. 1 (2019): 165–188, https://doi.org/10.1093/isle/isz004.

18. David J. Alworth, *Site Reading: Art, Fiction, Social Form* (Princeton: Princeton University Press, 2015), 52.

19. Ibid.

20. Qtd. in Michael Fried, "Art and Objecthood," *Art and Objecthood: Essays and Reviews* (Chicago: University of Chicago Press, 1998), 158.

21. Ibid., 159.

22. Robert Smithson, "Towards the Development of an Air Terminal Site," in *Robert Smithson: The Collected Writings*, ed. Jack Flam (Berkeley: University of California Press), 59.

23. Robert Smithson, "Letter to the Editor," in *Robert Smithson: The Collected Writings*, ed. Jack Flam (Berkeley: University of California Press, 1996), 67.

24. Robert Smithson, "A Museum of Language in the Vicinity of Art," in *Robert Smithson: The Collected Writings*, ed. Jack Flam (Berkeley: University of California Press, 1996), 91.

25. Jennifer L. Roberts, "Landscapes of Indifference: Robert Smithson and John Lloyd Stephens in Yucatán," *The Art Bulletin* 82, no. 3 (2000): 544, https://www.jstor.org/stable/3051401.

26. Don DeLillo, *Ratner's Star* (New York: Vintage, 1989), 218.

27. Qtd. in Robert A. Sobieszek, "Robert Smithson's *Proposal for a Monument at Antarctica*," in *Robert Smithson*, ed. Eugenie Tsai and Cornelia Butler (Berkeley: University of California Press, 2004), 143.

28. Smithson, "Aerial Art," 116.

29. Ibid., 117.

30. This isn't to say that textuality is unimportant for Smithson, as critics from Craig Owens to Lytle Shaw have demonstrated. Rather, Smithson's interest in textuality is largely non-conceptual and non-narrative, as it attempts to surpass hermeneutics for an intimate and immediate perceptual experience. See Craig Owens, "Earthwords," *October* 10 (1979): 120–130, http://doi.org/10.2307/778632; and Lytle Shaw, *Fieldworks: From Place to Site in Postwar Poetics* (Tuscaloosa: University of Alabama Press, 2013), 192–209.

31. Phillip E. Wegner, "October 3, 1951 to September 11, 2001: Periodizing the Cold War in Don DeLillo's *Underworld*," *Amerikastuiden/American Studies* 49, no. 1 (2004): 54.

32. Stéphane Bou and Jean-Baptiste Thoret, "A Conversation with Don DeLillo: Has Terrorism Become the World's Main Plot?," *Panic* 1 (2005), http://perival.com/delillo/interview_panic_2005.html. Patrick O'Donnell goes so far as to suggest that the "antimonies of [. . .] system and waste are visible everywhere in *Underworld*, and their interaction constitutes what might be termed the novel's dialectic." See Patrick O'Donnell, "*Underworld*," in *The Cambridge Companion to Don DeLillo*, ed. John N. Duvall (Cambridge: Cambridge University Press, 2008), 113.

33. There is also a connection here to DeLillo's *Ratner's Star*, which takes place in a secluded think tank and features a character who lives in a hole in the ground.

34. Robert Smithson, "Language to Be Looked at, and/or Things to Be Read," in *Robert Smithson: The Collected Writings*, ed. Jack Flam (Berkeley: University of California Press, 1996), 61.

35. Don DeLillo, *Great Jones Street* (New York: Penguin, 1994), 74–75 and 209.

36. DeLillo, *Ratner's*, 221.

37. An acknowledgment is owed here to David Cowart's exemplary reading of De-Lillo's work, which foregrounds the sense of gravity that the author's prose communicates. According to Cowart, *Underworld* presents its readers with "a kind of agon [. . .] between the wordable and the unwordable." See David Cowart, *Don DeLillo: The Physics of Language* (Athens: University of Georgia Press, 2003), 182. Although the Anthropocene is not the subject of Cowart's study, he nonetheless offers an extended examination of how DeLillo's approach to language raises an ambiguity between signification and materiality.

38. Don DeLillo, *The Names* (New York: Vintage, 1989), 294.

39. Jussi Parikka, *The Geology of Media* (Minneapolis: University of Minnesota Press, 2015), 81.

40. For a brief and sharp diagnosis of this blurring, see Bernadette Wegenstein, "Body," in *Critical Terms for Media Studies*, ed. W.J.T. Mitchell and Mark B. N. Hansen (Chicago: University of Chicago Press, 2010), 27–29. For a longer treatment of the cybernetic paradigm, see N. Katherine Hayles, *How We Became Posthuman: Virtual Bodies in Cybernetics, Literature, and Informatics* (Chicago: University of Chicago Press, 1999).

41. McGurl, "Gigantic," 420.

42. Ursula K. Heise, *Imagining Extinction: The Cultural Meanings of Endangered Species* (Chicago: University of Chicago Press, 2016), 219.

43. Ibid., 219–220.

44. Qtd. in Heise, *Imagining*, 67.

45. Evans, "Nomenclature," 490.

46. Shaw, *Fieldworks*, 199.

Chapter 2: Plot Holes

An earlier version of Chapter 2 appeared in *Contemporary Literature*, Volume 62, No, 3, Fall 2021. ©2021 by the Board of Regents of the University of Wisconsin System. All rights reserved.

1. Don DeLillo, *Ratner's Star* (New York: Vintage, 1989). Page numbers are cited in the text.

2. John Steinbeck, "High Drama of Bold Thrust Through Ocean Floor: Earth's Second Layer Is Tapped in Prelude to Mohole," *Life*, April 14, 1961, 111–122.

3. Ibid., 118.

4. "Kola Superdeep Borehole," *Atlas Obscura*, February 21, 2018, https://www.atlasobscura.com/places/kola-superdeep-borehole.

5. Kenneth Jinghwa Hsü, *Challenger at Sea: A Ship That Revolutionized Earth Science* (Princeton: Princeton University Press, 2014), 12–14.

6. Project Mohole never reached the mantle. The geological debate would come to a virtual end in 1966, however, when data confirmed key explanations for seafloor spreading, a foundational component of the currently favored theory of plate tectonics. See Henry Frankel, "Plate Tectonics," in *The Cambridge History of Science*, vol. 6, ed. Peter J. Bowler and John V. Pickstone (Cambridge: Cambridge University Press, 2009), 393.

7. Despite the specificity of the name, no scholarly examinations of DeLillo's novel mention the relevance of Project Mohole; there is also no explicit evidence that DeLillo lifted the name from the geological project. Given the novel's engagement with deep time, however, and its references to digging deep into the earth, it's highly likely the author was invoking the failed attempt to drill down to the mantle.

8. *Speculative geology* is not a term of art, but it isn't my coinage either. It appeared in *Geological Magazine* as early as 1886 regarding the establishment of an intercontinental model of geological history. See R. D. Oldham, "Essays on Speculative Geology: 1. On Homotaxis and Contemporaneity," *Geological Magazine* 3, no. 7 (1886): 293–300; and "Essays on Speculative Geology: 2. Probable Changes of Latitude," *Geological Magazine* 3, no. 7 (1886): 300–308.

9. Joseph Masco, *The Future of Fallout, and Other Episodes in Radioactive World-Making* (Durham: Duke University Press, 2021), 221.

10. Karen Barad, *Meeting the Universe Halfway: Quantum Physics and the Entanglement of Matter and Meaning* (Durham: Duke University Press, 2007), 140.

11. Timothy Morton, *Dark Ecology: For a Logic of Future Coexistence* (New York: Columbia University Press, 2016), 64.

12. Stephanie Wakefield, *Anthropocene Back Loop: Experimentation in Unsafe Operating Space* (London: Open Humanities Press, 2020), 29–32.

13. Robert MacFarlane, *Underland: A Deep Time Journey* (New York: Norton, 2019), 312.

14. Qtd. in Jussi Parikka, *The Geology of Media* (Minneapolis: University of Minnesota Press, 2015), 32.

15. Ibid., 33.

16. Reza Negarestani, *Cyclonopedia: Complicity with Anonymous Materials* (Melbourne: re.press, 2008) . Page numbers are cited in the text.

17. Mark McGurl, "The New Cultural Geology," *Twentieth-Century Literature* 57, no. 3–4 (2011): 381, http://doi.org/10.1215/0041462X-2011-4011.

18. Hugh Walters, *The Mohole Menace* (New York: Criterion, 1968). Page numbers are cited in the text. In this chapter, I refer to the novel by its original title; however, I'm quoting from the U.S. edition, published as *The Mohole Menace*.

19. McGurl, "New," 384.

20. For more on the cultural connections between geology, epistemology, and legibility, see Kate Rigby, *Dancing with Disaster: Environmental Histories, Narratives, and Ethics for Perilous Times* (Charlottesville: University of Virginia Press, 2015), 26.

21. Lucy R. Lippard, *Undermining: A Wild Ride Through Land Use, Politics, and Art in the Changing West* (New York: New Press, 2014), 2.

22. Klaus Hasselmann, "Mohole 1957–1964," in *Seventy Years of Exploration in Oceanography: A Prolonged Weekend Discussion with Walter Munk*, ed. Hans von Storch and Klaus Hasselmann (Berlin: Springer, 2010), 68.

23. Steinbeck, "High," 118.

24. Hasselmann, "Mohole," 68.

25. Hollis D. Hedberg, "Petroleum and Progress in Geology," *Journal of the Geological Society* 127 (1971): 3, https://doi.org/10.1144/gsjgs.127.1.0003.

26. Ibid., 5.

27. Ibid., 6.

28. Ibid., 6–7.

29. Ibid., 7.

30. Andreas Malm, *Fossil Capital: The Rise of Steam Power and the Roots of Global Warming* (London: Verso, 2016), 9.

31. Daniel S. Greenberg, "Mohole: The Project That Went Awry (II)," *Science* 143, no. 3603 (1964): 224, https://www.jstor.org/stable/1712431.

32. Ibid., 224–225.

33. One such record was set by the infamous *Deepwater Horizon* rig in the Keathley Canyon, one year before the explosion for which it is best known. See "*Deepwater Horizon* Drills World's Deepest O&G Well," *Rigzone*, September 2, 2009, https://www.rigzone.com/news/oil_gas/a/79954/transoceans_deepwater_horizon_drills_worlds

_deepest_og_well/. For those interested in Project Mohole's contentious history, Greenberg's three-part exposé (1964) outlines numerous organizational and political ambiguities within the project, although Hedberg (1964) and Willard Bascom (1964) dispute some of its suggestions in letters to the journal *Science*. For two accounts of the scientific aspirations of the project, see Willard Bascom, "The Mohole," *Scientific American* 200, no. 4 (1959): 41–49, https://www.jstor.org/stable/10.2307/26172027; and H. H. Hess, "The AMSOC Hole to the Earth's Mantle," in *Study of the Earth: Readings in Geological Science*, ed. J. F. White (Englewood Cliffs: Prentice-Hall, 1962), 79–88.

34. Imre Szeman, "System Failure: Oil, Futurity, and the Anticipation of Disaster," in *Energy Humanities: An Anthology*, ed. Imre Szeman and Dominic Boyer (Baltimore: Johns Hopkins University Press, 2017), 59.

35. Timothy Mitchell, *Carbon Democracy: Political Power in the Age of Oil* (London: Verso, 2013), 112–113.

36. Roger Revelle et al, *Restoring the Quality of Our Environment: Report of the Environmental Pollution Panel, President's Science Advisory Committee* (Washington, DC: The White House, 1965), 126.

37. Rachel Carson, "Of Man and the Stream of Time," in *Silent Spring and Other Writings on the Environment*, ed. Sandra Steingraber (New York: Library of America, 2018), 425.

38. Claire Colebrook, *Death of the PostHuman: Essays on Extinction*, vol. 1 (London: Open Humanities Press, 2014), 39.

39. Kim Stanley Robinson, *Red Mars* (New York: Del Rey, 2017). Page numbers are cited in the text.

40. For more on the sociopolitical history of conservationism, see Bram Büscher and Robert Fletcher, *The Conservation Revolution: Radical Ideas for Saving Nature Beyond the Anthropocene* (London: Verso, 2020), 13–46. For more on convivial conservation, see ibid., 158–198.

41. See Elizabeth Leane, "Chromodynamics: Science and Colonialism in Kim Stanley Robinson's Mars Trilogy," *Ariel* 33, no. 1 (2002): 88, ProQuest; and Eric Otto, "Kim Stanley Robinson's *Mars* Trilogy and the Leopoldian Land Ethic," *Utopian Studies* 14, no. 2 (2003): 118–135, EBSCOhost. Heise has argued that Robinson's trilogy stages conflicting and politically motivating definitions of nature, offering a provocative thought experiment on twentieth-century environmentalist movements. See Ursula K. Heise, "Martian Ecologies and the Future of Nature," *Twentieth-Century Literature* 57, no. 3–4 (2011): 461–462, http://doi.org/10.1215/0041462X-2011-4003. Finally, for a foundational account of Robinson's utopianism and literary intervention, see Fredric Jameson, "'If I Can Find One Good City I Will Spare the Man': Realism and Utopia in Kim Stanley Robinson's *Mars* Trilogy," in *Archaeologies of the Future: The Desire Called Utopia and Other Science Fictions* (London: Verso, 2007), 393–416.

42. Dipesh Chakrabarty, *The Climate of History in a Planetary Age* (Chicago: University of Chicago Press, 2021), 67.

43. Elizabeth A. Povinelli, *Geontologies: A Requiem to Late Liberalism* (Durham: Duke University Press, 2016), 45.

44. Kim Stanley Robinson, *Green Mars* (New York: Bantam, 1995), 376.

45. Ursula K. Heise, "Realism, Modernism, and the Future: An Interview with Kim Stanley Robinson," *ASAP/Journal* 1, no. 1 (2016): 30, http://doi.org/10.1353/asa.2016.0001.

46. Amitav Ghosh, "Petrofiction: The Oil Encounter and the Novel," in *Energy Humanities: An Anthology*, ed. Imre Szeman and Dominic Boyer (Baltimore: Johns Hopkins University Press, 2017), 432.

47. For a formal analysis of *Cyclonopedia*, see Kate Marshall, "*Cyclonopedia* as Novel (a meditation on complicity as inauthenticity)," in *Leper Creativity*: Cyclonopedia *Symposium*, ed. Ed Keller, Nicola Masciandaro, and Eugene Thacker (Santa Barbara: punctum books, 2012), 147–157.

48. Abdelrahman Munif, *Cities of Salt*, trans. Peter Theroux (New York: Vintage, 1989), 140.

49. Rob Nixon, *Slow Violence and the Environmentalism of the Poor* (Cambridge, MA: Harvard University Press, 2011), 93.

50. Timothy Morton, *Hyperobjects: Philosophy and Ecology After the End of the World* (Minneapolis: University of Minnesota Press, 2013), 31.

51. Melanie Doherty, "Oil and Dust: Theorizing Reza Negarestani's *Cyclonopedia*," in *Oil Culture*, ed. Ross Barrett and Daniel Worden (Minneapolis: University of Minnesota Press, 2014), 373.

52. Robin MacKay, "A Brief History of Geotrauma," in *Leper Creativity*: Cyclonopedia *Symposium*, ed. Ed Keller, Nicola Masciandaro, and Eugene Thacker (Santa Barbara: punctum books, 2012), 29.

53. Timothy Mitchell offers a nuanced account of the complex dynamic between the oil market, as dictated largely by the pressures of Western capitalism, and Jihadi movements in the Middle East—a dynamic that he calls McJihad, signaling Islam's indispensable role in securing petroleum reserves for Western countries. See Mitchell, *Carbon*, 214: "Seen as a process of McJihad, oil-based industrial capitalism no longer appears self-sufficient. Its success depends on other forces, which are both essential to and disjunctive with the process we call capitalist development."

54. See Matthew T. Huber, *Lifeblood: Oil, Freedom, and the Forces of Capital* (Minneapolis: University of Minnesota Press, 2013), 103.

55. See Thomas Pynchon, *Gravity's Rainbow* (New York: Penguin, 2006), 600; and Robert Smithson, "Strata: A Geophotographic Fiction," in *Robert Smithson: The Collected Writings*, ed. Jack Flam (Berkeley: University of California Press, 1996), 75–77.

56. Gilles Deleuze and Félix Guattari, *A Thousand Plateaus: Capitalism and Schizophrenia*, trans. Brian Massumi (Minneapolis: University of Minnesota Press, 2011), 67.

57. Gregory Flaxman, *Gilles Deleuze and the Fabulation of Philosophy* (Minneapolis: University of Minnesota Press, 2012), 89.

58. Karen Tei Yamashita, *Through the Arc of the Rain Forest* (Minneapolis: Coffee House Press, 2017). Page numbers are cited in the text.

59. Parikka, *Geology*, 102.

60. Ursula K. Heise, *Sense of Place and Sense of Planet: The Environmental Imagination of the Global* (Oxford: Oxford University Press, 2008), 102.

61. Andrew Rose, "Insurgency and Distributed Agency in Karen Tei Yamashita's *Through the Arc of the Rain Forest*," *ISLE: Interdisciplinary Studies in Literature and Environment* 26, no. 1 (2019): 133–134, http://doi.org/10.1093/isle/isy076.

62. Stephen Graham, *Vertical: The City from Satellites to Bunkers* (London: Verso, 2016), 283.

63. Jan Zalasiewicz et al., "The Geological Cycle of Plastics and Their Use As a Stratigraphic Indicator," *Anthropocene* 13 (2016): 10, http://doi.org/10.1016/j.ancene.2016.01.002.

64. For more on Yamashita's engagements with plastic, see Jennifer A. Wagner-Lawlor, "Plastic's 'Untiring Solicitation': Geographies of Myth, Corporate Alibis, and the Plaesthetics of the Matacão," in *Life in Plastic: Artistic Responses to Petromodernity*, ed. Caren Irr (Minneapolis: University of Minnesota Press, 2021), 259–280.

65. Heather Swan, "What Counts as Environmental Storytelling: A Conversation with Karen Tei Yamashita," *Edge Effects*, May 21, 2019, https://edgeeffects.net/karen-tei-yamashita/.

66. Min Hyoung Song, "Becoming Planetary," *American Literary History* 23, no. 3 (2011): 557, http://doi.org/10.1093/alh/ajr020.

67. For a perceptive reading of the challenges in comparing oil culture and the Matacão, see Treasa De Loughry, "Petromodernity, Petro-Finance and Plastic in Karen Tei Yamashita's *Through the Arc of the Rain Forest*," *Journal of Postcolonial Writing* 53, no. 3 (2017): 331, http://doi.org/10.1080/17449855.2017.1337685. See also Song, "Becoming," 569–571.

68. Claire Colebrook, "What Is the Anthropo-Political?," in *Twilight of the Anthropocene Idols*, by Tom Cohen, Claire Colebrook, and J. Hillis Miller (London: Open Humanities Press, 2016), 124.

69. Colebrook, *Death*, 35.

70. See also Claire Colebrook, "The Context of Humanism," *New Literary History* 42, no. 4 (2011): 710, http://doi.org/10.1353/nlh.2011.0035: "literary texts are possible because of a more general textuality: bodies and 'life' are textual, not because we only know them through language or textuality, but because all the features of textuality—such as dispersal, nonlinear causality, nonidentity, and an ongoing instability—mark life as such."

71. Colebrook, *Death*, 26.

Chapter 3: Overview Effects

1. Tim O'Brien, *The Nuclear Age* (New York: Penguin, 1996). Page numbers are cited in the text.

2. Don DeLillo, "Human Moments in World War III," in *American Gothic Tales*, ed. Joyce Carol Oates (New York: Plume, 1996). Page numbers cited in the text.

3. See Jessica Hurley, *Infrastructures of Apocalypse: American Literature and the Nuclear Complex* (Minneapolis: University of Minnesota Press, 2020); Joseph Masco, *The Theater of Operations: National Security Affect from the Cold War to the War on*

Terror (Durham: Duke University Press, 2016); Daniel Grausam, *On Endings: American Postmodern Fiction and the Cold War* (Charlottesville: University of Virginia Press, 2011); and Daniel Cordle, *State of Suspense: The Nuclear Age, Postmodernism, and United States Fiction and Prose* (London: Palgrave, 2008).

4. Fredric Jameson, *The Geopolitical Aesthetic: Cinema and Space in the World System.* (Bloomington: Indiana University Press, 1992), 1.

5. Jerry Aline Flieger, "Postmodern Perspective: The Paranoid Eye," *New Literary History* 28, no. 1 (1997): 90, http://doi.org/10.1353/nlh.1997.0008.

6. Fredric Jameson, *Postmodernism, or, the Cultural Logic of Late Capitalism* (Durham: Duke University Press, 1991), 44.

7. Emily Apter, "On Oneworldedness: Or Paranoia as a World System," *American Literary History* 18, no. 2 (2006): 370, http://doi.org/10.1093/alh/ajj022.

8. Thomas Pynchon, *Gravity's Rainbow* (New York: Penguin, 2006). Page numbers are cited in the text.

9. Dipesh Chakrabarty, *The Climate of History in a Planetary Age* (Chicago: University of Chicago Press, 2021), 79.

10. Fred Kaplan, *The Wizards of Armageddon* (Stanford: Stanford University Press, 1991), 286.

11. Rebecca Solnit, *Savage Dreams: A Journey into the Hidden Wars of the American West* (Berkeley: University of California Press, 2014), 96.

12. Ralph Sanders, *Project Plowshare: The Development of the Peaceful Use of Nuclear Explosions* (New York: Public Affairs Press, 1962), 32.

13. Ibid., 35.

14. Joseph Masco, *The Future of Fallout, and Other Episodes in Radioactive World-Making* (Durham: Duke University Press, 2021), 142.

15. See Ally Ireson and Nick Barley, eds., *City Levels* (Basel: Birkhäuser, 2000), 7.

16. For more on Pynchon's contextual relationship to the environmental movement, see Thomas Schaub, "The Environmental Pynchon: *Gravity's Rainbow* and the Ecological Context," *Pynchon Notes*, no. 42–43 (1998): 59–72, http://doi.org/10.16995/pn.140; and Magda Majewska, "Immanence Is Bliss: The Ecological Imagination in Thomas Pynchon's *Gravity's Rainbow*," in *An Eclectic Bestiary: Encounters in a More-Than-Human World*, ed. Birgit Spengler and Babette B. Tischleder (Bielefeld: Verlag, 2019): 225–240.

17. Brian McHale identifies 1973 as the definitive year of high postmodernism, ushering in what he calls its "major phase." See Brian McHale, "Period, Break, Interregnum," in *Postmodern/Postwar—and After: Rethinking American Literature*, ed. Jason Gladstone, Andrew Hoberek, and Daniel Worden (Iowa City: University of Iowa Press, 2016), 62.

18. Stephen Graham, *Vertical: The City from Satellites to Bunkers* (London: Verso, 2016), 57.

19. Masco, *Future*, 140–141.

20. Ibid., 24.

21. Ibid., 147.

22. McKenzie Wark, *Molecular Red: Theory for the Anthropocene* (London: Verso, 2015), 180.

23. Qtd. in Frank White, *The Overview Effect: Space Exploration and Human Evolution* (Boston: Houghton Mifflin Harcourt, 1987), 196.

24. White, *Overview*, 4.

25. Ibid., 3.

26. Donna J. Haraway, "Situated Knowledges: The Science Question in Feminism and the Privilege of Partial Perspective," in *Simians, Cyborgs, and Women: The Reinvention of Nature* (London: Free Association Books, 1991), 188. For a critique of objectivity in the development of scientific instrumentation (specifically, satellites), see Ronald N. Giere, *Scientific Perspectivism* (Chicago: University of Chicago Press, 2010), 41–58.

27. Hurley, *Infrastructures*, 132.

28. Vollmer's question is a close paraphrase of Enrico Fermi's legendary question. See Jim Al-Khalili, "Introduction: Where Is Everybody?," in *Aliens: The World's Leading Scientists on the Search for Extraterrestrial Life*, ed. Jim Al-Khalili (New York: Picador, 2016), 1–2. For more on climate change as one possible answer to the Fermi paradox, see David Wallace-Wells, "The Uninhabitable Earth," *New York Magazine*, July 10, 2017, https://nymag.com/intelligencer/2017/07/climate-change-earth-too-hot-for-humans.html.

29. Qtd. in White, *Overview*, 197.

30. White, *Overview*, 21.

31. Claire Colebrook, *Death of the PostHuman: Essays on Extinction*, vol. 1 (London: Open Humanities Press, 2014), 225.

32. White, *Overview*, 201.

33. U.S. Atomic Energy Commission and U.S. Geological Survey, *Prospecting for Uranium*, rev. ed. (Washington DC: U.S. Government Printing Office, 1957).

34. See Joseph Masco, "The Age of (a) Man," in *Future Remains: A Cabinet of Curiosities for the Anthropocene*, ed. Gregg Mitman, Marco Armiero, and Robert S. Emmett (Chicago: University of Chicago Press, 2018), 47.

35. Ibid., 47.

36. Ibid., 45.

37. Daniel Cordle, "In Dreams, In Imagination: Suspense, Anxiety and the Cold War in Tim O'Brien's *The Nuclear Age*," *Critical Survey* 19, no. 2 (2007): 102, http://doi.org/10.3167/cs.2007.190207.

38. See Cordle, "Dreams," 114–115.

39. Daniel Grausam, "Games People Play: Metafiction, Defense Strategy, and the Cultures of Simulation," *ELH* 78 (2011): 509, http://doi.org/10.1353/elh.2011.0027.

40. Qtd. in Robert Smithson, "A Thing Is a Hole in a Thing It Is Not," in *The Collected Writings*, ed. Jack Flam (Berkeley: University of California Press, 1996), 95.

41. Timothy Morton, *Hyperobjects: Philosophy and Ecology After the End of the World* (Minneapolis: University of Minnesota Press, 2013), 108.

42. Timothy Clark, *The Value of Ecocriticism* (Cambridge: Cambridge University Press, 2019), 84.

43. Hurley, *Infrastructures*, 137.

44. For one such gloss on Fukuyama, see Hurley, *Infrastructures*, 138–139.

45. For definitive postmodernist readings of Pynchon, see Brian McHale, *Postmodernist Fiction* (London: Routledge, 1987), 21–25; and Brian McHale, *Constructing Postmodernism* (London: Routledge, 1992), 61–114. For historical, or historically inflected, readings, see David Cowart, *Thomas Pynchon and the Dark Passages of History* (Athens: University of Georgia Press, 2012), 57–81; Luc Herman and Steven Weisenburger, Gravity's Rainbow, *Domination, and Freedom* (Athens: University of Georgia Press, 2013); and Paul K. Saint-Amour, *Tense Future: Modernism, Total War, Encyclopedic Form* (Oxford: Oxford University Press, 2015), 307–312.

46. Ursula K. Heise, *Chronoschisms: Time, Narrative, and Postmodernism* (Cambridge: Cambridge University Press, 1997), 180.

47. For Norbert Wiener's discussion of cybernetics, see Norbert Wiener, *Cybernetics: or Control and Communication in the Animal and the Machine* (Cambridge, MA: MIT Press, 1948).

48. See Hunter Heyck, *Age of System: Understanding the Development of Modern Social Science* (Baltimore: Johns Hopkins University Press, 2015).

49. Kathryn Hume, "Views from Above, Views from Below: The Perspectival Subtext in *Gravity's Rainbow*," *American Literature* 60, no. 4 (1988): 625, http://doi.org/10.2307/2926661.

50. Steven C. Weisenburger, *A Gravity's Rainbow Companion: Sources and Contexts for Pynchon's Novel*, 2nd ed. (Athens: University of Georgia Press, 2006), 20.

51. See Andreas Malm and the Zetkin Collective, *White Skin, Black Fuel: On the Danger of Fossil Fascism* (London: Verso, 2021), 430.

52. See John Johnston, *Information Multiplicity: American Fiction in the Age of Media Saturation* (Baltimore: Johns Hopkins University Press, 1998), 62.

53. Friedrich Kittler, "Media and Drugs in Pynchon's Second World War," trans. Michael Wutz and Geoffrey Winthrop-Young, in *Reading Matters: Narratives in the New Media Ecology*, ed. Joseph Tabbi and Michael Wutz (Ithaca: Cornell University Press, 1997), 162.

54. See Thomas P. Hughes, *Human-Built World: How to Think About Technology and Culture* (Chicago: University of Chicago Press, 2004), 79–83.

55. See Weisenburger, *Companion*, 37.

56. See Cecil Rhodes, *The Last Will and Testament of Cecil John Rhodes*, ed. W. T. Stead (London: "Review of Reviews" Office, 1902), 190.

Chapter 4: Fossil Labor

1. For more on Pynchon's Herero, including a structural treatment of their role in the text, see Paul A. Bové, "History and Fiction: The Narrative Voices of Pynchon's *Gravity's Rainbow*," *Modern Fiction Studies*, 50, no. 3 (2004): 662–664, http://doi.org/10.1353/mfs.2004.0057.

2. Ralph Ellison, *Invisible Man* (New York: Vintage, 1995), 7.

3. Kate Marshall, *Corridor: Media Architectures in American Fiction* (Minneapolis: University of Minnesota Press, 2013), 80.

4. Chester Himes, *Plan B* (Jackson: University of Mississippi Press, 1993), 185.

5. Ibid., 186–187.

6. Joanna Freer has written on the influence of the Black Panthers for Pynchon's novel, specifically the concept of "revolutionary suicide," which manifests in the Zone Hereros but was also a tenet of the Black Panther Party. See Joanna Freer, "Thomas Pynchon and the Black Panther Party: Revolutionary Suicide in *Gravity's Rainbow*," *Journal of American Studies* 47, no. 1 (2013): 171–188, http://doi.org/10.1017/S0021875812000758.

7. Nigel Clark, "Politics of Strata," *Theory, Culture & Society* 34, no. 2–3 (2016): 214, http://doi.org/10.1177/0263276416667538.

8. See Nicholas Mirzoeff, "It's Not the Anthropocene, It's the White Supremacy Scene; or, The Geological Color Line," in *After Extinction*, ed. Richard Grusin (Minneapolis: University of Minnesota Press, 2018), 123–149; Elizabeth A. Povinelli, *Geontologies: A Requiem to Late Liberalism* (Durham: Duke University Press, 2016), 57–91; and Kathryn Yusoff, *A Billion Black Anthropocenes or None* (Minneapolis: University of Minnesota Press, 2018).

9. Achille Mbembe, *Necropolitics* (Durham: Duke University Press, 2019), 78–87.

10. Karl Marx, *Capital*, vol. 1: *A Critical Analysis of Capitalist Production*, ed. Frederick Engels (New York: International Publishers, 1967), 224.

11. Martín Arboleda, *Planetary Mine: Territories of Extraction Under Late Capitalism* (London: Verso, 2020), 78.

12. Yusoff, *Billion*, 9.

13. For more on the historical development from chattel slavery to the modern prison and other managerial institutions centered on racial discrimination, see Dan Berger and Toussaint Losier, *Rethinking the American Prison Movement* (London: Routledge, 2017), 15–43.

14. Ibid., 33.

15. Kathryn Yusoff, "Geologic Realism: On the Beach of Geologic Time," *Social Text* 37, no. 1 (2019): 11, https://doi.org/10.1215/01642472-7286240.

16. For an account of Fanon's work as ecologically oriented, see Romy Opperman, "A Permanent Struggle Against an Omnipresent Death: Revisiting Environmental Racism with Frantz Fanon," *Critical Philosophy of Race* 7, no. 1 (2019): 57–80, http://doi.org/10.5325/critphilrace.7.1.0057. In addition to works of Mirzoeff, Povinelli, and Yusoff (see note 8 in this chapter), see Katherine McKittrick, *Demonic Grounds: Black Women and the Cartographies of Struggle* (Minneapolis: University of Minnesota Press, 2006); and Monique Allewaert, *Ariel's Ecology: Plantations, Personhood, and Colonialism in the American Tropic* (Minneapolis: University of Minnesota Press, 2013).

17. Frantz Fanon, *The Wretched of the Earth*, trans. Constance Farrington (New York: Grove Press, 1963), 238.

18. Gavin Arnall, *Subterranean Fanon: An Underground Theory of Radical Change* (New York: Columbia University Press, 2020), 16.

19. Kathryn Yusoff, "The Inhumanities," *Annals of the American Association of Geographers* 111, no. 3 (2021): 665, http://doi.org/10.1080/24694452.2020.1814688.

20. Fred Moten, "Blackness and Nothingness (Mysticism in the Flesh)," *South Atlantic Quarterly* 112, no. 4 (2013): 742, http://doi.org/10.1215/00382876-2345261.

21. Colson Whitehead, *The Nickel Boys* (New York: Anchor, 2019), 77.

22. See Cara New Daggett, *The Birth of Energy: Fossil Fuels, Thermodynamics, and the Politics of Work*. Durham: Duke University Press, 2019, 135.

23. The imagination of colonial spaces as empty is well-documented and has been discussed by scholars. See Rebecca Solnit, *Savage Dreams: A Journey into the Hidden Wars of the American West* (Berkeley: University of California Press, 2014), 153–154; Rob Nixon, *Slow Violence and the Environmentalism of the Poor* (Cambridge, MA: Harvard University Press, 2011), 152–153; and Joseph Masco, *The Future of Fallout, and Other Episodes in Radioactive World-Making* (Durham: Duke University Press, 2021), 83–112.

24. For a notable exception to the paucity of ecocritical readings, see Shouhei Tanaka, "Fossil Fuel Fiction and the Geologies of Race," *PMLA* 137, no. 1 (2022): 36–51, https://doi.org/10.1632/S0030812921000717. For treatments of history and literary tradition in Whitehead's fiction, see Jeffrey Allen Tucker, "'Verticality Is Such a Risky Enterprise': The Literary and Paraliterary Antecedents of Colson Whitehead's *The Intuitionist*," *Novel: A Forum on Fiction* 43, no. 1 (2010): 148–156, http://doi.org/10.1215/00295132-2009-075; Madhu Dubey, "Museumizing Slavery: Living History in Colson Whitehead's *The Underground Railroad*," *American Literary History* 32, no. 1 (2019): 111–139, http://doi.org/10.1093/alh/ajz056; and Alexander Manshel, "Colson Whitehead's History of the United States," *MELUS* 45, no. 4 (2020): 22–45, http://doi.org/10.1093/melus/mlaa051.

25. Michael Bérubé, "Race and Modernity in Colson Whitehead's *The Intuitionist*," in *The Holodeck in the Garden: Science and Technology in Contemporary American Fiction*, ed. Peter Freese and Charles B. Harris (Funks Grove: Dalkey Archive Press, 2004), 163.

26. Rebecca Evans, "Geomemory and Genre Friction: Infrastructural Violence and Plantation Afterlives in Contemporary African American Novels," *American Literature* 93, no. 3 (2021): 454, http://doi.org/10.1215/00029831-9361265. See also Kirsten Dillender, "Land and Pessimistic Futures in Contemporary African American Speculative Fiction," *Extrapolation* 60, no. 1–2 (2020): 131–150, http://doi.org/10.3828/extr.2020.9; Henry Ivry, "'Improbable Metaphor': Jesmyn Ward's Asymmetrical Anthropocene," *European Review* 29, no. 3 (2021): 383–396, http://doi.org/10.1017/S1062798720000708; and Sara Stephens Loomis, "The Sound of All Water: Petro-Culture and Black Modernity in Jesmyn Ward's *Sing, Unburied, Sing*," *Contemporary Literature* 62, no. 2 (2021): 177–206, http://doi.org/10.3368/cl.62.2.177.

27. See Heather Houser, *Ecosickness in Contemporary U.S. Fiction: Environment*

and Affect (New York: Columbia University Press, 2014), 1–30; and Priscilla Wald, *Contagious: Cultures, Carriers, and the Outbreak Narrative* (Durham: Duke University Press, 2008), 11–20.

28. Ian Baucom, *History 4° Celsius: Search for a Method in the Age of the Anthropocene* (Durham: Duke University Press, 2020), 23.

29. Colson Whitehead, *The Underground Railroad* (New York: Doubleday, 2016), 12. Page numbers are cited in the text.

30. Dubey, "Museumizing," 111.

31. Tanaka, "Fossil Fuel," 48.

32. Timothy Mitchell, *Carbon Democracy: Political Power in the Age of Oil* (London: Verso, 2013), 4.

33. For more on slave gardens as sites of agency, see Judith A. Carney and Richard Nicholas Rosomoff, *In the Shadow of Slavery: Africa's Botanical Legacy in the Atlantic World* (Berkeley: University of California Press, 2011), 125.

34. Anna Kornbluh, "We Have Never Been Critical: Toward the Novel as Critique," *Novel* 50, no. 3 (2017): 406. http://doi.org/10.1215/00295132-4195016.

35. Hari Kunzru, *White Tears* (New York: Knopf, 2017). Page numbers are cited in the text.

36. Ellison, *Invisible*, 443.

37. For more on good use gardening, see Janae Davis, Alex A. Moulton, Levi Van Sant, and Brian Williams, "Anthropocene, Capitalocene, . . . Plantationocene? A Manifesto for Ecological Justice in an Age of Global Crises," *Geography Compass* 13, no. 5 (2019): 8, http://doi.org/10.1111/gec3.12438.

38. Jesmyn Ward, *Sing, Unburied, Sing* (New York: Scribner, 2017). Page numbers are cited in the text.

39. Katherine McKittrick, "Plantation Futures," *Small Axe* 17, no. 3 (2013): 2–3. http://doi.org/10.1215/07990537-2378892.

40. Loomis, "Sound," 180.

41. See Ryan C. Edwards, "Convicts and Conservation: Inmate Labor, Fires and Forestry in Southernmost Argentina," *Journal of Historical Geography* 56 (2017): 1–13. https://doi.org/10.1016/j.jhg.2017.01.005; and Clarence Jefferson Hall, *A Prison in the Woods: Environment and Incarceration in New York's North Country* (Amherst: University of Massachusetts Press, 2020).

42. For an alternative take on the importance of trees in *Sing, Unburied, Sing*, see Loomis, "Sound," 200.

43. Left out of this discussion are the history of vinyl's relationship to the fossil fuel industry and its perceptual effects on the human experience of time. For a succinct and insightful overview of these dynamics, see Loren Glass, "The Album Era," in *Life in Plastic: Artistic Responses to Petromodernity*, ed. Caren Irr (Minneapolis: University of Minnesota Press, 2021): 59–76.

44. For more on environmental controversies in Hunts Point and other at-risk communities, see Don Ryan and Ralph Scott, "Viewpoint: The Promise of Environ-

mental Sampling and Right-to-Know Laws for At-Risk Communities," *Public Health Reports (1947-)* 115, no. 6 (2000): 511–520.

45. Qtd. in Keiko Morris, "Affordable Housing Coming to Jail Site in the Bronx's Hunts Point," *Dow Jones Institutional News*, October 26, 2016, n.p., ProQuest.

46. Qtd. in Matthew Haag, "A Floating Jail Was Supposed to Be Temporary. That Was 27 Years Ago," *The New York Times*, October 10, 2019, https://www.nytimes.com/2019/10/10/nyregion/a-floating-jail-was-supposed-to-be-temporary-that-was-27-years-ago.html.

47. Jackie Wang, *Carceral Capitalism* (Los Angeles: Semiotext(e), 2018), 114.

48. Yusoff, *Billion*, 88.

49. For more on vertical modernity, see Nigel Clark and Bronislaw Szerszynski, *Planetary Social Thought: The Anthropocene Challenge to the Social Sciences* (Cambridge, UK: Polity, 2021), 103–106.

50. Colson Whitehead, *The Intuitionist: A Novel* (New York: Anchor, 2000). Page numbers are cited in the text.

51. Madhu Dubey, *Signs and Cities: Black Literary Postmodernism* (Chicago: University of Chicago Press, 2003), 238.

52. Manshel, "Colson," 26.

53. Frank White, *The Overview Effect: Space Exploration and Human Evolution* (Boston: Houghton Mifflin Harcourt, 1987), 92.

54. Stephen Graham, *Vertical: The City from Satellites to Bunkers* (London: Verso, 2016), 136.

55. Heyck, *Age*, 51–80.

56. Arboleda is here invoking Gray Brechin's use of the phrase "inverted mines." See Arboleda, *Planetary*, 61.

57. Graham, *Vertical*, 370–371. For more on the ways that late capitalist extraction constitutes a new form of transnational planetarity, see Arboleda, *Planetary*, 1–34.

58. Graham, *Vertical*, 136.

59. Tucker, " 'Verticality," 152.

60. Bruno Latour, *Science in Action: How to Follow Scientists and Engineers Through Society* (Cambridge: Harvard University Press, 1997), 131.

Underview: Writing Our Resilience

1. Octavia E. Butler, *Parable of the Sower* (New York: Grand Central, 2019), 222.

2. Ibid., 20.

3. Shelley Streeby, *Imagining the Future of Climate Change: World-Making Through Science Fiction and Activism* (Oakland: University of California Press, 2018), 81.

4. Butler, *Parable*, 21.

5. Qtd. in Nick Estes, *Our History Is the Future: Standing Rock Versus the Dakota Access Pipeline, and the Long Tradition of Indigenous Resistance* (London: Verso, 2019), 13.

6. Anna Lowenhaupt Tsing, *The Mushroom at the End of the World: On the Possibility of Life in Capitalist Ruins* (Princeton: Princeton University Press, 2015), 29.

References

Agar, Jon. *Science in the Twentieth Century and Beyond.* Cambridge, UK: Polity, 2012.

Al-Khalili, Jim. "Introduction: Where Is Everybody?" In *Aliens: The World's Leading Scientists on the Search for Extraterrestrial Life,* edited by Jim Al-Khalili, 1–10. New York: Picador, 2016.

Allewart, Monique. *Ariel's Ecology: Plantations, Personhood, and Colonialism in the American Tropic.* Minneapolis: University of Minnesota Press, 2013.

Alworth, David J. *Site Reading: Art, Fiction, Social Form.* Princeton: Princeton University Press, 2015.

Anker, Elizabeth S., and Rita Felski, eds. *Critique and Postcritique.* Durham: Duke University Press, 2017.

Apter, Emily. "On Oneworldedness: Or Paranoia as a World System." *American Literary History* 18, no. 2 (2006): 365–389. http://doi.org/10.1093/alh/ajj022.

Arboleda, Martín. *Planetary Mine: Territories of Extraction under Late Capitalism.* London: Verso, 2020.

Arendt, Hannah. *The Human Condition.* Chicago: University of Chicago Press, 1998.

Arnall, Gavin. *Subterranean Fanon: An Underground Theory of Radical Change.* New York: Columbia University Press, 2020.

Barad, Karen. *Meeting the Universe Halfway: Quantum Physics and the Entanglement of Matter and Meaning.* Durham: Duke University Press, 2007.

Bascom, Willard. "Letters." *Science* 143 (March 1964): 1275–1276.

———. "The Mohole." *Scientific American* 200, no. 4 (1959): 41–49. https://www.jstor.org/stable/10.2307/26172027.

Baucom, Ian. *History 4° Celsius: Search for a Method in the Age of the Anthropocene.* Durham: Duke University Press, 2020.

Benjamin, Walter. "Theses on the Philosophy of History." In *Illuminations: Essays and Reflections,* translated by Harry Zohn, edited by Hannah Arendt, 253–264. New York: Schocken Books, 2007.

Berger, Dan, and Toussaint Losier. *Rethinking the American Prison Movement*. London: Routledge, 2017.

Bérubé, Michael. "Race and Modernity in Colson Whitehead's *The Intuitionist*." In *The Holodeck in the Garden: Science and Technology in Contemporary American Fiction*, edited by Peter Freese and Charles B. Harris, 163–178. Funks Grove: Dalkey Archive Press, 2004.

Bjornerud, Marcia. *Timefulness: How Thinking Like a Geologist Can Help Save the World*. Princeton: Princeton University Press, 2018.

Bou, Stéphane, and Jean-Baptiste Thoret. "A Conversation with Don DeLillo: Has Terrorism Become the World's Main Plot?" *Panic* 1 (2005). http://perival.com/delillo/interview_panic_2005.html.

Bould, Mark. *The Anthropocene Unconscious: Climate Catastrophe Culture*. London: Verso, 2021.

Bové, Paul A. "History and Fiction: The Narrative Voices of Pynchon's *Gravity's Rainbow*." *Modern Fiction Studies* 50, no. 3 (2004): 657–680. http://doi.org/10.1353/mfs.2004.0057.

Brand, Stewart. *Whole Earth Catalog: Access to Tools*. Fall 2018. https://archive.org/details/1stWEC-complete/mode/2up.

Brassier, Ray. *Nihil Unbound: Enlightenment and Extinction*. London: Palgrave, 2010.

Büscher, Bram, and Robert Fletcher. *The Conservation Revolution: Radical Ideas for Saving Nature Beyond the Anthropocene*. London: Verso, 2020.

Butler, Octavia E. *Parable of the Sower*. New York: Grand Central, 2019.

Canavan, Gerry. "Science Fiction and Utopia in the Anthropocene." *American Literature* 93, no. 2 (2021): 255–282. https://doi.org/10.1215/00029831-9003582.

Carney, Judith A., and Richard Nicholas Rosomoff. *In the Shadow of Slavery: Africa's Botanical Legacy in the Atlantic World*. Berkeley: University of California Press, 2011.

Carson, Rachel. "Of Man and the Stream of Time." In *Silent Spring and Other Writings on the Environment*, edited by Sandra Steingraber, 421–427. New York: Library of America, 2018.

Carter, Dale. *The Final Frontier: The Rise and Fall of the American Rocket State*. London: Verso, 1988.

Chakrabarty, Dipesh. *The Climate of History in a Planetary Age*. Chicago: University of Chicago Press, 2021.

"Chasing the Moon Transcript: Part Two." *American Experience*, WGBH Educational Foundation, July 10, 2019. https://www.pbs.org/wgbh/americanexperience/films/chasing-moon/#transcript.

Chow, Rey. *The Age of the World Target: Self-Referentiality in War, Theory, and Comparative Work*. Durham: Duke University Press, 2006.

Clark, Nigel. "Politics of Strata." *Theory, Culture & Society* 34, no. 2–3 (2016): 211–231. http://doi.org/10.1177/0263276416667538.

Clark, Nigel, and Bronislaw Szerszynski. *Planetary Social Thought: The Anthropocene Challenge to the Social Sciences*. Cambridge, UK: Polity, 2021.

Clark, Timothy. *The Value of Ecocriticism*. Cambridge: Cambridge University Press, 2019.

Clarke, Bruce. *Gaian Systems: Lynn Margulis, Neocybernetics, and the End of the Anthropocene*. Minneapolis: University of Minnesota Press, 2020.

———. *Posthuman Metamorphosis: Narrative and Systems*. New York: Fordham University Press, 2008.

Colebrook, Claire. "The Context of Humanism." *New Literary History* 42, no. 4 (2011): 701- 718. http://doi.org/10.1353/nlh.2011.0035.

———. *Death of the PostHuman: Essays on Extinction*, Vol. 1. London: Open Humanities Press, 2014.

———. "Extinguishing Ability: How We Became Postextinction Persons." In *Eco-Deconstruction: Derrida and Environmental Philosophy*, edited by Matthias Fritsch, Philippe Lynes, and David Wood, 261–275. Cambridge: Cambridge University Press, 2018.

———. "We Have Always Been Post-Anthropocene: The Anthropocene Counterfactual." In *Anthropocene Feminism*, edited by Richard Grusin, 1–20. Minneapolis: University of Minnesota Press, 2017.

———. "What Is the Anthropo-Political?" In *Twilight of the Anthropocene Idols*, by Tom Cohen, Claire Colebrook, and J. Hillis Miller, 81–125. London: Open Humanities Press, 2016.

Cordle, Daniel. "In Dreams, In Imagination: Suspense, Anxiety and the Cold War in Tim O'Brien's *The Nuclear Age*." *Critical Survey* 19, no. 2 (2007): 101–120. http://doi.org/10.3167/cs.2007.190207.

———. *State of Suspense: The Nuclear Age, Postmodernism, and United States Fiction and Prose*. London: Palgrave, 2008.

Cowart, David. *Don DeLillo: The Physics of Language*. Athens: University of Georgia Press, 2003.

———. *Thomas Pynchon and the Dark Passages of History*. Athens: University of Georgia Press, 2012.

Crutzen, Paul J. "Geology of Mankind." *Nature* 415 (January 2002): 23. http://doi.org/10.1038/415023a.

Crutzen, Paul J., and Eugene Stoermer. "The 'Anthropocene.'" *IGPB Newsletter* 41 (2000): 17-18.

Daggett, Cara New. *The Birth of Energy: Fossil Fuels, Thermodynamics, and the Politics of Work*. Durham: Duke University Press, 2019.

Dango, Michael. *Crisis Style: The Aesthetics of Repair*. Stanford: Stanford University Press, 2021.

Davis, Janae, Alex A. Moulton, Levi Van Sant, and Brian Williams. "Anthropocene, Capitalocene . . . Plantationocene? A Manifesto for Ecological Justice in an Age of Global Crises." *Geography Compass* 13, no. 5 (2019): e12438-n/a. http://doi.org/10.1111/gec3.12438.

Dawson, Ashley. *Extinction: A Radical History*. New York: OR Books, 2016.

De Loughry, Treasa. "Petromodernity, Petro-Finance and Plastic in Karen Tei Ya-mashita's *Through the Arc of the Rain Forest.*" *Journal of Postcolonial Writing* 53, no. 3 (2017): 329–341. http://doi.org/10.1080/17449855.2017.1337685.

"*Deepwater Horizon* Drills World's Deepest O&G Well." *Rigzone.* September 2, 2009. https://www.rigzone.com/news/oil_gas/a/79954/transoceans_deepwater_horizon _drills_worlds_deepest_og_well/.

Deleuze, Gilles, and Félix Guattari. *A Thousand Plateaus: Capitalism and Schizophrenia.* Translated by Brian Massumi. Minneapolis: University of Minnesota Press, 2011.

DeLillo, Don. *Great Jones Street.* New York: Penguin, 1994.

———. "Human Moments in World War III." In *American Gothic Tales,* edited by Joyce Carol Oates, 325–338. New York: Plume, 1996.

———. *The Names.* New York: Vintage, 1989.

———. *Ratner's Star.* New York: Vintage, 1989.

———. *Underworld.* New York: Scribner, 1998.

Derrida, Jacques. "No Apocalypse, Not Now (Full Speed Ahead, Seven Missiles, Seven Missives)." Translated by Catherine Porter and Philip Lewis. *Diacritics* 14, no. 2 (1984): 20–31. http://doi.org/10.2307/464756.

DiCaglio, Joshua. *Scale Theory: A Nondisciplinary Inquiry.* Minneapolis: University of Minnesota Press, 2021.

Dillender, Kirsten. "Land and Pessimistic Futures in Contemporary African American Speculative Fiction." *Extrapolation* 60, no. 1–2 (2020): 131–150. http://doi.org/ 10.3828/extr.2020.9.

Dini, Rachele. "'What We Excrete Comes Back to Consume Us': Waste and Reclamation in Don DeLillo's *Underworld.*" *ISLE: Interdisciplinary Studies in Literature and the Environment* 26, no. 1 (2019): 165–188. https://doi.org/10.1093/isle/isz004.

Dmochowski, Jane E., and David A. D. Evans. "Earth's Changing Climate: A Deep-Time Geoscience Perspective." In *Time Scales: Thinking Across Ecological Temporalities,* edited by Bethany Wiggin, Carolyn Fornoff, and Patricia Eunji Kim, 27–37. Minneapolis: University of Minnesota Press, 2020.

Doherty, Melanie. "Oil and Dust: Theorizing Reza Negarestani's *Cyclonopedia.*" In *Oil Culture,* edited by Ross Barrett and Daniel Worden, 366–383. Minneapolis: University of Minnesota Press, 2014.

Dubey, Madhu. "Museumizing Slavery: Living History in Colson Whitehead's *The Underground Railroad,*" *American Literary History* 32, no. 1 (2019): 111–139. http:// doi.org/10.1093/alh/ajz056.

———. *Signs and Cities: Black Literary Postmodernism.* Chicago: University of Chicago Press, 2003.

Duvall, John N. "Baseball as Aesthetic Ideology: Cold War History, Race, and DeLillo's 'Pafko at the Wall.'" *Modern Fiction Studies* 41, no. 2 (1995): 285–313. http://doi .org/10.1353/mfs.1995.0091.

Edwards, Paul. *A Vast Machine: Computer Models, Climate Data, and the Politics of Global Warming.* Cambridge, MA: MIT Press, 2010.

Edwards, Ryan C. "Convicts and Conservation: Inmate Labor, Fires and Forestry in Southernmost Argentina." *Journal of Historical Geography* 56 (2017): 1–13. https://doi.org/10.1016/j.jhg.2017.01.005.

Ellison, Ralph. *Invisible Man*. New York: Vintage, 1995.

Estes, Nick. *Our History Is the Future: Standing Rock Versus the Dakota Access Pipeline, and the Long Tradition of Indigenous Resistance*. London: Verso, 2019.

Evans, Rebecca. "Geomemory and Genre Friction: Infrastructural Violence and Plantation Afterlives in Contemporary African American Novels." *American Literature* 93, no. 3 (2021): 445–472. http://doi.org/10.1215/00029831-9361265.

———. "Nomenclature, Narrative, and Novum: 'The Anthropocene' and/as Science Fiction." *Science Fiction Studies* 45, no. 3 (2018): 484–499. http://doi.org/10.5621/sciefictstud.45.3.0484.

Fanon, Frantz. *The Wretched of the Earth*. Translated by Constance Farrington. New York: Grove Press, 1963.

Flaxman, Gregory. *Gilles Deleuze and the Fabulation of Philosophy*. Minneapolis: University of Minnesota Press, 2012.

Flieger, Jerry Aline. "Postmodern Perspective: The Paranoid Eye." *New Literary History* 28, no. 1 (1997): 87–109. http://doi.org/10.1353/nlh.1997.0008.

Frank, Adam. "Earth Will Survive. We May Not." *The New York Times*, June 12, 2018. https://www.nytimes.com/2018/06/12/opinion/earth-will-survive-we-may-not.html.

Frankel, Henry. "Plate Tectonics." In *The Cambridge History of Science*, Vol. 6, edited by Peter J. Bowler and John V. Pickstone, 385–394. Cambridge: Cambridge University Press, 2009.

Freer, Joanna. "Thomas Pynchon and the Black Panther Party: Revolutionary Suicide in *Gravity's Rainbow*." *Journal of American Studies* 47, no. 1 (2013): 171–188. http://doi.org/10.1017/S0021875812000758.

Freud, Sigmund. *Beyond the Pleasure Principle*. Translated by James Strachey. New York: W. W. Norton, 1989.

Fried, Michael. "Art and Objecthood." In *Art and Objecthood: Essays and Reviews*, 148–172. Chicago: University of Chicago Press, 1998.

Ganguly, Debjani. "Catastrophic Form and Planetary Realism." *New Literary History* 51, no. 2 (2020): 419–453. https://doi.org/10.1353/nlh.2020.0025.

Ghosh, Amitav. *The Great Derangement: Climate Change and the Unthinkable*. Chicago: University of Chicago Press, 2016.

———. "Petrofiction: The Oil Encounter and the Novel." In *Energy Humanities: An Anthology*, edited by Imre Szeman and Dominic Boyer, 431–440. Baltimore: Johns Hopkins University Press, 2017.

Giere, Ronald N. *Scientific Perspectivism*. Chicago: University of Chicago Press, 2010.

Glass, Loren. "The Album Era." In *Life in Plastic: Artistic Responses to Petromodernity*, edited by Caren Irr, 59–76. Minneapolis: University of Minnesota Press, 2021.

Goossen, Benjamin W. "A Benchmark for the Environment: Big Science and 'Artificial' Geophysics in the Global 1950s." *Journal of Global History* 15, no. 1 (2020): 149–168. http://doi.org/10.1017/S1740022819000378.

Gould, Stephen Jay. *Time's Arrow, Time's Cycle: Myth and Metaphor in the Discovery of Geological Time*. Cambridge, MA: Harvard University Press, 1987.

Graham, Stephen. *Vertical: The City from Satellites to Bunkers*. London: Verso, 2016.

Grausam, Daniel. "Games People Play: Metafiction, Defense Strategy, and the Cultures of Simulation." *ELH* 78 (2011): 507–532. http://doi.org/10.1353/elh.2011.0027.

———. *On Endings: American Postmodern Fiction and the Cold War*. Charlottesville: University of Virginia Press, 2011.

Greenberg, Daniel S. "Mohole: The Project That Went Awry (II)." *Science* 143, no. 3603 (1964): 223–227. https://www.jstor.org/stable/1712431.

Greene, John. "Humanity's Temporal Range." In *The Anthropocene Reviewed*, 13–21. New York: Dutton, 2021.

Griffiths, Devin. "The Ecology of Form." *Critical Inquiry* 48, no. 1 (2021): 68–93. https://doi.org/10.1086/715980.

Haag, Matthew. "A Floating Jail Was Supposed to Be Temporary. That Was 27 Years Ago." *The New York Times*, October 10, 2019. https://www.nytimes.com/2019/10/10/nyregion/a-floating-jail-was-supposed-to-be-temporary-that-was-27-years-ago.html.

Hall, Clarence Jefferson. *A Prison in the Woods: Environment and Incarceration in New York's North Country*. Amherst: University of Massachusetts Press, 2020.

Haraway, Donna J. "Situated Knowledges: The Science Question in Feminism and the Privilege of Partial Perspective." In *Simians, Cyborgs, and Women: The Reinvention of Nature*, 183–202. London: Free Association Books, 1991.

———. *Staying with the Trouble: Making Kin in the Chthulucene*. Durham: Duke University Press, 2016.

Hasselmann, Klaus. "Mohole 1957–1964." In *Seventy Years of Exploration in Oceanography: A Prolonged Weekend Discussion with Walter Munk*, edited by Hans von Storch and Klaus Hasselmann, 67–70. Berlin: Springer, 2010.

Hayles, N. Katherine. *How We Became Posthuman: Virtual Bodies in Cybernetics, Literature, and Informatics*. Chicago: University of Chicago Press, 1999.

Hedberg, Hollis D. "Letters." *Science*, 143 (March 1964): 1274–1275.

———. "Petroleum and Progress in Geology." *Journal of the Geological Society* 127 (1971): 3–16. https://doi.org/10.1144/gsjgs.127.1.0003.

———. "The Stratigraphic Panorama." In *Study of the Earth: Readings in Geological Science*, edited by J. F. White, 171–201. Englewood Cliffs: Prentice-Hall, 1962.

Heidegger, Martin. "'Only a God Can Save Us': *Der Spiegel*'s Interview with Martin Heidegger." In *The Heidegger Controversy: A Critical Reader*, edited by Richard Wolin, 91–116. Cambridge, MA: MIT Press, 1992.

Heise, Ursula K. *Chronoschisms: Time, Narrative, and Postmodernism*. Cambridge: Cambridge University Press, 1997.

———. *Imagining Extinction: The Cultural Meanings of Endangered Species*. Chicago: University of Chicago Press, 2016.

————. "Martian Ecologies and the Future of Nature." *Twentieth-Century Literature* 57, no. 3–4 (2011): 447–471. http://doi.org/10.1215/0041462X-2011-4003.

————. "Realism, Modernism, and the Future: An Interview with Kim Stanley Robinson." *ASAP/Journal* 1, no. 1 (2016): 17–33. http://doi.org/10.1353/asa.2016.0001.

————. *Sense of Place and Sense of Planet: The Environmental Imagination of the Global*. Oxford: Oxford University Press, 2008.

Hensley, Nathan K., and Philip Steer, eds. *Ecological Form: System and Aesthetics in the Age of Empire*. New York: Fordham University Press, 2019.

Herman, Luc, and Steven Weisenburger. Gravity's Rainbow, *Domination, and Freedom*. Athens: University of Georgia Press, 2013.

Hess, H. H. "The AMSOC Hole to the Earth's Mantle." In *Study of the Earth: Readings in Geological Science*, edited by J. F. White, 79–88. Englewood Cliffs: Prentice-Hall, 1962.

Heyck, Hunter. *Age of System: Understanding the Development of Modern Social Science*. Baltimore: Johns Hopkins University Press, 2015.

Himes, Chester. *Plan B*. Jackson: University of Mississippi Press, 1993.

Houser, Heather. *Ecosickness in Contemporary U.S. Fiction: Environment and Affect*. New York: Columbia University Press, 2014.

————. *Infowhelm: Environmental Art and Literature in an Age of Data*. New York: Columbia University Press, 2020.

Hsü, Kenneth Jinghwa. *Challenger at Sea: A Ship That Revolutionized Earth Science*. Princeton: Princeton University Press, 2014.

Huber, Matthew T. *Lifeblood: Oil, Freedom, and the Forces of Capital*. Minneapolis: University of Minnesota Press, 2013.

Hughes, Thomas P. *Human-Built World: How to Think About Technology and Culture*. Chicago: University of Chicago Press, 2004.

Hume, Kathryn. "Views from Above, Views from Below: The Perspectival Subtext in *Gravity's Rainbow*." *American Literature* 60, no. 4 (1988): 625–642. http://doi.org/10.2307/2926661.

Hurley, Jessica. *Infrastructures of Apocalypse: American Literature and the Nuclear Complex*. Minneapolis: University of Minnesota Press, 2020.

Ireson, Ally, and Nick Barley, eds. *City Levels*. Basel: Birkhäuser, 2000.

Ivry, Henry. "'Improbable Metaphor': Jesmyn Ward's Asymmetrical Anthropocene." *European Review* 29, no. 3 (2021): 383–396. http://doi.org/10.1017/S1062798720000708.

Jameson, Fredric. *The Geopolitical Aesthetic: Cinema and Space in the World System*. Bloomington: Indiana University Press, 1995.

————. "'If I Can Find One Good City I Will Spare the Man': Realism and Utopia in Kim Stanley Robinson's *Mars* Trilogy." In *Archaeologies of the Future: The Desire Called Utopia and Other Science Fictions*, 393–416. London: Verso, 2007.

————. *Postmodernism, or, the Cultural Logic of Late Capitalism*. Durham: Duke University Press, 1991.

Johnston, John. *Information Multiplicity: American Fiction in the Age of Media Saturation*. Baltimore: Johns Hopkins University Press, 1998.

Kaplan, Fred. *The Wizards of Armageddon*. Stanford: Stanford University Press, 1991.

Kennedy, Eugene. "Earthrise: The Dawning of a New Spiritual Awareness." *New York Times*, April 15, 1979. https://www.nytimes.com/1979/04/15/archives/earthrise-the -dawning-of-a-new-spiritual-awareness.html.

Kittler, Friedrich. "Media and Drugs in Pynchon's Second World War," translated by Michael Wutz and Geoffrey Winthrop-Young. In *Reading Matters: Narratives in the New Media Ecology*, edited by Joseph Tabbi and Michael Wutz, 157–172. Ithaca: Cornell University Press, 1997.

Klinke, Ian. "On the History of a Subterranean Geopolitics." *Geoforum* 127 (2021): 356–363. http://doi.org/10.1016/j.geoforum.2019.10.010.

Knight, Les U. "The Voluntary Human Extinction Movement." VHEMT. http://vhemt .org/.

Knight, Peter. "Everything Is Connected: *Underworld*'s Secret History of Paranoia." *Modern Fiction Studies* 45, no. 3 (1999): 811–836. http://doi.org/10.1353/mfs.1999 .0052.

"Kola Superdeep Borehole." *Atlas Obscura*, February 21, 2018. https://www.atlasobscura .com/places/kola-superdeep-borehole.

Kolbert, Elizabeth. *The Sixth Extinction: An Unnatural History*. New York: Henry Holt, 2014.

Konstantinou, Lee. "Neorealist Fiction." In *American Literature in Transition, 2000–2010*, edited by Rachel Greenwald Smith, 109–124. Cambridge: Cambridge University Press, 2018.

Kornbluh, Anna. "Extinct Critique." *South Atlantic Quarterly* 119, no. 4 (2020): 767–777. https://doi.org/10.1215/00382876-8663675.

———. *The Order of Forms: Realism, Formalism, and Social Science*. Chicago: University of Chicago Press, 2019.s

———. "We Have Never Been Critical: Toward the Novel as Critique." *Novel* 50, no. 3 (2017): 397–408. http://doi.org/10.1215/00295132-4195016.

Kunzru, Hari. *White Tears*. New York: Knopf, 2017.

Latour, Bruno. *Science in Action: How to Follow Scientists and Engineers Through Society*. Cambridge, MA: Harvard University Press, 1997.

Lazier, Benjamin. "Earthrise; or, the Globalization of the World Picture." *American Historical Review* 116, no. 3 (2011): 602–630. http://doi.org/10.1086/ahr.116.3.602.

Leane, Elizabeth. "Chromodynamics: Science and Colonialism in Kim Stanley Robinson's Mars Trilogy." *Ariel* 33, no. 1 (2002): 83–104. ProQuest.

LeClair, Tom. *In the Loop: Don DeLillo and the Systems Novel*. Champaign: University of Illinois Press, 1987.

Lesjak, Carolyn. *The Afterlife of Enclosure: British Realism, Character, and the Commons*. Stanford: Stanford University Press, 2021.

Levine, Caroline. *Forms: Whole, Rhythm, Hierarchy, Network*. Princeton: Princeton University Press, 2015.

Lippard, Lucy R. "Coming Clean." In *Nonstop Metropolis: A New York City Atlas*, edited by Rebecca Solnit and Joshua Jelly-Schapiro, 142–146. Berkeley: University of California Press, 2016.

———. *Undermining: A Wild Ride Through Land Use, Politics, and Art in the Changing West*. New York: The New Press, 2014.

Loomis, Sara Stephens. "The Sound of All Water: Petro-Culture and Black Modernity in Jesmyn Ward's *Sing, Unburied, Sing*." *Contemporary Literature* 62, no. 2 (2021): 177–206. http://doi.org/10.3368/cl.62.2.177.

MacFarlane, Robert. *Underland: A Deep Time Journey*. New York: Norton, 2019.

MacKay, Robin. "A Brief History of Geotrauma." In *Leper Creativity*: Cyclonopedia *Symposium*, edited by Ed Keller, Nicola Masciandaro, and Eugene Thacker, 1–37. Santa Barbara: punctum books, 2012.

Majewska, Magda. "Immanence Is Bliss: The Ecological Imagination in Thomas Pynchon's *Gravity's Rainbow*." In *An Eclectic Bestiary: Encounters in a More-Than-Human World*, edited by Birgit Spengler and Babette B. Tischleder, 225–240. Bielefeld: Bielefelder Verlag, 2019.

Malm, Andreas. *Fossil Capital: The Rise of Steam Power and the Roots of Global Warming*. London: Verso, 2016.

Malm, Andreas, and the Zetkin Collective. *White Skin, Black Fuel: On the Danger of Fossil Fascism*. London: Verso, 2021.

Manshel, Alexander. "Colson Whitehead's History of the United States." *MELUS* 45, no. 4 (2020): 22–45. http://doi.org/10.1093/melus/mlaa051.

Marshack, Alexander. *The World in Space: The Story of the International Geophysical Year*. New York: Dell, 1958.

Marshall, Kate. *Corridor: Media Architectures in American Fiction*. Minneapolis: University of Minnesota Press, 2013.

———. "*Cyclonopedia* as Novel (a meditation on complicity as inauthenticity)." In *Leper Creativity*: Cyclonopedia *Symposium*, edited by Ed Keller, Nicola Masciandaro, and Eugene Thacker, 147–157. Santa Barbara: punctum books, 2012.

———. "New Wave Fabulism and Hybrid Science Fictions." In *American Literature in Transition, 2000–2010*, edited by Rachel Greenwald Smith, 76–87. Cambridge: Cambridge University Press, 2018.

———. "What Are the Novels of the Anthropocene? American Fiction in Geological Time." *American Literary History* 27, no. 3 (2015): 523–538. http://doi.org/10.1093/alh/ajv032.

Marx, Karl. *Capital*, Vol. 1: *A Critical Analysis of Capitalist Production*. Edited by Frederick Engels. New York: International Publishers, 1967.

Masco, Joseph. "The Age of (a) Man." In *Future Remains: A Cabinet of Curiosities for the Anthropocene*, edited by Gregg Mitman, Marco Armiero, and Robert S. Emmett, 40–49. Chicago: University of Chicago Press, 2018.

———. *The Future of Fallout, and Other Episodes in Radioactive World-Making*. Durham: Duke University Press, 2021.

———. "The Six Extinctions: Visualizing Planetary Ecological Crisis Today." In *After*

Extinction, edited by Richard Grusin, 71–105. Minneapolis: University of Minnesota Press, 2018.

———. *The Theater of Operations: National Security Affect from the Cold War to the War on Terror.* Durham: Duke University Press, 2016.

Mbembe, Achille. *Necropolitics.* Durham: Duke University Press, 2019.

McBrien, Justin. "Accumulating Extinction: Planetary Catastrophism in the Necrocene." In *Anthropocene or Capitalocene? Nature, History, and the Crisis of Capitalism*, edited by Jason W. Moore, 116–137. Oakland: PM Press, 2016.

McGurl, Mark. "Gigantic Realism: The Rise of the Novel and the Comedy of Scale." *Critical Inquiry* 43 (2017): 403–430. https://www.journals.uchicago.edu/doi/full/10.1086/689661.

———. "The New Cultural Geology." *Twentieth-Century Literature* 57, nos. 3 and 4 (2011): 380–390. http://doi.org/10.1215/0041462X-2011-4011.

McHale, Brian. *Constructing Postmodernism.* London: Routledge, 1992.

———. "Period, Break, Interregnum." In *Postmodern/Postwar—and After: Rethinking American Literature*, edited by Jason Gladstone, Andrew Hoberek, and Daniel Worden, 59–72. Iowa City: University of Iowa Press, 2016.

———. *Postmodernist Fiction.* London: Routledge, 1987.

McKittrick, Katherine. *Demonic Grounds: Black Women and the Cartographies of Struggle.* Minneapolis: University of Minnesota Press, 2006.

———. "Plantation Futures." *Small Axe* 17, no. 3 (2013): 1–15. https://doi.org/10.1215/07990537-2378892.

McNeill, J. R., and Peter Engelke. *The Great Acceleration: An Environmental History of the Anthropocene since 1945.* Cambridge, MA: Belknap Press of Harvard University Press, 2014.

Meillassoux, Quentin. *After Finitude: An Essay on the Necessity of Contingency.* Translated by Ray Brassier. London: Continuum, 2008.

Mirzoeff, Nicholas. "It's Not the Anthropocene, It's the White Supremacy Scene; or, The Geological Color Line." In *After Extinction*, edited by Richard Grusin, 123–149. Minneapolis: University of Minnesota Press, 2018.

Mitchell, Timothy. *Carbon Democracy: Political Power in the Age of Oil.* London: Verso, 2013.

Morris, Keiko. "Affordable Housing Coming to Jail Site in the Bronx's Hunts Point." *Dow Jones Institutional News.* October 26, 2016, n.p. ProQuest.

Morton, Timothy. *Dark Ecology: For a Logic of Future Coexistence.* New York: Columbia University Press, 2016.

———. *Hyperobjects: Philosophy and Ecology After the End of the World.* Minneapolis: University of Minnesota Press, 2013.

Moten, Fred. "Blackness and Nothingness (Mysticism in the Flesh)." *South Atlantic Quarterly* 112, no. 4 (2013): 737–780. http://doi.org/10.1215/00382876-2345261.

Munif, Abdelrahman. *Cities of Salt.* Translated by Peter Theroux. New York: Vintage, 1989.

Negarestani, Reza. *Cyclonopedia: Complicity with Anonymous Materials*. Melbourne: re.press, 2008.

Nixon, Rob. *Slow Violence and the Environmentalism of the Poor*. Cambridge, MA: Harvard University Press, 2011.

O'Brien, Tim. *The Nuclear Age*. New York: Penguin, 1996.

O'Donnell, Patrick. "*Underworld*." In *The Cambridge Companion to Don DeLillo*, edited by John N. Duvall, 108–121. Cambridge: Cambridge University Press, 2008.

Oldham, R. D. "Essays on Speculative Geology: 1. On Homotaxis and Contemporaneity." *Geological Magazine* 3, no. 7 (1886): 293–300.

———. "Essays on Speculative Geology: 2. Probable Changes of Latitude." *Geological Magazine* 3, no. 7 (1886): 300–308.

Opperman, Romy. "A Permanent Struggle Against an Omnipresent Death: Revisiting Environmental Racism with Frantz Fanon." *Critical Philosophy of Race* 7, no. 1 (2019): 57–80. http://doi.org/10.5325/critphilrace.7.1.0057.

Otto, Eric. "Kim Stanley Robinson's *Mars* Trilogy and the Leopoldian Land Ethic." *Utopian Studies* 14, no. 2 (2003): 118–135. EBSCOhost.

Owens, Craig. "Earthwords." *October* 10 (1979): 120–130. http://doi.org/10.2307/778632.

Parikka, Jussi. *The Geology of Media*. Minneapolis: University of Minnesota Press, 2015.

Poe, Edgar Allan. "The Domain of Arnheim." In *The Complete Tales and Poems of Edgar Allan Poe*, 604–615. New York: Vintage, 1975.

Povinelli, Elizabeth A. *Geontologies: A Requiem to Late Liberalism*. Durham: Duke University Press, 2016.

Pynchon, Thomas. *Gravity's Rainbow*. New York: Penguin, 2006.

Raffles, Hugh. *The Book of Unconformities: Speculations on Lost Time*. New York: Pantheon, 2020.

Rampino, Michael R. *Cataclysms: A New Geology for the Twenty-First Century*. New York: Columbia University Press, 2017.

Rasmussen, Knud. *Across Arctic America: Narrative of the Fifth Thule Expedition*. 1927. Reprint, College: University of Alaska Press, 1999.

Ravindranathan, Thangam. "The Rise of the Sea and the Novel." *differences* 30, no. 3 (2019): 1-33. http://doi.org/10.1215/10407391-7973974.

Revelle, Roger, et al. *Restoring the Quality of Our Environment: Report of the Environmental Pollution Panel, President's Science Advisory Committee*. Washington, DC: The White House, 1965.

Rhodes, Cecil. *The Last Will and Testament of Cecil John Rhodes: With Elucidatory Notes to Which Are Added Some Chapters Describing the Political and Religious Ideas of the Testator*. Edited by W. T. Stead. London: "Review of Reviews" Office, 1902.

Rigby, Kate. *Dancing with Disaster: Environmental Histories, Narratives, and Ethics for Perilous Times*. Charlottesville: University of Virginia Press, 2015.

Roberts, Jennifer L. "Landscapes of Indifference: Robert Smithson and John Lloyd

Stephens in Yucatán," *The Art Bulletin* 82, no. 3 (2000): 544–567. https://www.jstor.org/stable/3051401.

Robinson, Kim Stanley. *Green Mars*. New York: Bantam, 1995.

———. *Red Mars*. New York: Del Rey, 2017.

Rose, Andrew. "Insurgency and Distributed Agency in Karen Tei Yamashita's *Through the Arc of the Rain Forest*." *ISLE: Interdisciplinary Studies in Literature and Environment* 26, no. 1 (2019): 125–144. http://doi.org/10.1093/isle/isy076.

Ryan, Don, and Ralph Scott. "Viewpoint: The Promise of Environmental Sampling and Right-to-Know Laws for At-Risk Communities." *Public Health Reports (1947-)* 115, no. 6 (2000): 511–520.

Saint-Amour, Paul K. *Tense Future: Modernism, Total War, Encyclopedic Form*. Oxford: Oxford University Press, 2015.

Sanders, Ralph. *Project Plowshare: The Development of the Peaceful Use of Nuclear Explosions*. New York: Public Affairs Press, 1962.

Schaub, Thomas. "The Environmental Pynchon: *Gravity's Rainbow* and the Ecological Context," *Pynchon Notes*, no. 42–43 (1998): 59–72. http://doi.org/10.16995/pn.140.

Schneider-Mayerson, Matthew. "Climate Change Fiction." In *American Literature in Transition, 2000–2010*, edited by Rachel Greenwald Smith, 309–321. Cambridge: Cambridge University Press, 2018.

Scranton, Roy. "Learning How to Die in the Anthropocene." In *Energy Humanities: An Anthology*, edited by Imre Szeman and Dominic Boyer, 384–388. Baltimore: Johns Hopkins University Press, 2017.

Shaw, Lytle. *Fieldworks: From Place to Site in Postwar Politics*. Tuscaloosa: University of Alabama Press, 2013.

Smith, Rachel Greenwald, ed. *American Literature in Transition, 2000–2010*. Cambridge: Cambridge University Press, 2018.

Smithson, Robert. "Aerial Art." In *Robert Smithson: The Collected Writings*, edited by Jack Flam, 116–118. Berkeley: University of California Press, 1996.

———. "Language to Be Looked at, and/or Things to Be Read." In *Robert Smithson: The Collected Writings*, edited by Jack Flam, 61. Berkeley: University of California Press, 1996.

———. "Letter to the Editor." In *Robert Smithson: The Collected Writings*, edited by Jack Flam, 66-67. Berkeley: University of California Press, 1996.

———. "A Museum of Language in the Vicinity of Art." In *Robert Smithson: The Collected Writings*, edited by Jack Flam, 78–94. Berkeley: University of California Press, 1996.

———. "Strata: A Geophotographic Fiction." In *Robert Smithson: The Collected Writings*, edited by Jack Flam, 75–77. Berkeley: University of California Press, 1996.

———. "A Thing Is a Hole in a Thing It Is Not." In *Robert Smithson: The Collected Writings*, edited by Jack Flam, 95–96. Berkeley: University of California Press, 1996.

———. "Towards the Development of an Air Terminal Site." In *Robert Smithson: The Collected Writings*, edited by Jack Flam, 52–60. Berkeley: University of California Press, 1996.

Sobieszek, Robert A. "Robert Smithson's *Proposal for a Monument at Antarctica*," in *Robert Smithson*, edited by Eugenie Tsai and Cornelia Butler, 142–147. Berkeley: University of California Press, 2004.

Solnit, Rebecca. *Savage Dreams: A Journey into the Hidden Wars of the American West.* Berkeley: University of California Press, 2014.

Song, Min Hyoung. "Becoming Planetary." *American Literary History* 23, no. 3 (2011): 555-573. http://doi.org/10.1093/alh/ajr020.

———. *Climate Lyricism*. Durham: Duke University Press, 2022.

Steffen, Will, Paul J. Crutzen, and John R. McNeill. "The Anthropocene: Are Humans Now Overwhelming the Great Forces of Nature?" *Ambio* 36, no. 8 (2007): 614–621. https://doi.org/10.1579/0044-7447(2007)36[614:TAAHNO]2.0.CO;2.

Steinbeck, John. "High Drama of Bold Thrust Through Ocean Floor: Earth's Second Layer Is Tapped in Prelude to Mohole." *Life*, April 14, 1961.

Steyerl, Hito. "In Free Fall: A Thought Experiment on Vertical Perspective." *e-flux Journal*, no. 24 (April 2011). https://www.e-flux.com/journal/24/67860/in-free-fall-a-thought-experiment-on-vertical-perspective/.

Streeby, Shelley. *Imagining the Future of Climate Change: World-Making Through Science Fiction and Activism*. Oakland: University of California Press, 2018.

Swan, Heather. "What Counts as Environmental Storytelling: A Conversation with Karen Tei Yamashita." *Edge Effects*, May 21, 2019, https://edgeeffects.net/karen-tei-yamashita/.

Szeman, Imre. "System Failure: Oil, Futurity, and the Anticipation of Disaster." In *Energy Humanities: An Anthology*, edited by Imre Szeman and Dominic Boyer, 55–70. Baltimore: Johns Hopkins University Press, 2017.

Tanaka, Shouhei. "Fossil Fuel Fiction and the Geologies of Race." *PMLA* 137, no. 1 (2022): 36-51. https://doi.org/10.1632/S0030812921000717.

Thomas, Julia Adeney, Mark Williams, and Jan Zalasiewicz. *The Anthropocene: A Multidisciplinary Approach*, 69–86. Cambridge, UK: Polity, 2020.

Trexler, Adam. *Anthropocene Fictions: The Novel in a Time of Climate Change*. Charlottesville: University of Virginia Press, 2015.

Tsing, Anna Lowenhaupt. *The Mushroom at the End of the World: On the Possibility of Life in Capitalist Ruins*. Princeton: Princeton University Press, 2015.

Tucker, Jeffrey Allen. "'Verticality Is Such a Risky Enterprise': The Literary and Paraliterary Antecedents of Colson Whitehead's *The Intuitionist*." *Novel: A Forum on Fiction* 43, no. 1 (2010): 148–156. http://doi.org/10.1215/00295132-2009-075.

U.S. Atomic Energy Commission and U.S. Geological Survey. *Prospecting for Uranium*. Rev. ed. Washington, DC: U.S. Government Printing Office, 1957.

Vergès, Françoise. "Racial Capitalocene." In *Futures of Black Radicalism*, edited by Gaye Theresa Johnson and Alex Lubin, chap. 4. London: Verso, 2017. ProQuest Ebrary.

Virilio, Paul. *Open Sky*. Translated by Julie Rose. London: Verso, 2008.

Wagner-Lawlor, Jennifer A. "Plastic's 'Untiring Solicitation': Geographies of Myth, Corporate Alibis, and the Plaesthetics of the Matacão." In *Life in Plastic: Artistic*

Responses to Petromodernity, edited by Caren Irr, 259–280. Minneapolis: University of Minnesota Press, 2021.

Wakefield, Stephanie. *Anthropocene Back Loop: Experimentation in Unsafe Operating Space*. London: Open Humanities Press, 2020.

Wald, Priscilla. *Contagious: Cultures, Carriers, and the Outbreak Narrative*. Durham: Duke University Press, 2008.

Wallace-Wells, David. "The Uninhabitable Earth." *New York Magazine*, July 10, 2017, https://nymag.com/intelligencer/2017/07/climate-change-earth-too-hot-for-humans.html.

Walters, Hugh. *The Mohole Menace*. New York: Criterion, 1968.

Wang, Jackie. *Carceral Capitalism*. Los Angeles: Semiotext(e), 2018.

Ward, Jesmyn. *Sing, Unburied, Sing*. New York: Scribner, 2017.

Wark, McKenzie. *Molecular Red: Theory for the Anthropocene*. London: Verso, 2015.

Wasserman, Sarah. *The Death of Things: Ephemera and the American Novel*. Minneapolis: University of Minnesota Press, 2020.

Wegenstein, Bernadette. "Body." In *Critical Terms for Media Studies*, edited by W.J.T. Mitchell and Mark B. N. Hansen, 19–34. Chicago: University of Chicago Press, 2010.

Wegner, Phillip E. *Life Between Two Deaths, 1989–2001: U.S. Culture in the Long Nineties*. Durham: Duke University Press, 2020.

———. "October 3, 1951 to September 11, 2001: Periodizing the Cold War in Don DeLillo's *Underworld*." *Amerikastuiden/American Studies* 49, no. 1 (2004): 51–64.

Weisenburger, Steven C. *A Gravity's Rainbow Companion: Sources and Contexts for Pynchon's Novel*. 2nd ed. Athens: University of Georgia Press, 2006.

White, Frank. *The Overview Effect: Space Exploration and Human Evolution*. Boston: Houghton Mifflin Harcourt, 1987.

Whitehead, Colson. *The Intuitionist: A Novel*. New York: Anchor, 2000.

———. *The Nickel Boys*. New York: Anchor, 2019.

———. *The Underground Railroad*. New York: Doubleday, 2016.

Wiener, *Cybernetics: or Control and Communication in the Animal and the Machine*. Cambridge, MA: MIT Press, 1948.

Wolfe, Cary. *Critical Environments: Postmodern Theory and the Pragmatics of the "Outside."* Minneapolis: University of Minnesota Press, 1998.

Wright, Michelle M. *Physics of Blackness: Beyond the Middle Passage Epistemology*. Minneapolis: University of Minnesota Press, 2015.

Yamashita, Karen Tei. *Through the Arc of the Rain Forest*. Minneapolis: Coffee House Press, 2017.

Yusoff, Kathryn. *A Billion Black Anthropocenes or None*. Minneapolis: University of Minnesota Press, 2018.

———. "Epochal Aesthetics: Affectual Infrastructures of the Anthropocene." In *Accumulation: The Art, Architecture, and Media of Climate Change*, edited by Nick Axel, Daniel A. Barber, Nikolaus Hirsch, and Anton Vidokle, 13–25. An *e-flux* Architecture volume. Minneapolis: University of Minnesota Press, 2022.

———. "Geologic Realism: On the Beach of Geologic Time." *Social Text* 37, no. 1 (2019): 1–26. https://doi.org/10.1215/01642472-7286240.

———. "The Inhumanities." *Annals of the American Association of Geographers* 111, no. 3 (2021): 663–676. http://doi.org/10.1080/24694452.2020.1814688.

Zalasiewicz, Jan. *The Earth After Us: What Legacy Will Humans Leave in the Rocks?* Oxford: Oxford University Press, 2008.

Zalasiewisz, Jan, Colin N. Waters, Juliana A. Ivar do Sul, Patricia L. Corcoran, Anthony D. Barnosky, Alejandro Cearreta, Matt Edgeworth, et al. "The Geological Cycle of Plastics and Their Use As a Stratigraphic Indicator." *Anthropocene* 13 (2016): 4–17. http://doi.org/10.1016/j.ancene.2016.01.002.

Index

scale, 33, 35–36, 39, 45, 47, 49; and science fiction, 52–53; and vertical perspective, 31, 35–36, 37–39; and visual art, 37, 42–43, 46. *See also* DeLillo, Don
uniformitarianism, 15, 168n31
uranium, 29, 90, 104–5, 113–14

Vergès, Françoise, 22
Verne, Jules, 60
Vernon C. Bain Correctional Center, 134, 142, 149
vertical science, 10–11, 26–27, 30, 36, 91, 95–96, 99, 116, 119, 162, 164; definition of, 10–11; and race, 128, 132–34, 146, 151, 153, 157. *See also* verticality
verticality, 4, 8–12, 15, 18, 19–20, 23, 25, 37, 45, 53, 100, 123, 131, 163, 167n16; and Black planetarity, 128–129, 133–134; and modernity, 151–55, 157–58, 185n49; and the orbital field, 91–93, 97–98, 102–3; and speculative geologies, 71, 106–7
Virilio, Paul, 11–12, 15
Voluntary Human Extinction Movement (VHEMT), 12–13. *See also* Knight, Les
Vostok program, 8

Wakefield, Stephanie, 59
Wald, Priscilla, 22, 133
Walters, Hugh, 67; *The Mohole Mystery*, 27–28, 56–57, 64–67
Wang, Jackie, 150
Ward, Jesmyn, 12, 23, 25, 129, 132–33, 161; *Salvage the Bones*, 143; *Sing,*

Unburied, Sing, 29, 133–34, 140–47, 151
Wark, McKenzie, 98, 166n2
Wasserman, Sarah, 32, 41, 171n4, 172n17
waste, 11–12, 26, 30, 33, 40–42, 52, 133, 148, 154, 173n32; and the Moholean Anthropocene, 58–59; and speculative geologies, 82–87. *See also* Fresh Kills landfill
Weather Underground, 107, 109
Wegener, Alfred, 56
Wegner, Phillip E., 32, 46, 171n4
Weisenburger, Steven, 116, 118
White, Frank, 100, 103, 153. *See also* overview effect
Whitehead, Colson, 12, 25, 132–33, 161, 183n24; *The Intuitionist*, 29, 128–29, 132, 134, 151–59; *The Nickel Boys*, 131 *The Underground Railroad*, 19, 29, 128–30, 132, 134–41, 151, 152, 154
Wiener, Norbert, 116, 181n47
Wolfe, Cary, 22
World War II, 6, 7–9, 27, 38, 40, 57–58, 67, 97–98, 117, 119, 124; and extinction, 13–14; and vertical science, 11–12; and World War I, 3
Wright, Richard: *The Man Who Lived Underground*, 125–27, 129

Yamashita, Karen Tei, 12, 25, 90; *Through the Arc of the Rain Forest*, 23, 28, 57–59, 61, 74, 81–88, 97, 178n64, 178n67
Yusoff, Kathryn, 18, 128–31, 151

Zalasiewicz, Jan, 10, 167n11
Zapruder film, 51